The Decorative Arts of the Mariner

Seventeenth-century navigational instruments

The Decorative Arts of the Mariner

Edited by
Gervis Frere-Cook

LITTLE, BROWN AND COMPANY
Boston   Toronto

LIBRARY OF CONGRESS CATALOG CARD NO. 66-20998

FIRST AMERICAN EDITION

PRINTED IN GREAT BRITAIN

CONTENTS

INTRODUCTION

The purpose of this book is very simple. It is to show how the sea has provided the opportunity and inspiration for sailors and craftsmen to produce works of art. Its scope encompasses the maritime world and goes back in time as far as recorded history.

Inevitably the material available for illustration is uneven in quality and erratic in time and place. The natural materials of the seafarer are wood and canvas, rope and paint, and none of these readily endures the passage of time, least of all when exposed to wind and sea. Sometimes, however, the craftsmanship was in ivory, metal or stone and survived better, and the earliest examples we have are connected with funerary rites: the models from the Pharaohs' tombs in Egypt and the Gokstad ship in Norway. Of the great artistic period of the European Renaissance little trace remains except through pictures, models and ornamental pieces. Of these ample exist to show the glorious decoration lavished on the vessels of the sixteenth and seventeenth centuries, indicating, especially in the state barges and 'wagoners' (or chart portfolios), how the wonderful opulence and imagination of the time spread from the land across the waterfront and afloat.

For the sailors themselves, making long, monotonous voyages or serving interminable sentences as prisoners-of-war in the hulks, passing the time became a vital problem. These men made the beautiful bone models, intricate rope-work and sentimental scrimshaw etching and carving, this last an art with a noticeable family feminine influence.

These then are the sources from which the illustrations have been derived; their inspiration, the ever-changing, ever-challenging sea.

As it is the Editor's duty to write an introduction to his book, so it is his privilege to give thanks to all who have helped him in its preparation. I must firstly express my gratitude to the Directors of Cassell & Co. Ltd, but for whose faith in me this volume would have remained a dream, and to all the contributors, men of high standing in their particular subjects, who have so generously given of their time and knowledge to make its compilation possible; secondly, to the designer and editorial team who were responsible for its presentation; and thirdly, to all those unnamed persons behind the scenes in libraries, museums and offices who have helped it on its way. To see it finally in print gives me that same contentment as tying up in harbour after a successful spell at sea. Sailors will understand what I mean.

GERVIS FRERE-COOK

CHAPTER I

VESSELS OF THE ANCIENT WORLD

LEONARD COTTRELL

It all began of course in Egypt, birthplace of the oldest civilization in the Mediterranean region; vying only with Sumer as the most ancient civilization on earth. At a time, three thousand years B.C., when the inhabitants of latter-day Phoenicia, Asia Minor, Crete and Greece had hardly progressed, nautically, beyond the small boat, Egypt was building ships of considerable size and burthen, decked, with tall masts made from Lebanon cedars, sails and banks of oars, capable, even before the time of the earliest pyramid-builders, of sea-voyages along the coast of the Levant. The only known representations of these ships, alas, are crude drawings on *ostraka*, or scratched on rock-faces, or (very rarely) carved on royal ceremonial objects—such as the famous Narmer palette of 3200 B.C.

Since written records of this 'pre-dynastic' period of Egyptian history do not exist, the evidence is mainly archaeological, but there are crude drawings of ships of this period shown with oars (not paddles), a rudder or steering-oar, tall masts which must have been imported from the Lebanon, cabins and forecastles, sails and yards. Even if these drawings did not exist, the existence of such ships can be argued from the fact that articles were being imported at this time from Syria, the Lebanon and even Asia Minor and objects of Egyptian manufacture were being exported to these lands, and the size and weight-carrying capacity of these ancient Egyptian vessels estimated from the fact that heavy slabs of granite have been found in early-dynastic tombs in northern (i.e. Lower) Egypt which could only have come from Assuan, some seven hundred miles to the south. Only ships or possibly tower rafts could have supported them.

Later, from sculptured reliefs in the Old Kingdom and Middle Kingdom tombs, we know that ships of great size were built capable of carrying granite obelisks weighing as much as two hundred tons and more. In this epoch (*circa* 2000 B.C.) and in the New Kingdom (*circa* 1600 to 1100 B.C.) the skill of the Ancient Egyptian shipwright reached its peak, as can be seen from the beautiful detailed models of such craft made by the Egyptians themselves for burial in their tombs. Among the finest examples are those discovered in the Eleventh Dynasty sepulchre of an official called Meket-Re, and the fine ceremonial model ships discovered in the sumptuously furnished tomb of the Pharaoh Tutankhamun.

Egyptian ships were produced in a great variety of types, from warships and large merchantmen to private yachts and ships designed specifically for hippopotamus hunting, an aristocratic sport in Pharaonic times. Owing to the scarcity of large trees in Egypt, these ships had to be built of relatively small planks made from such trees as persea and sycamore. Masts had to be imported.

Crete, the second oldest civilization in the Mediterranean and the oldest in Europe, was the legendary kingdom of Minos of whom Thucydides wrote that he was 'the earliest ruler we know of who possessed a fleet, and controlled most of what are now Greek waters'. Unfortunately, though archaeologists can trace the origin of Cretan or 'Minoan' civilization as far back as 3000 B.C., and we know from the evidence of ancient harbours, for example the dry docks at Nirou Khani, that Crete was a great maritime power, there is not one detailed picture of a Minoan vessel. Those that exist are mere sketches, sometimes painted on potsherds, or engraved on diminutive 'bead-seals'.

Though doubtless the design of these ships was influenced by Egypt, the Cretan vessels were certainly not mere imitations of Egyptian sea-going ships. When, in the fifteenth century B.C., the Mycenaeans (Homer's 'bronze-clad Achaeans') took to the sea, conquered Crete and ruled the Aegean in their turn, their ships naturally followed Minoan models, to judge from the few crude sketches which survive. Presumably it was vessels such as these which bore the Greek army to Troy. One interesting point is raised by Professor R. C. Anderson in his *Oared Fighting Ships*. He points out that in the well-known sculptured relief depicting the victory of Rameses III over the 'sea-peoples' in a naval battle off Alexandria, neither the Egyptian nor the enemy vessels are shown with rams. As the date of the battle can be fixed at about the same time as the siege of Troy we can assume that this type of vessel was known to Agamemnon, Odysseus and their companions.

The ram later became a deadly weapon of naval warfare, but Anderson in his book comments on the ships shown in the Egyptian relief, 'They have oars and they have their bows finished off by heavy carved heads, but these are set at such an angle and carried so high above the water that they would be quite useless as rams; while the number of oars shown would not give sufficient speed to make even a well-placed ram at all effective.'

In the days when naval artillery did not exist, and the most powerful projectile which could be fired from a ship was an arrow, the ram was a mighty development in naval armament and one which vitally affected the design and appearance of warships. It was well established in the Mediterranean by 800 B.C. Greek pottery of this period shows galleys equipped with rams, and Phoenician ships depicted in Assyrian sculptures also show the ram.

From 800 B.C. onwards the Greeks developed a variety of vessels ranging from merchantmen to swift men-of-war. The names of some are familiar—trireme, bireme, penteconter, and in the 'classical' and 'Hellenistic' periods, roughly between 500 B.C. down to 300 B.C., these ships are delineated in some detail, sometimes in sculpture (of which the famous 'Winged Victory of Samothrace' is an instance), but more often as decorative elements on pottery. But none of their artists produced a detailed study of a Greek ship, let alone made a model of one, as the Ancient Egyptians did, so the models illustrated in this book are painstaking modern reconstructions based on vase-paintings and sculptured bas-reliefs.

The Phoenicians and Etruscans, rivals of the Greeks, were even less well served; few representations of their craft have survived, though there are some in Assyrian sculpture of the eighth century B.C. and a relief of an Etruscan galley.

Also, in the tomb of Kenamun, Thebes, there is a painting of 'deep-bellied' freighters with curved ends terminating in short straight stems and sternposts. They had flush decks surrounded by high railings permitting them to carry a substantial deck load as well.

There is little pictorial evidence of Etruscan ships, nor indeed of anything Etruscan save their tomb-furnishings, so thorough were their Roman enemies in stamping out their memory. However, from Greek records it is known that they were doughty seamen and pirates, whom the Greeks called the Tyrrhenians.

Before the trireme, with its three banks of oars, was introduced, the standard Greek fighting-ship was the penteconter of fifty oars. Most probably Homer's larger ships were of this class, although he says they carried fifty-two men or in some

2 *From the tomb of Tiyi, a high official of the Fifth Dynasty (2560–2420 B.C.). These skiffs were used in Pharaonic times mainly for hunting and fishing, as depicted in this superb relief. Note how the reed-boats were bound together; also the fish and animals depicted in the Nile, and the wildfowl in the reeds above. In this highly conventionalized art the river was represented by vertical squiggles and the papyrus which grew along its banks by vertical flutings*

cases 120. These were almost certainly penteconters with fifty rowers, a steersman and a 'boatswain of the oars'—the *keleustes* or time-beater. The 120-man ship may have had an additional bank of oars, making a bireme, or it may have had two men to each oar.

Later came the true trireme with three banks of oars. The ingenious model designed by Admiral Serre shows how the oarsmen were placed.

There are a few representations, for example the Leonormant relief in the Acropolis Museum in Athens, showing a ship of 400 B.C., and the much more interesting and exciting relief from the Palazzo Spada shown in Fig. 19. But again we have to rely more on literature than on pictures to get an idea of what a Greek warship looked like.

In Roman times, at the time of the first Punic War (264–241 B.C.), the standard fighting-ship was the quinquereme, with five banks of oars against the trireme's three, or so it would appear. The Romans had to learn the art of naval warfare from the Carthaginians, and the sculptured reliefs of Roman galleys show how expert the Romans became at shipbuilding and ship-handling. Nevertheless, despite the grace of the galleys depicted in the Pompeian frescoes no Roman warship can compare with those of Greece in her golden age. The Romans were shrewd imitators, and fine disciplinarians at sea as well as on land, but they lacked that indefinable quality of original artistry, and this shows both in the design of their vessels and the unimaginative accounts of their naval engagements, and one recognizes the difference. But, from the viewpoint of ship design and decorative art, we certainly know more about Roman craft than that of any other ancient civilization—with the sole exception of Egypt.

2

3

In the Eleventh and Twelfth Dynasties (2100–1790 B.C.) it was customary for noblemen to have buried in their tombs models of the objects they used in their earthly life, including boats and ships. Full-size boats were buried beside the pyramids of the Pharaohs but these may have been intended either for the journey of the king's spirit to the holy city of Abydos, or across the sky with the sun-god Re. Non-royal personages, however, were content with models such as these from the tomb of Meket-Re, an official of the Eleventh Dynasty (c. 2000 B.C.) and they give us an accurate and fascinating picture of the boats which a great nobleman of this period regularly used

3 is a fishing or fowling-skiff, in which Meket-Re sits in front of his cabin to the sides of which are lashed the spreaders and anchor-posts for a bird-net. Note the alert stance of the harpooner, the eager oarsmen with blades poised and the boy and girl handing strings of ducks to their master

4 depicts another boat in Meket-Re's flotilla. It is one of his travelling boats with cabin; inside, not visible in the picture, are his bed and cabin trunk. This, a twelve-oared boat with a cabin extending from gunwale to gunwale, was intended, possibly, for leisurely journeys. But he had a longer, faster boat (4a) with eighteen oars and a smaller cabin. Each has a mast, spars and a square sail

4

4b A kitchen tender on which Meket-Re's meals were prepared. Between the rowers women are grinding flour while men mix dough. The area contains beer and wine jars and joints of meat. Notice the crutch for the mast in each craft

4a

5 A large ocean-going ship with thirty oars, one of the vessels which Queen Hatshepsut (Eighteenth Dynasty, c. 1500 B.C.) sent down the Red Sea to the 'Land of Punt' (probably Somaliland) on a trading venture. Note the large square sail, the yard of which was pushed up (the pulley-block being unknown), the sailors hauling on the rigging, the man near the poop beating time for the rowers, the steering-oar, and the stern shaped like a lotus, a favourite Egyptian emblem. The general shape of this large wooden ship is still reminiscent of the pre-Dynastic papyrus-skiff

6 A twenty-four-oared rivercraft belonging to Rekh-mi-re, Vizier (Prime Minister) under Hatshepsut's successor Tuthmosis III (Eighteenth Dynasty, c. 1450 B.C.). It has a highly decorated forecastle and stern-castle, the large structure amidships, and the man in the bows taking soundings. Sandbanks are still a hazard on the Nile. Judging by the straining, standing oarsmen and the fact that the huge sail is spread, the vessel is pulling upstream, probably at flood time. (From the paintings in Rekhmire's tomb in Thebes)

4b

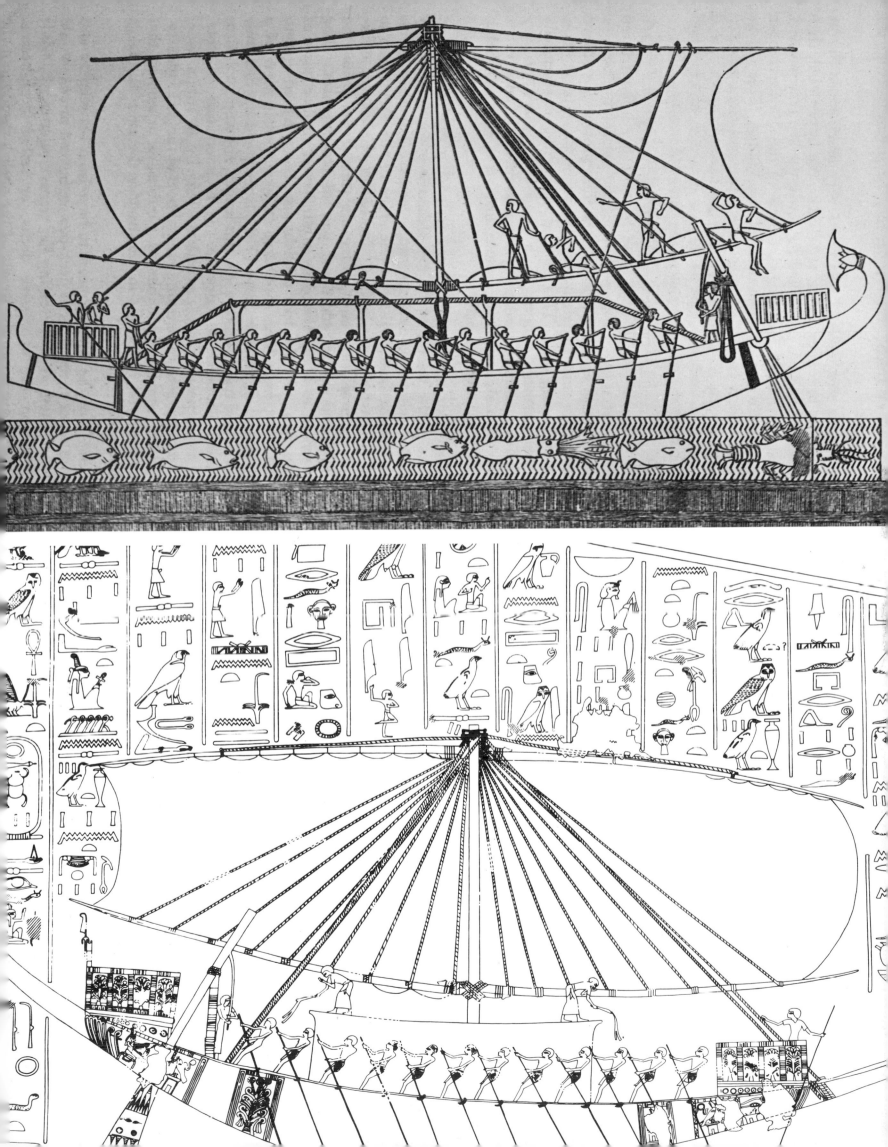

7 One of the earliest pictures in the world of a combined land and naval engagement; the historic battle between the forces of Rameses III (1198–1166 B.C.) and the 'Peoples of the Sea', who came down from the Aegean area by sea and land, ravaging the coast and threatening Egypt. The subject, depicted on a gigantic wall-relief, was clearly beyond the powers of the artist, and the original (from which this line drawing is taken) is very indistinct. Note the round shields of the enemy and their flowerpot-shaped headdress (?helmet), the capsized enemy vessel with its crew falling into the water, and the captured prisoners below. The ships of the Egyptians and those of the 'Sea-peoples' can be distinguished, the former being of half-moon shape and apparently more streamlined. The vessels of the Aegean peoples are more square-ish and have cumbersome forecastles and stern-castles. On the right Rameses III shoots with his archers

8 *Formal representation of an Egyptian 'sacred barque' from the temple of Rameses II at Abu Simbel. It is unlikely that this ever sailed, but was carried in processions on the shoulders of priests, with the god's image under the shrine in the centre. Note the figure of the falcon-headed god Horus on the stern, the fans, and the stone platform on which it rested in the temple sanctuary*

9 *Another sacred barque, of Ptolemaic date (332–330 B.C.) again showing the shrine, and the figure of the deity—in this case Hat-hor, goddess of love and beauty—surmounting bows and stern. This relief shows how the barque was carried (see 8 and accompanying description). As in Ancient Egypt ships were the normal mode of travel, it was natural to assume that the gods also used them. (From the temple of Hat-hor at Denderah)*

8

9

10 *Very few representations of the far-famed ships of the Phoenicians exist, and even these are poor. The vessel illustrated is from an Assyrian relief and dates from the eighth century B.C. Note the ram (this was a warship) and heavy superstructure with the warriors aloft. The sculptor seems to have been more interested in the marine life, of which the octopus and fishes are amusing examples*

11 *Another Phoenician galley, also from an Assyrian relief of the time of Sennacherib (c. 700 B.C.). This shows more detail, including the mast and rigging, the steering-oars, and the curious incurved stern*

12 *A Greek merchant-ship from a vase painting. It has forty-eight oars in two banks, a square-rigged sail and a forecastle. The steersman is comfortably seated. Compare the Egyptian examples, in which the steersman is standing*

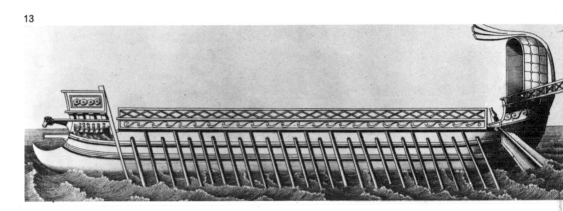

13 *A bireme of fifty-four oars shown without mast, sail or crew (the figures near the bows appear to be painted on the forecastle). Nevertheless this old print, presumably derived from a vase painting (like 12), shows some interesting details, including the raised, covered-in platform for the steersman. Ships such as these would have conveyed the Greeks to Troy*

14 *Another print showing an oar-driven ship of early classical times, with a lamp and decorative pattern on the bows and stern-castle*

15 *Sketch of a Greek war-galley of classical times, of the type which took part in the Battle of Salamis (480 B.C.). Observe the ram which was used with such deadly effect (the only woman commander rammed one of her own ships), the graceful lines of the craft and the high forecastle*

16

17

18

19

16 *An eighteenth-century print depicting the great war-galley of Pyrrhus, King of Epirus (c. 318–272 B.C.). As a royal ship it is highly and somewhat horribly decorated. It has the 'eye' below the figurehead, which also appears on the vessel shown in 14. It may have been a charm, comparable with the Egyptian 'eye of Horus'*

17 *A highly imaginative reconstruction of a war-galley in action. Note the eagle and the SPQR banner, and the sword-shaped ram, which looks highly impractical*

18 *Derived from a painting at Pompeii, this print shows a ship of ninety-six oars, mainsail and foresail, and a figurehead in the form of a bird. Strongly reinforced bows, the ram, armed men standing on deck and a figure standing to attention outside the cabin can all be seen*

19 *Another warship in action, from a relief depicting the Battle of Actium, in which the combined fleets of Antony and Cleopatra were defeated by the Romans. This was one of Cleopatra's vessels, hence her sign, the crocodile, which appears below the bows. The prow has heavy decoration, including a female figure, probably that of the queen*

20 *How the Roman fleet appeared in action. Though the Roman ships were heavier and more cumbersome than the Greek, they were highly seaworthy and battleworthy vessels. The decoration of the bows is prominent, coarse and florid. Note the different figureheads, the covered-in quarters near the stern and the profusion of banners*

21 *A two-masted Roman galley with banks of forty oars, ram and lion figurehead. Note the SPQR banner above the bows and the eagle standards on each side of the cabin. The heavy spearheads projecting from the figurehead and above it were probably decorative, though Roman warships of this size did carry* ballistae (*spring-guns*)

20, 21

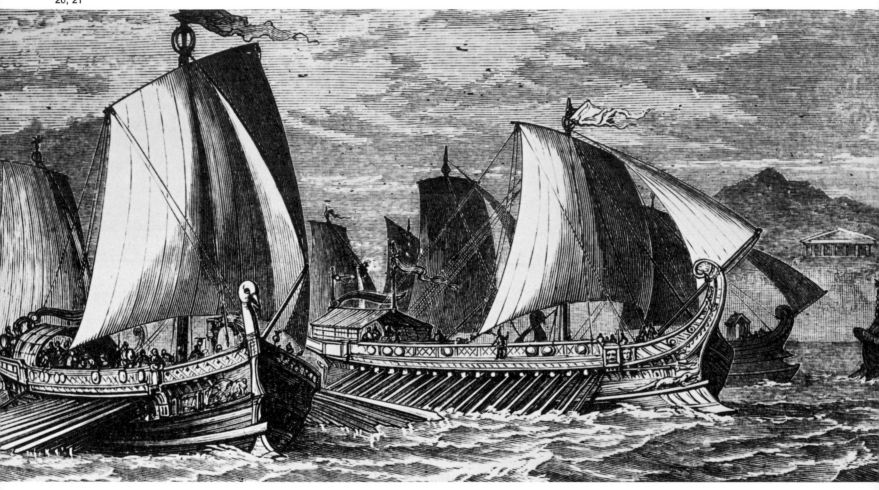

CHAPTER II

THE VIKING LONGSHIPS

ARNE EMIL CHRISTENSEN JR.

In Scandinavia are preserved eight ships and three small boats from the Viking Age, a period which can be approximately dated between the years A.D. 800 and A.D. 1050. Of these, the three ships and three small boats preserved in the Viking Ship Museum in Oslo, Norway, have been known to the public for a long time. They all come from royal pagan burials dating from the ninth century. In Denmark, five ships were excavated in 1962. They had been sunk, probably early in the eleventh century, to block a sailing channel. A few other finds exist, but in a very fragmentary state.

Out of these eight ships and three boats, only the Oseberg ship carries much decoration, but the decorations, composed of animals and humans, carved in relief or in the round (Figs. 2 and 3), are lavish.

From the late Viking Age we have written sources dealing with ships and their ornaments. From these we know that the most common piece of ornament for a ship was a 'dragon's head' on the prow, sometimes with a corresponding tail, or another head, on the stempost. Other kinds of ornament mentioned in the written sources or known from archaeological finds are painting, relief carving, decorative iron mounts and bronze weathervanes. The last were carried either at the masthead, or more often, on the prow (Fig. 9).

Apart from the Oseberg ship, only two 'dragon's heads' are known from Scandinavia, both carved on fragmentary stems found in west Norwegian peat-bogs. Judging from the size, they were intended for small boats. As can be seen, the type of head is different from the one in the Oseberg ship (Fig. 4). A 'dragon's head' from the river Schelde, now in the British Museum, may come from a Viking ship, but there has been some disagreement as to its function, and the head is rather small for a stem ornament.

From contemporary pictures of ships, we see that two different forms of 'dragon's head' occur regularly. The snake, coiled and ready to strike, as in the Oseberg ship, and the fierce animal showing its teeth, like the one in Fig. 11.

The 'picture-stones' on the Swedish island of Gotland, which give us many detailed pictures of ships, sometimes show the ships with the shields hung along the side. The shields were painted in different colours, and gave additional splendour to the ship. From the written sources, the sagas, we know that this was generally done only when the ship was in harbour. When the Gokstad ship was excavated, the shields still hung along both sides. There were sixty-four shields, painted alternately black and yellow.

Most ships were evidently undecorated, but the excellent workmanship and sweeping elegant lines are proof that the sailor and shipwright both had a keen sense of what a beautiful ship should look like (Figs. 5, 6). The Gokstad ship, and the three small boats found with it, are sufficient proof of this. The owner of the Gokstad ship must have had an excellent woodcarver at his disposal. The tent found with the ship is decorated with fierce-looking animal heads carved on the ends of the tentpoles. A similar head may have decorated the prow, but this part of the ship had been destroyed by rot, so nothing definite can be said. The only part of the ship which carries decoration is the tiller (Fig. 11). The carving seems to have been executed by the same artist who carved the tentpoles. On the tiller the carving is further embellished with colours, which were still visible during the excavation. The small Gokstad boats are undecorated, except for some carving on the rowlocks (Fig. 7).

From two Viking graves we have the remnants of decorative iron mounts from the ship. One of these graves is situated on the coast of France, the other in Denmark. In both cases, there is very little left of the ship itself. The sternpost ornament on a ship from a Swedish carved stone shows a close resemblance to the iron mounts from the French grave. It is fairly certain that this is what the iron mounts looked like when in use (Fig. 8).

The Oseberg ship shows us what the Viking Age woodcarver could achieve at his very best. The elaborate carvings are concentrated near the stem and stern. The coiled snake on the stem was found in fragments during the excavation, while the tail on the stern is a reconstruction. On the stem and sternpost, and on the upper strake near stem and stern, are carved a series of animals. These animals, four-legged with a body shaped like the figure eight, are all of the same main form, but no two are exactly alike. They twist together to form a rhythmic frieze (Fig. 2). On the inside of the stem are depicted three small men thoughtfully stroking their beards (Fig. 3).

In the sagas, golden vanes shining on the prow of the ship are sometimes spoken of, and vanes can be seen in several contemporary ship pictures. A few of these vanes are still preserved, having done service on church towers after being removed from the ships. One of the Norwegian ones, made of copper with rich gilding, probably dates from the first part of the eleventh century. On one side are engraved a couple of animals, probably lions, on the other an eagle (Fig. 9).

Very few traces of painting are preserved on the ships, but the written sources often speak of ships with red or golden 'dragons' heads' gleaming in the sun, and of one ship it is said that it is painted all over. This ship probably looked like the ships on the Bayeux tapestry, where the strakes seem to be painted in different colours.

Many modern artists have depicted Viking ships, often with great skill and care for correct detail, but in my opinion it has never been done better than by the nameless medieval artist in Bergen who carved a fleet of ships on a piece of wood. He lived a little later than the Viking Age, but the ships he shows us are surely warships, and they had not changed much since the Viking Age. This is the way a Viking fleet looked in all its splendour, most of the ships plain and businesslike, but with lovely lines, and some, probably the ships of the king and nobility, with 'dragon's heads' and weathervanes shining in the sun, red and golden.

1

1 *The Oseberg ship, built* c. *A.D. 800. Probably the ship was originally built as a yacht for the noblewoman for whose burial it was used* c. *A.D. 850*

2 *Detail of the prow of the Oseberg ship. The animals forming the frieze along the stem do not resemble any zoological species; they are the offspring of the artist's imagination*

3 *Human figures on the stem of the Oseberg ship*

2

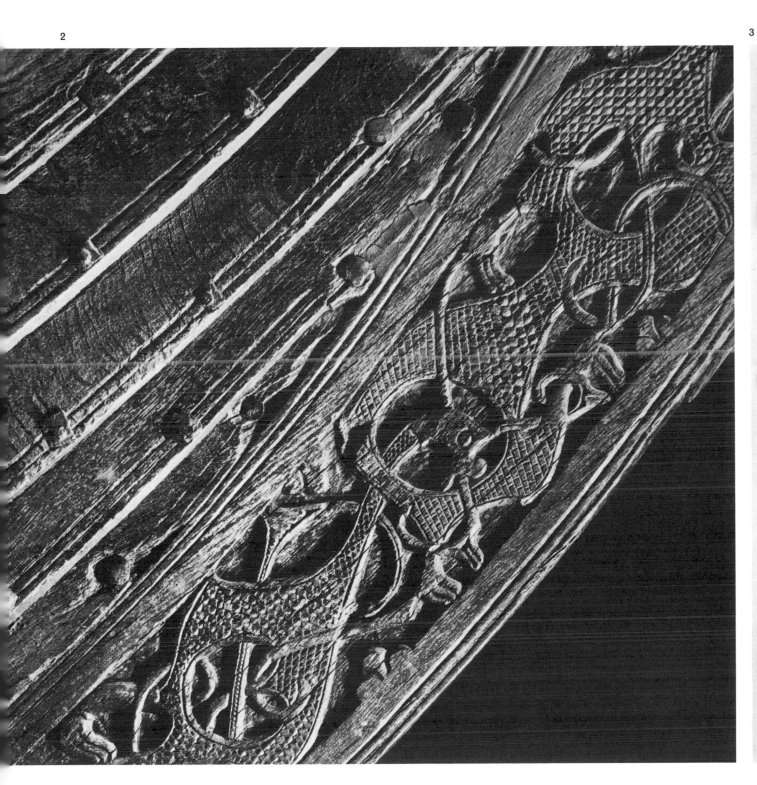

3

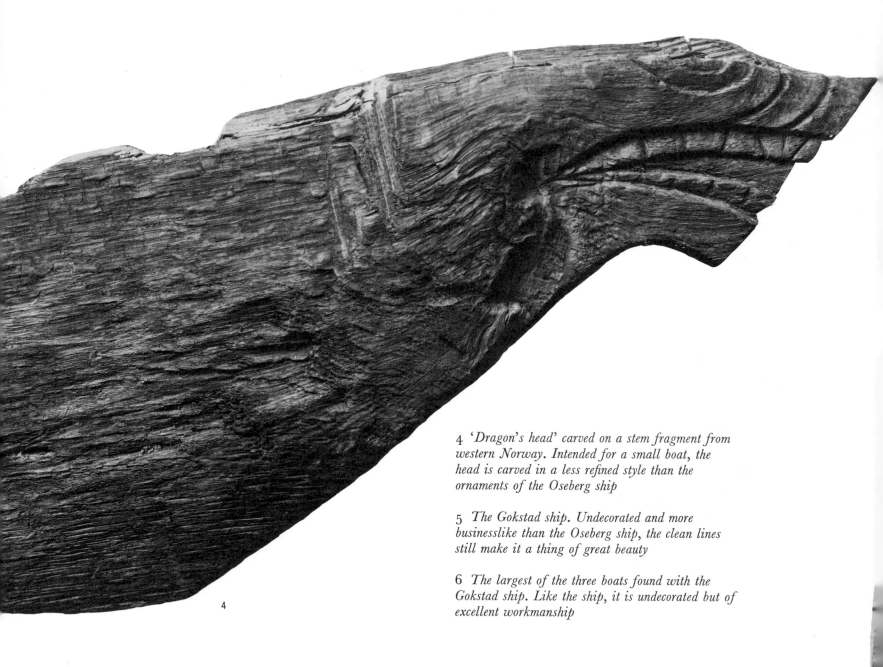

4

4 'Dragon's head' carved on a stem fragment from western Norway. Intended for a small boat, the head is carved in a less refined style than the ornaments of the Oseberg ship

5 The Gokstad ship. Undecorated and more businesslike than the Oseberg ship, the clean lines still make it a thing of great beauty

6 The largest of the three boats found with the Gokstad ship. Like the ship, it is undecorated but of excellent workmanship

5

6

7 *Stylized human mask on a rowlock from one of the small Gokstad boats. Some of the rowlocks carry different patterns*

8 *Ship carved on one of the 'picture-stones' from the island of Gotland, Sweden. The 'dragon's tail' on the stern probably carried decorative ironwork like the ones found in some Viking graves*

9 *Weathervane of richly gilded copper with engraved decorations, made during the first half of the eleventh century. It stood on the tower of Heggen Church, eastern Norway, until c. 1900. The holes along the curved edge were intended for fringes of cloth or sheet metal*

10 *A Viking fleet. This picture, carved on a scrap of wood by a medieval artist, gives a vivid impression of a fleet arranged in battle order*

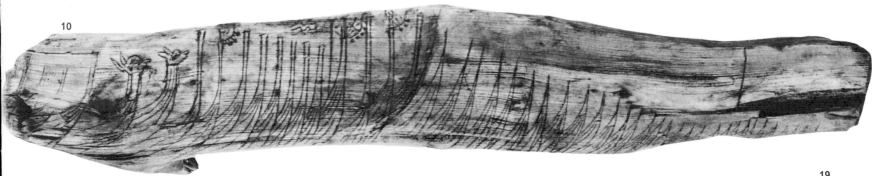

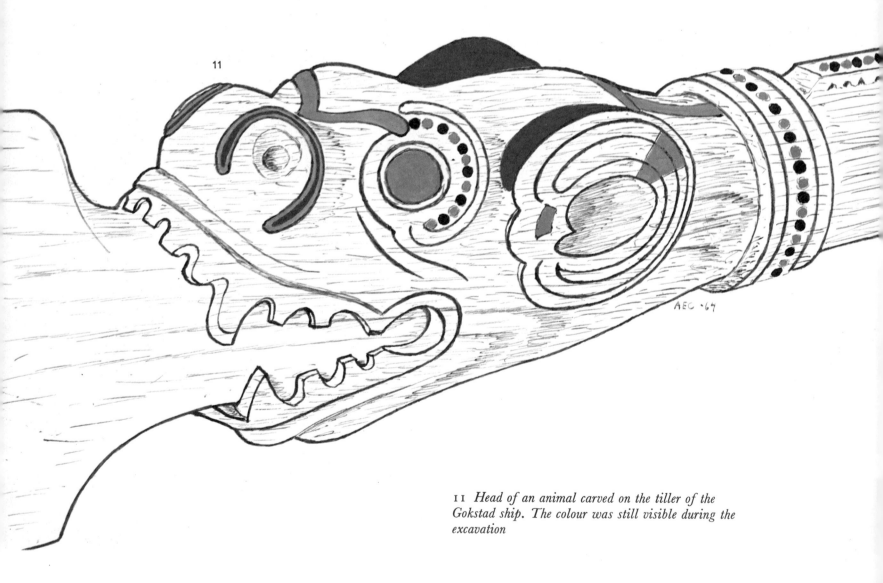

11 *Head of an animal carved on the tiller of the Gokstad ship. The colour was still visible during the excavation*

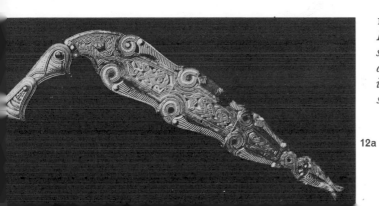

12 and 12a *Provisional reconstruction by the British Museum of the original shield buried in the ship-burial mound at Sutton Hoo, c. A.D. 650, and detail of the gilt bronze ornament, set with garnets, in the form of a winged dragon, on the front of the shield*

12a

13 and 14 *The Viking influence extended over much of Europe and these two scenes from the Bayeux tapestry show how the design of their longships continued into the eleventh and twelfth centuries, especially for war vessels with their high, decorated stem and sternposts*

13

14

CHAPTER III

VESSELS OF THE MEDITERRANEAN

ERNLE BRADFORD

Shipbuilders, ship-decorators and mariners themselves are among the most conservative people in the world. Once a design for a hull, or a device for decorating it, has proved satisfactory or acceptable by the sailors of the boat, it is very likely to continue in use not only for years but for centuries.

In that cradle of Western maritime art, the Mediterranean, it is only within recent years that hull-shapes and decorative devices have begun to alter in conformity with the new mechanical, or technological age. To give but one instance: when I first revisited the islands of Malta and Gozo shortly after the Second World War, I found that the two-masted lateen-rigged Gozo boats still made their way down to Valetta, Malta, laden with fruit and vegetables for the principal market—under sail.

Returning in 1964, I found that the boats were now powered by diesel engines—with short masts that could carry only steadying sails. But in respect of overall design, and indeed of decoration, they had changed hardly at all. Their elaborate gingerbread work and beautiful colours might be described by a 'time-and-motion' expert as unnecessary, and their hulls would be much more efficient for mechanical power if they were radically altered. But fortunately, in my opinion, the Mediterranean shipbuilder and craftsman retain too many memories of their past to discard them over-night.

If one remembers that ships have been active about this sea for some three thousand years, one is in a position to realize that it is not just innate conservatism which makes shipwrights and artificers, from Spain to Greece and the Levant, cling to ancient traditions. To them the twentieth century is no more than a wink of the eye—and it is 'The Eye' which still serves as a reminder on so many Mediterranean craft that it was from Crete, via Egypt and the East, that the craft of the boatbuilder and the mariner developed.

All along the North African shores, in the Maltese islands, the Aegean and southern Italy, and as far west as the Spanish peninsula, the *oculus* or 'Eye' is to be found carved—and often elaborately painted—on the bows of schooners, small motor vessels and rowing-boats. The usual reason given for its presence is that it enables the vessel to see her way. Up to a point there can be little doubt that it is this anthropomorphic aspect of 'The Eye' which has preserved it in popular favour

Gomppolder: Shotte of yron Sh

of Stert Bowes Bowestrynge

Men
mary
Gonn

Mbnici

for so many centuries. There is also good reason to believe that the *oculus* on a ship derives from the ancient Egyptian civilization, and that it is the eye of the hawk-god Horus which still preserves Mediterranean vessels while at sea. Few creatures are more keen-sighted than a hawk, and it was natural that the Egyptians should so grace their Nile barges, as well as their sea-going vessels which made the—for those days—'long' voyage down the Red Sea to Somaliland.

It is worth remarking that eyes on the bows of boats are more commonly found today in the Maltese islands and Sicily than anywhere else. This may well be ascribed to the immense residue of Phoenician craft and tradition—particularly in Malta and Gozo—to be found in these areas. (Malta was an important Phoenician colony, and the evidence of the island's ancestry is to be found not only in the decoration of its boats, but in the Phoenician roots of the language.)

Moving eastward to Greece and the Levant one finds that the style and decoration of the boats is considerably different. The Greeks, with that instinctive feeling for line and shape which has never deserted them, still produce some of the best-shaped hulls in the Mediterranean—as they have done for many centuries. They have at the same time something of the reticence and classical decorum of their ancestors when it comes to decoration. The Baroque has never belonged to Greece, and a working vessel will not attempt the decorative extravagances that are considered normal in the central part of this sea. Some schooners (powered, but using steadying sails) still have carved figureheads, but they are comparatively few. The attractive quality of Greek coastal traders, marred though it has been by the transition from sail to diesel power, lies very largely in their lines. Separated by the continent of Europe from those great seafarers, the Dutch, the Greeks in their almost equally short and obstinate seas have evolved a dish-shaped type of craft that is more picturesque than beautiful. They have been practical sailors first, and decorators second.

Throughout the whole history of Mediterranean sea-going craft it is essential to realize that, until the advent of mechanical power, all shape and design—and therefore, decoration—has been conditioned by the windless summer months when sail is useless. The galley, which had altered

relatively little since the days of Greece and Rome, survived in the Mediterranean into the nineteenth century.

The success of the sailing ship, as evolved in northern waters, put a final end to the galley, that lean greyhound of the sea. The design of a galley was basically that of a fast rowing-boat. Its long beak or ram in the bows, with its overhanging walk for gunners and raiding parties, gave this section of the ship a particular importance. At the same time, the steersman's position aft had hardly altered since the days of the Homeric heroes. It was here that the officers had their living place. From Roman times onwards, this after-end of a ship was carved into an elegant swan's neck shape. It was for these reasons, then, that the bows and the stern of oared galleys, as well as oared-and-sailing vessels such as galleasses, were the focal point of interest. They received most of the attention of the decorators.

The sides of a boat, subject to chafing and rubbing when she is lying alongside in a harbour or when she is working nets or other gear, remain simple and practical to this day. A gilded or painted line may continue the decoration of the fore-end of the ship to the after-end, but the working part of the boat is almost invariably left plain. Acanthus-leaf patterns, foliage generally, dolphins, snakes, dragons, squid and mythical sea-monsters are still found delineated on the bows and quarters of central Mediterranean boats.

In Greece and the Levant, as has been suggested, there is more instinct for form and line, and in the West—from the Balearics to Spain itself—the contact with the Atlantic and the pragmatic North has long since tended to efface a native instinct for decorative non-essentials. This is not to suggest that the northern countries of Europe did not, in their time, contribute greatly to the decorative art of the mariner. But it is interesting to note that their contribution, here as elsewhere in the 'purer arts', was more in the direction of baroque-style carving and, at any rate in the nineteenth century, the craft of decorative ropework. In the Mediterranean, on the other hand, one finds well-kept craft—in terms of paint and woodwork—but little or no attempt at fancy ropework.

In Sicily, southern Italy, Sardinia and Corsica there are still a number of traditional Mediterranean schooners. None of them relies any more upon its sails for anything except steadying canvas, but many of them still retain the decorative features of their ancestors. An athwartship bulkhead abaft the stubby bowsprit is not uncommon, while wooden bitts and cat-heads for securing the anchors still provide a place for the carver and painter to exercise their crafts. Most of these descendants of the sailing schooners still retain the graceful bow of their type. In the central Mediterranean especially, these are still decorated with cut-in lines of paint that accentuate their shark's mouth shape. Bright primary colours—red, yellow and blue—are as popular as they must have been in Homeric days, when we read of the 'blue' ships of the heroes. (Indigo has been one of the principal decorative colours used in the Mediterranean since pre-classical times.)

Quite apart from the decorations of the carver, many Mediterranean vessels still preserve purely magical ornaments which are placed aboard by the sailors. In Sicily, for instance, it is quite common to find branches of palm fixed to the mastheads—relics of Palm Sunday which are kept there throughout the year. Here, too, as well as in some parts of the Levant, one can still see bull's horns fixed to the mast. These are as ancient in origin as the *oculus*; deriving from 'the Horns of the Altar', and from the symbolism of the horns in ancient Minoan and Near Eastern art. Today, sailors consider them to be a preservative against the evil eye, and it is as such that they are found in ships along the North African coast.

Among the smaller craft in the Mediterranean, the Maltese *dghaisa* is one of the most colourful and unusual. With its stempost extended high in the air (so that it can be used for mooring-ropes), and its elegant lines, it is in every way as graceful as its near relative, the better-known Venetian gondola. One characteristic of the *dghaisa* must be remarked, since it is found in rowing-boats throughout the length and breadth of this sea: this is the fact that the oarsman rows standing up, facing the direction in which he is going. This rowing position possibly evolved in the Mediterranean because in its tideless waters there is far less chop and swell. This position would be almost impossible for a ferryman in a Channel port, but in a quiet Mediterranean harbour it is perfectly efficient, as well as being easier on the rower. In *dghaisas*, and indeed nearly all Mediterranean rowing-boats, the thole-pin and grommet is still in everyday use—in preference to the northern rowlock—just as it was in ancient Greece. This has inevitably led to the strengthening of the bulwarks of boats at this point, and often enough the cushion-pads in which the thole-pins sit have become minor decorative objects. In some boats, particularly those to be found in Gozo, this cushion and a permanent thole-pin in the bows have become part of the integral bulwark design: the forward thole-pins being used as secondary bitts or mooring-posts to the elevated stem itself.

Until comparatively recent years some of the most practical, wood-built schooners were to be found in the western Mediterranean—running often between the Balearic Islands and ports such as Barcelona. These had little of the decorative beauty of their central and eastern sisters. They had, however, a sturdy quality, sometimes bore figureheads, and quite often had gingerbread and carved work around their sterns. Unfortunately for the traditionalist, new Spanish shipping laws have frowned on the construction of any further wooden vessels. The sail has disappeared from Spanish waters almost as rapidly as from the French coast. The galley—something which had dominated the Mediterranean for so many centuries—is hardly even reflected in rowing-boats or small local fishing craft in this part of the sea today.

On the west coast of Italy, as well as around parts of Sicily, there still remain a few unique types of vessel. Most unusual of all these is the sword-fishing boat evolved for work in the Messina Strait, with its immensely tall mast and its bowsprit and catwalk that are often longer than the vessel itself. The lateen rig and even the standing gaff (with its mainsail that is hauled out along the gaff by a tricing line) are still sometimes to be found in northern Italy, but nowadays these are usually old and poorly kept boats: the decoration that once embellished them has long since been forgotten. On the east coast of Italy, the Yugoslavian shores, and occasionally in the Aegean, one still meets the *trabacola*: shallow-draughted, broad-beamed, and the Mediterranean equivalent of a Dutch *boeier*. When these are well kept, they can display elaborate carving on bulwarks and bows and stern. In the main, sad to say, they have become second-grade local cargo-carriers and are disappearing from the scene.

The past twenty-five years have witnessed the decline and

disappearance of much that was beautiful and unusual in the decoration of Mediterranean sailing-boats and oared craft. Only in comparatively few places can one still find the traditional skills, patterns and usages of colour being applied to hulls that have hardly changed since Phoenician, Greek or Roman times. Happily, on the other hand, so attractive are many of these traditional craft that the advent of tourism in the Mediterranean islands and seaboard—far from banishing these traditional skills—is helping to preserve them.

2

2 *The* Salamander, *also from the roll of ships drawn by Anthony Anthony for Henry VIII*

3 *Portuguese caravels of the fifteenth century. The lateen rig was developed from the lateen used for centuries by the Arabs but the hull shape was largely determined by Atlantic conditions, as the Portuguese were just beginning to open up the Atlantic coasts of Africa*

3

4 *Neapolitan galleys as shown in part of the Armada tapestry. Detail of the painting on p. 43*

5 *A Turkish carrack. From a medieval drawing in the St Peter papers in Karlsruhe*

Die waffen stund herussen vor   modon sagt man das sin sin
acht hundert moern so al   von den türken erkoufft
warent für aichw elend   lüt / der türke stattz ma
hie hundet sinsi türra   gen modon vn kostend vil
                                       ergsen vnd and ding das tö
                                       glich türe ward ze mace

RESENTATION de la Galere Reale
ce, Et de son Armement

CANONS

rance a Sept Canons de Prouë qui sont le -
uez au Milieu de 4 Bastardes et 2 Perriers

Perriers, a chaque Escale Vn

BANCZ

Bancz desquelz il n'y en a que 28 Fournis de
quatre d'Vn costé Seruans a mettre le Fougon ou
ne, et les 4 de l'autre costé a mettre la cage

FORCATZ

ame ayant Sept Forcats chaque Banc, qui sont
nes .... 392 Forcatz

OFFICIERS

aux 28
arance 10
igation 14
les 70

e total tant des Officiers Principaux Et
que de Mariniers 128

SOLDATS

alestilles a deux Soldats chacune 128
ve 26
ë 20
Bateau 12
fort 40

total des Soldats. 226

des Hommes qui sont sur lace 746
415 pour la Vogue Et nauigation - Et
mbat

REPRESENTATION de la Galere, com
d'Espagne, Et de son Armement

CANONS

La Galere commune d'Espagne a cinq Canons de Prouë q
le canon de courcier entre 4 Bastardes

FORCATZ

Elle a 26 Bancz a 5 forçatz pour Banc estant QuinqueRa
de l'Arbre a poupe faisant .... 130 fo
Elle a 26 Bancs a 4 forcatz pour banc estant Quadriram
l'Arbre a proue faisant 104

Nombre total des Forçatz 234

OFFICIERS

Officiers Principaux 26
Mariniers 60

Nombre total des Officiers
Et Mariniers 86

SOLDATZ

Pour les 52 Arbalestilles .... 52 Soldatz
Soldatz de Pouppe 16
Soldatz pour la Rambade de Proue 12
Soldatz de Reserue 26

Nombre total des Soldatz 106

Nombre total des hommes qui sont Sur Vne Galere
commune d'Espagne 426. desquelz il y en a 260 pou
Vogue, et Nauigation, Et 166 pour le Combat

6 and 6a *A Galley Royal of France and a common galley of Spain. The vessels are very similar except that the Galley Royal is more ornately decorated and carries the larger complement as befits her exalted station*

7 *Venetian gondola with a single rower. The laws of Venice required that all gondolas should be unornamented and painted black*

7

8 *The Annual Regatta on the Grand Canal in Venice, by Canaletto*

9 *The galley of the Grand Master of the Knights of St John under oars. This is the galley of the brothers Rafaele and Nicolo Cottoner, successively Grand Masters, 1660–3 and 1663–80*

10 *The Grand Galley of Grand Master Pinto (1741–73) under oars and sail*

11 *The Grand Galley of Grand Master de Rohan (1775–97) under full sail*

8

Gran Galera dei Gran Maestri Rafaele e Nicolò Cottoner.

9

Gran Galione del Gran Maestro dell'Ordine G.º F. Emmanuel Pinto.

10

11

Gran Galione del Gran Maestro dell'Ordine Ger.º Fr. Emmanuel de Rohan.

12 *A tartan, with a view of Europa Point,
Gibraltar*

13 *Maltese dghaisas in Grand Harbour; a dying race of craft now that the Mediterranean Fleet is no more*

14 *A flying fish with a bird's head decorates the bow of this working boat*

13

14

15 *A Royal Tapestry of Spain depicting the Spanish galleys off Tunis*

16 *The distinctive bright colours, decorative paintwork and* oculus *on the bows of a Maltese rowing-boat*

15

17 *The elaborately carved and decorated* San Giorgio *is run ashore in the same manner that Mediterranean craft have been beached since Homeric days*

18 *Fishing boats in Marsa Sirocco, Malta*

17

18

CHAPTER IV

SAILING SHIPS OF THE ATLANTIC SEAS

Lt.-Cdr. P. K. KEMP, R.N.

It would be easy to suggest that the art of decoration in ships, when it reached the Atlantic, was inherited from the earlier vessels of the Mediterranean. Egyptian, Greek and Roman ships had a long tradition of elaborate decoration, and at first sight it seems reasonable to suppose that the practice spread naturally from ocean to ocean. In fact, however, there is no substantial evidence that this is so, and the decoration of contemporary Mediterranean ships and of medieval Atlantic ships has remarkably few points in common.

It is more probable that early Atlantic ship decoration sprang naturally from two main causes, and quite irrespective of the Mediterranean precedents. One was the contemporary love of pageantry which swept the European nations in the earlier centuries of their development; the other was the inherent beauty of the ship herself in her functional aspect, which lent itself to natural embellishment in the form of gay colours, elaborate carving and gold leaf to enhance an already beautiful shape. Subsidiary causes probably arose from religious fervour, expressed in carvings of saints and other Biblical motifs; from the love of allegory, which expressed itself in representations of gods and goddesses whose virtues would thus be incorporated into the ship herself; and from superstition, giving rise to the use of decorative designs to placate the spirits of the sea who, though acknowledged by the educated even in medieval days as mythical, yet found a wide measure of belief among seafaring men.

This chapter deals mainly with ship decoration in the Atlantic sailing ships, taking note of other decorative aspects such as votive offerings, china and glass and the like. If in the main it illustrates British practice in ship decoration, this is because the chief and most important source of contemporary information lies in the vast mass of Navy Board papers and Admiralty draughts now preserved in the Public Record Office and the National Maritime Museum, the most considerable and detailed archive on this subject in existence in the world. This, however, is not as exclusive as it may appear, for in the great days of ship decoration, British fashions were widely copied in the ships of France, Holland, Spain and Sweden. Thus there appeared a considerable degree of universality among the ships of those nations which used the Atlantic in their search for maritime supremacy.

The earliest form of ship decoration took the shape of painted sails, hulls and pavesses. The painting of sails developed from the simple striped sails of the Norse ships to the heraldic mainsails of the fourteenth and fifteenth centuries. One of the ships shown in the Bayeux tapestry carries a sail decorated with a Sun in Splendour, the emblem adopted a century later by Richard Cœur-de-Lion to decorate the sails of his ships. Another two centuries on, and the whole area of the sail is being used to display armorial bearings. The Rous Roll in the British Museum gives evidence of this, and one of its illustrations shows the Earl of Warwick, 'Kingmaker' and Lord High Admiral of England, leading his fleet to sea. The entire mainsail of his ship is charged with the Neville arms, in blue, red, gold and white, while an immense pendant flutters from the masthead. The ship herself is the contemporary high-charged ship with fore and after-castles decorated in the traditional manner with pavesses.

Hulls were usually painted in horizontal stripes, one stripe to each strake. Again the Bayeux tapestry provides the evidence, although it is not possible to be certain that the colours there are necessarily correct, for the Queen and her ladies were obviously limited by the colours of their wools. It was not until carvel construction superseded clench that an entire body colour was used for the hull. And even then, a painted frieze was almost invariably introduced above the main body colour along the upper wale. The effect of this can be seen in the reproductions of Elizabethan ship designs from the *Fragments of Ancient English Shipwrightry*, among the Pepysian MSS in Magdalene College, Cambridge.

Pavesses, which in earlier ships were normally limited to the sides of fore and after-castles only, and only later were extended to the waists, descend directly from the shield bulwarks of the Viking ships. They were wooden shields made from poplar, which did not splinter when hit by a musket ball. Their purpose originally was to afford some protection to the archers massed on the fore and after-castles, but later their sole use was decorative. They were painted with the arms of the knights or other notable persons on board, or else displayed national or local insignia.

Flags, pendants and immensely long streamers were a natural form of decoration which lasted well into the eigh-teenth century. The illustration of the *Henry Grace à Dieu*, launched in 1514, which appears in the Anthony Roll, shows her flying no fewer than twenty flags and nine pendants or streamers. No expense was spared when it came to the pro-vision of flags, as an account in the Sloane MSS (BM2450) shows: 'To Lewis Lydgard of London, painter, the 28 January 1587 for the price of 102 yards of calico had for the making of two great flags, stained in colours with Her Majesty's arms, to be worn at sea in the ship the Lord Admiral sails in, at 9d. every yard, 3l. 16s. 6d. More for the sewing and making up of them, 10s. And more to him for the stain-ing of the said flags with colours, and the charge for bringing the same from London to Queenborough, 6l. 16s. 8d. Summa, 11l. 1s. 2d.' Eleven pounds was a very considerable sum in Elizabeth I's reign, the equivalent of some hundreds of pounds today.

Apart from painted sails, which in any case were usually limited to ships actually carrying important noblemen, painted hulls, pavesses, and a large number of flags, banners and pendants, the early Atlantic ships had little external decoration. Sometimes, on occasions of state, a gaily coloured pavilion was erected on the quarterdeck, usually with striped awnings, but this was not a usual feature unless an expression of temporary magnificence was to be made. Royal ships always carried a gilt crown on the masthead, and sometimes on the beakhead. These were relatively expensive decorations, and in the Exchequer Warrants for 1492 there is mention of a payment of £5 10s. to Robert Duke of Greenwich for new gilding 'a corone of laten [a compound of copper and brass] which shalbe sett upon our shippe called the *Regent*'. Also in royal ships, usually on the capstan but sometimes on the bowsprit, were gilt fleurs-de-lis, an indication that the King also held sovereignty over parts of France. In the Augmen-tation Office book containing the accounts of Robert Brygandyne between 1495 and 1497, there is an item for three 'fflowredelyeez gylte' for the 'Kynges Ship Ryall called the *Soueraigne*'. An earlier set of Exchequer accounts show that the *Holigost*, of some eighty years earlier, also carried three gilt fleurs-de-lis on her capstan. A note, quoted by Nicolas, says that she was painted with 'swans, antelopes and divers arms, also with the royal motto called *Une sanz pluis* in divers parts of the said shippe'. The cost of this

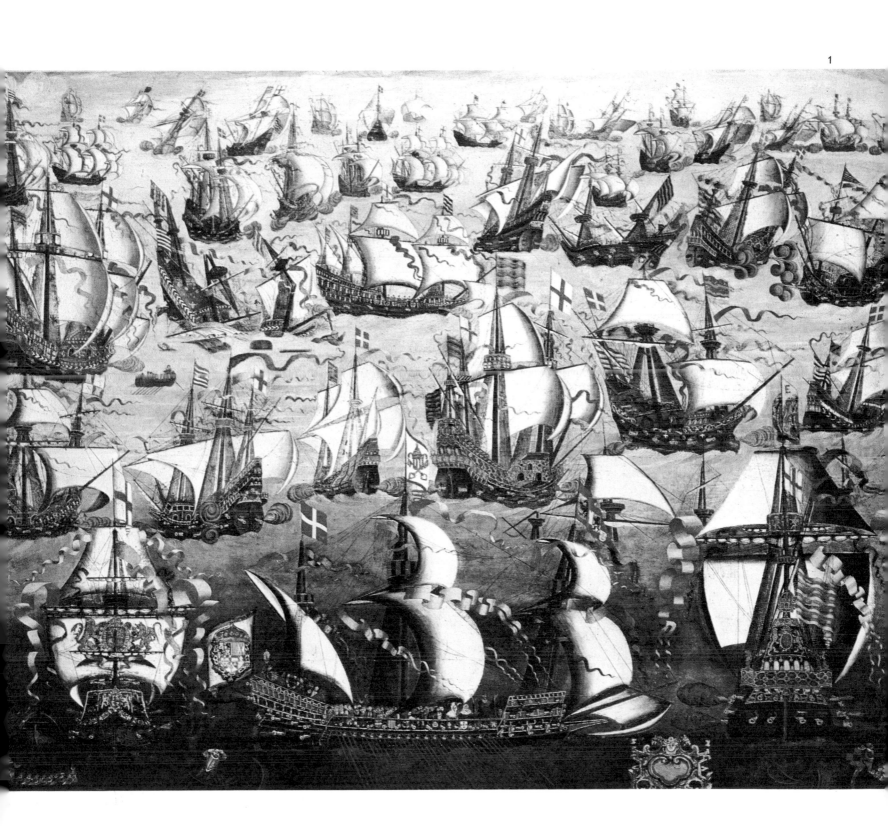

painting was £7 6s. 8d. This would make her one of the earliest ships in which the painted decoration departed from the conventional full body colour with a painted frieze above it.

One of the earliest known examples of a decorated stern is that of the royal ship, the *Trinity*, launched in 1400, which was ornamented with four carved figures of St George, St Anthony, St Catherine and St Margaret, together with four shields bearing the royal arms, all within a collar of gold. This degree of stern ornamentation was unusual at so early a date, particularly with carving taking the place of painting, though there are some examples of carved crowns placed on the counters of royal ships of the period. The *Trinity* was painted red externally, a body colour which seems to have been reserved for royal ships although not all of them were painted in it. Speaking generally, the sterns of European ships of the fifteenth and sixteenth centuries were not sufficiently large to carry much decoration (a poop deck above the quarterdeck was a comparatively late development) and most of them had no more than a little formal carving of a repeat pattern on the counter-brackets and the bulwark.

The great age of ship decoration began in England with the reign of Henry VIII, reached its peak with the magnificent carvings which decorated the ships of England, France, Holland and Spain during the seventeenth century, and declined slowly throughout the eighteenth and early nineteenth centuries. Not every ship, of course, carried the same lavish degree of carved ornamentation as, for instance, the *Prince Royal* or the *Sovereign of the Seas*, but all royal ships except the smallest, and most of the East Indiamen of England, France and Holland, had elaborately decorated sterns and quarter galleries and carved trailboards. The documentation of this period is immense, not only in the Navy Board papers mentioned above but also in the pictures of such great marine artists as the two Van de Veldes, Vroom, Puget and many others, and in the detailed models which exist in profusion in the maritime museums of the world.

The main feature of Elizabethan ship decoration was the gay painting of the fore and after-castles, often giving a Moorish impression of columns and arcades. Both castles, at the start of Elizabeth's reign, were open structures set on arches, designed partly as a tradition of ship ornament and partly to provide light and fresh air to the decks below. This open design lent itself admirably to highly coloured painting in geometric patterns, or to alternating armorial designs set in gilded frames. In the later Elizabethan ship designs, especially after Sir John Hawkins had eliminated the high forecastle to improve the ship's sailing qualities, the geometrical fashion in painting gave way to a much more elaborate system of decoration, in which carvings and gilded ornamentation took pride of place. Carvings were usually of religious figures or of the Queen's Beasts, with a generous proportion of the royal arms interspersed.

The shape of the stern had, of course, a profound effect on the type of decoration used. Until about 1615 the normal stern in English ships had a square tuck, the later examples having a succession of counters, each projecting a little further beyond the rudder head than the one below. The *Prince Royal*, Phineas Pett's masterpiece of 1610, has the square tuck and immensely high-built stern, but ships of only five or ten years later—the *Sovereign of the Seas* is an example—show the round stern which became such a feature of English sailing ships. These gave as much accommodation, because they were wider, on two decks as the high square stern did on four. French ships began to follow this new English design around 1670; the Dutch maintained the square stern until about 1720. Scandinavian ships closely followed the Dutch pattern throughout.

The ornamentation of the square stern, while always intricate and lavish, lost much of its majestic beauty because of the high narrow frame in which it had to be set. The round stern, on the other hand, with its better proportions and its wide bands of lights or its open galleries, presented a wonderful opportunity of merging purely decorative carving with the functional aspect of the lights along the stern and quarter galleries, which in themselves were things of beauty.

Stern galleries began to show themselves in the ships of Henry VIII and Edward VI, but they did not reach what might be called their maturity until the wider rounded stern arrived to displace the narrow square stern. Elizabethan ships almost invariably had only one gallery; two galleries only began to appear right at the end of her reign. Although the *Prince Royal* had three, this was an exception which never appeared as a general practice until, much later, the size

2 *King Richard's voyage to Ireland in 1399, with the* Sun in Splendour *emblem painted on the sail of his ship*

of the average first-rate rose from around 1,000 tons to more than double that figure. The great majority of ships throughout the seventeenth and eighteenth centuries were content with two galleries only.

Admiralty models and draughts illustrate how stern decoration developed. The *Sovereign of the Seas*, one of the earliest ships built with a rounded stern, is of course the choicest example of the intricate work expected of the carver during the reigns of the first two Stuart kings (Fig. 3). The Admiralty draughts of the sterns of HMS *Atlas*, of 1782, and of the Spanish *Phoenix*, launched thirty years earlier, both show the carver blending in his work with the natural beauty of stern lights and galleries. The same restraint in decoration and natural use of lights were also a feature of American ships, as the draught of the frigate *Raleigh*, launched in 1779, shows. The stern of the *Victory* is another fine example of the art of the carver in adapting his skill to the natural frame presented to him.

The cost of carving had, of course, a great deal to do with the decrease in elaboration which is so noticeable from the beginning of the eighteenth century. The Pipe Office accounts for the *Prince Royal* show that Sebastian Vicars was paid £441 for the carvings and Robert Beake and Paul Isackson £868 7s. for painting and gilding. Twenty-five years later the decoration of the *Sovereign of the Seas* was nearly six times as much, costing the King £6,691. The *Sovereign of the Seas*, however, was hardly a typical ship of the times. She was, to begin with, more than half as big again as the biggest ship yet built so far in England; she was a dream of Charles I brought to life by Phineas Pett; she was built as something of a showpiece of English naval architecture. All her carving was covered with gold leaf, and when she was finally launched there was more carving on her stern, sides and bulkheads than there was plain timber.

Obviously a halt would have to be called somewhere if so great a proportion of building costs was to be swallowed up by the carvers and gilders, and although ships built during the Commonwealth did not lack decoration, it was never on so lavish a scale as the *Prince Royal* and the *Sovereign of the Seas*. One of the economies discovered during the Commonwealth period was that gold paint looked just as effective as gold leaf at a fraction of the cost.

Costs naturally differed from ship to ship, but taking a broad average during the reign of William III, when naval ship decoration reached its peak of magnificence, they varied from £896 for a first-rate to £52 for a sixth-rate. These sums included the cost of painting, which was always higher than that of carving, possibly because of the painted frieze along the upper wale which was only just beginning to die out.

The continuing search for naval economies caused the Navy Board to step in with an order, dated 4 November 1700, placing a ceiling on the sums which could be spent on carving and painting. This varied from £500 for a first-rate to £25 for a sixth. At the current prices, this still allowed a profusion of decoration. Three years later, still looking for economies, the Navy Board tackled the problem from the other end. The axe fell with an order dated 16 June 1703:

> That the carved works be reduced to only a lion and trailboard for the head, with mouldings instead of brackets placed against the timbers; that the stern have only a tafferel and two quarterpieces, and in lieu of brackets between the lights of the stern, galleries and bulkheads, to have mouldings fixed against the timbers; that the joiners' works of the sides of the great cabin, coach, wardroom and round-house of each ship be fixed only with slip deals without any sort of moulding or cornice; and the painting to be only plain colour.

Oddly enough, this purely English order had an effect all over Europe. By 1700, English ships were being recognized by other European countries as models of naval architecture, and the fashions set in England were closely followed on the Continent.

Although this order sounds severe, it still left room for plenty of decoration. Figures applicable purely to carving and painting are not easy to discover in the immediately following years, but the few which have come to light suggest that no great savings were effected. The *Royal George*, first-rate of 100 guns launched in 1715, cost £323 7s. for carvings and £273 5s. 10½d. for painting; the figures for the *Britannia*, another 100-gun first-rate of 1719, were £290 5s. and £179 18s. 11d. respectively. Comparable costs for the *Princess Louisa*, a sixth-rate of forty guns, were £26 17s. and

£40 12s. 2d. In 1737 the Navy Board issued a new order, stabilizing the cost of carving at £166 12s. for a first-rate down to £37 2s. 4d. for a sixth. The cost of carving remained around these figures for the rest of the century.

What these Navy Board orders did was to put a ban on most of the extraneous pieces of carving which so typified the earlier ships. It can be said with a good deal of truth that the carvers employed on ship decoration in the sixteenth and seventeenth centuries never left a piece of timber bare that could in any way be carved. Now all these oddments were to disappear. The cat-heads, for example, which were projections from the bow on which the anchors were hung, were always decorated in the early ships, and when later the cat-heads were supported by brackets, these too carried a small amount of decorative carving.

The three great lanterns carried on the stern were another source of natural decoration, though English practice never reached the degree of elaboration which can be seen in French, Spanish and Dutch ships of the seventeenth and early eighteenth centuries. English ships were the first to adopt a standard pattern of stern lantern, and after about 1715 a hexagonal shape, with very occasionally an octagonal variant, was the rule.

Hancing pieces, which made their first appearance in ships of the Tudor period, were another obvious means of adding decoration to the ship. A hance is a step where the rail on a ship's side drops to a lower level. Such a step, if unfilled, is square and unsightly, and so a hancing piece is introduced to round it off. Up to about 1700, hancing pieces were usually combined with long drop carvings, often in the form of the human figure, but the Navy Board order of 1703 curbing excessive decoration effectively banished these long drop carvings, and hancing pieces became greatly simplified as a result.

The upper tier of gunports in naval ships were almost invariably wreathed, certainly on the half-deck and fore-castle, and frequently along the whole of the upper deck. Square wreaths were not uncommon in Commonwealth and Stuart ships, but with William III the round wreath became normal ship practice. This was an English design which was widely copied in several European nations, but it never achieved there quite the universal use which it enjoyed in England. The order of 1703 removed it from the upper-deck ports, but it was retained for the quarterdeck ports for another forty years or so.

As the size of warships grew from single-deckers to two or three-deckers, the necessity for an entering port gave yet another opportunity to the carvers to demonstrate their skill. In the earlier smaller ships it was a simple enough operation to mount the steps built into the ship's side and clamber in over the nettings, but in a three-decker this was a considerable undertaking. So an entering port was established on the middle deck, usually with a platform supported on a bracket at cill level and a canopy supported on pillars or brackets overhead. These were, of course, decorated, and remained so in spite of the 1703 order until well into the nineteenth century. The ornate pillars of the seventeenth century, usually carved in human form, gave way to square pillars in the eighteenth, but if the decoration in these years was more austere, it still remained there in a dignified simplicity.

Lights, or windows, were cut in the ship's side in the cabin spaces as early as the reign of James I, and increased in number over the next century or so. More often than not they were arched, with a simple decoration of a carved shell or the royal initials. Chesstrees, which were external timber fittings through which the main tack was led inboard, were invariably carved for as long as their use continued, sometimes in the form of a human face or a fox's mask, with the tack being led through the mouth, sometimes in the form of a Sun in Splendour.

Merchant ships largely followed naval fashions in decoration, though in general on a much reduced scale. Simple patterns were carved on the sterns as frames to the gallery lights; trailboards, which in the royal ships were often carved with Biblical scenes or allegorical figures, were decorated with mouldings of simple volute forms. Even quite small fishing craft usually had a little rudimentary carving on bow and stern. The exceptions were the lordly ships of the East India Companies, English, Dutch and French. They were usually as highly decorated as the royal ships of the same period, and Fig. 16 illustrates a good example of the elaborate carving with which these aristocratic merchant vessels were adorned.

So far in this chapter we have examined only the decoration

3 *Peter Pett and the* Sovereign of the Seas. *Attributed to Peter Lely.* The Sovereign of the Seas *was launched in 1637. After the Restoration in 1660 she was known as the* Royal Sovereign. *She was burnt by accident at Chatham in 1696*

1   2   3   4

4

carried by the ships themselves. But there was throughout the whole period under review just as flourishing and elaborate a maritime decorative movement ashore. This was only to be expected in countries whose history and wealth were bound up in the sea, a state which embraced most of Europe, with the exception of the central states of the Holy Roman Empire, and the eastern states of the American continent. Coming so late into the maritime field, of course, there is not the same richness and variety to be found in America as there is in Europe.

Silver and crystal models of ships, of the type known as nefs, were much prized on medieval tables to hold napkins and the salt—a commodity which in those days was rare and precious and thus thought worthy of a glittering receptacle. These nefs were mounted on wheels for ease of passing down the table, and were masterpieces of the art of the silversmith and the worker in glass. One of the most famous examples of these is the Burghley Nef, illustrated in Fig. 28.

Medieval ships were often used to form the seals of many English and Continental towns and boroughs, and buildings did not escape the urge for maritime decoration; the fouled Admiralty anchor, seal of the Lord High Admiral of England from the time of Howard of Effingham, can still be found sculpted on walls and gateways. Church fonts can show many examples of ships and other maritime decoration on their sides.

Perhaps the most famous of all such decoration used ashore is the Grinling Gibbons carving which adorns the fireplace of the old Admiralty Board Room. The main motif of this elaborate carving is based on the navigational instruments of the late seventeenth century, not only beautifully and accurately portrayed but also in full working order. Almost equally famous, though of a later period, is the immense suite of 'Dolphin' or 'Fish' furniture, made by William Collins of Tothill Fields, which was presented to Greenwich Hospital and is now in Admiralty House in Whitehall.

Of the more intimate forms of maritime decorative art, perhaps the votive offering is most worthy of notice. These range from elaborate stained-glass windows to crude models of ships, but behind them all lies the sailor's prayer for deliverance from the dangers of the sea, or his thanks for safe return from a voyage. In many churches along the

Atlantic seaboard, both east and west, hang models made by seamen of the ships in which they sailed, brought reverently for a blessing and left as an offering for divine protection. The famous church of Notre-Dame-de-la-Garde, which stands nobly above the port of Marseilles, is but one example of many. In it can be seen the offerings of seamen, often crude and simple models of their ships, which nevertheless take on a mysterious beauty in the setting in which they hang.

Table glass was another favourite medium for maritime

5

decoration. The earliest decorated glasses date back to the Stuart years, but this form of decoration persisted at least up to Napoleonic times. The occasion of much of this particular decoration was the practice of commemorating the commissioning of privateers with goblets on which was cut a representation of the ship, while around the rim was cut the legend 'Success to the Privateer . . . .' Decanters were similarly decorated.

One could go on almost for ever. Ships in glass bottles, decorated china and pottery, silver and glass models, binnacle lights, bells, dolphins and other fish, all owe their decorative origin to a deep-seated interest and love of the maritime affair in all its aspects. There is a basic beauty in the ship and in the sea that lends itself naturally to decorative purposes. The sailor's desire to beautify the ship in which he lives spreads naturally to a desire to repeat that beauty ashore. At sea, that desire reached its peak in the Restoration years and during the succeeding reign of William III; ashore the maritime influence still holds its place among the decorative arts of the nations.

6

7 *First Rate off Deptford, by John Cleveley the Elder. Signed and dated 1757. The ship is similar to the Royal George built in 1756, but there are variations from the known model which make identification doubtful. So far as is known, the* Royal George *never went up the river as far as Deptford*

8 *Elizabethan galleon, probably the* Ark Royal *of 1587. From* Ancient English Shipwrightry, *Pepys MSS Collection*

9 and 10 *Elizabethan galleons. From* Ancient English Shipwrightry, *Pepys MSS Collection*

11 *Elizabethan ship hull. From* Ancient English Shipwrightry, *Pepys MSS Collection*

7

12 *The* Henry Grace à Dieu *as she is shown in the Anthony Roll, with her flags and pennants flying*

13 *Stern and quarter-galleries of an English two-decker, probably the* Destiny, *34 guns, which was Raleigh's ship on his last voyage, and renamed* Convertine *before her sale to Portugal in 1650. From a drawing by Van de Velde the Younger*

12

14 *The stern carvings of the French ship* Royal Louis. *From a model in the Musée de la Marine, Paris*

15 *A Dutch decorated stern of 1664. This is the* Hollandia, *82 guns, flagship of De Ruyter and Tromp in the Second Dutch War*

16 *The decorated stern of an East Indiaman belonging to the Dutch Company. The date of the model is 1725* ˙

15

16

17 *Decorated cat-heads:* (a) *and* (b) *English;* (c) *Dutch*

18 *Dutch hancing pieces*

19 *English hancing pieces*

17

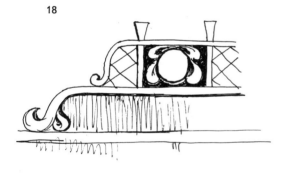

a

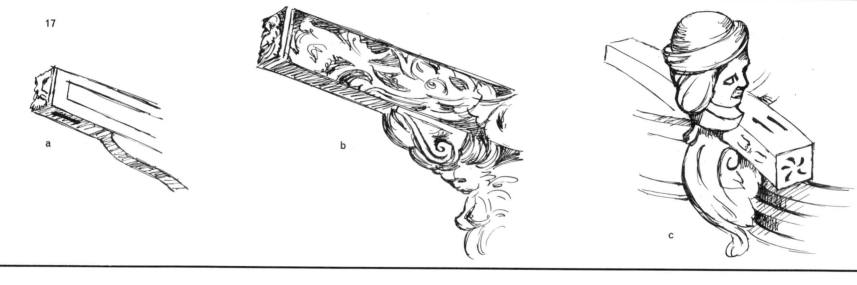

b

c

18

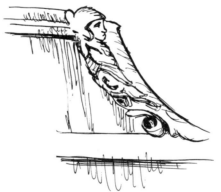

19

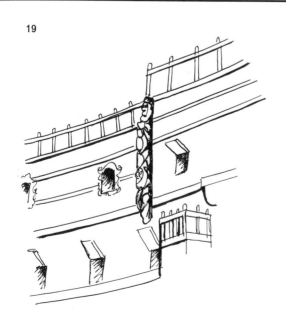

20 *English stern lanterns*

21 *English wreathed ports*

22 *English entering ports:* (a) *HMS* Prince, *launched in 1670;* (b) *HMS* Royal Anne, *launched in 1670 and rebuilt 1704;* (c) *HMS* Victory, *launched in 1765*

20

21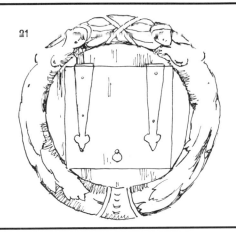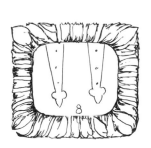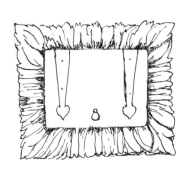

22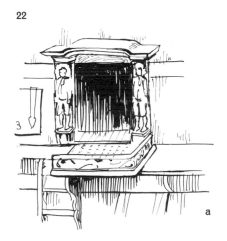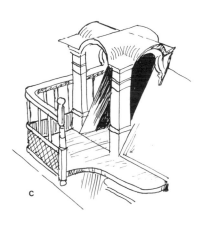

a   b   c

23 *Chesstrees:* (a) *English;* (b) *Dutch;* (c)
English

24 *English lights*

25 *French decorated sterns, eighteenth century*

26 *The Grinling Gibbons carving in the Board
Room, Old Admiralty Building. The navigational
instruments are all working models*

23

a

b

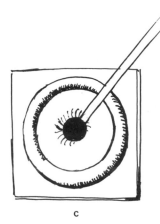

c

24

25

27 *A typical religious card showing a French sailor offering a model of his ship to Our Lady for divine protection. These religious cards were carried by many sailors*

28 *The Burghley Nef. These medieval nefs were used in lordly families to carry the salt and the napkins*

29 *A Portuguese carrack in gold filigree, presented to HMS* Dolphin *by the Portuguese submarine service*

27

28

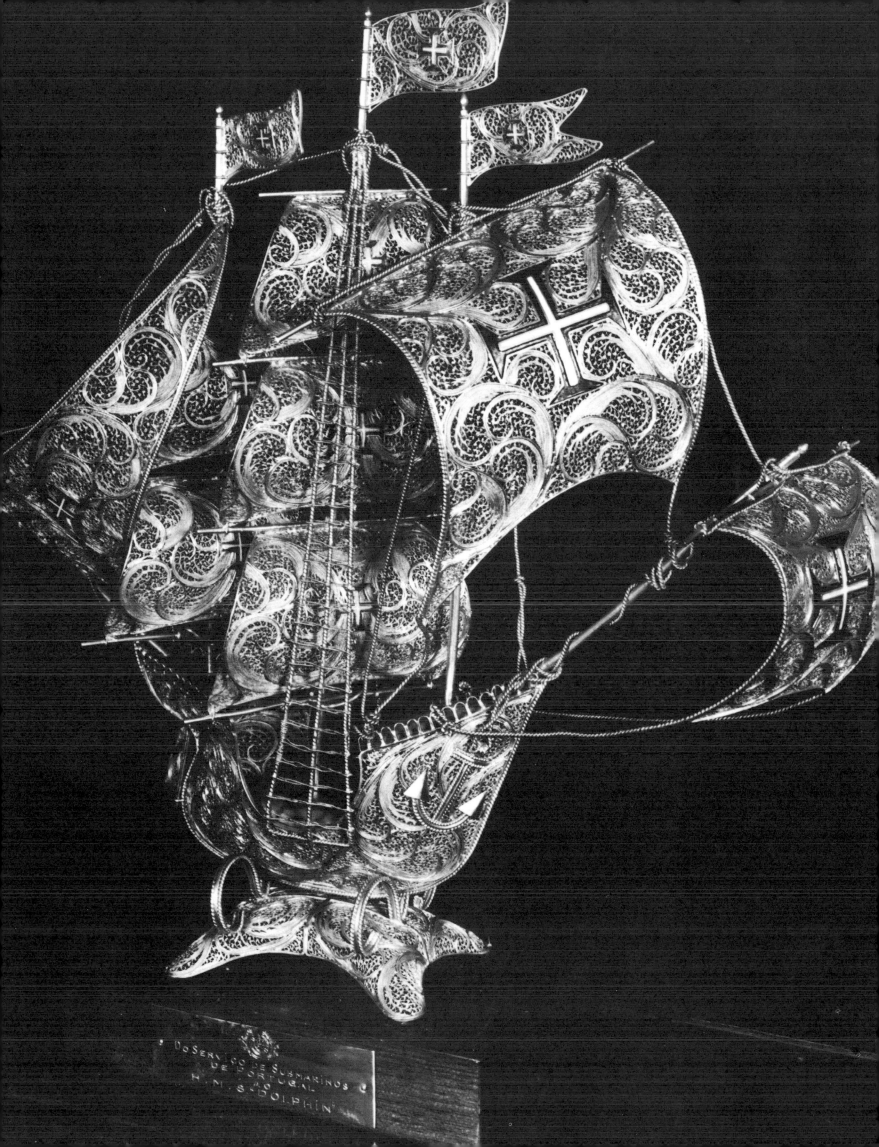

Do Serviço de Submarinos
de Portugal
H. M. S. "DOLPHIN"

30 *Stern and quarter gallery of the American frigate* Raleigh, *captured 1779. Admiralty draught*

31 *Stern and quarter gallery of the French third rate* Téméraire, *captured 1759. Admiralty draught*

30

31

32 English Third Rates in a Squall, c. *1675:*
studio of Van de Velde the Younger

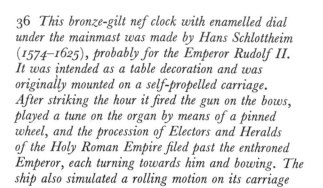

33 *Carved tiller of unknown origin*

34 *Stern of HMS* Atlas, *first rate of 98 guns, launched in 1782. Admiralty draught*

35 *Stern of Spanish second rate* Fenix, *launched in 1749 and captured in 1780, when she was renamed HMS Gibraltar. Admiralty draught*

36 *This bronze-gilt nef clock with enamelled dial under the mainmast was made by Hans Schlottheim (1574–1625), probably for the Emperor Rudolf II. It was intended as a table decoration and was originally mounted on a self-propelled carriage. After striking the hour it fired the gun on the bows, played a tune on the organ by means of a pinned wheel, and the procession of Electors and Heralds of the Holy Roman Empire filed past the enthroned Emperor, each turning towards him and bowing. The ship also simulated a rolling motion on its carriage*

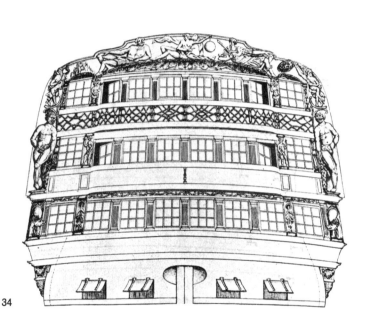

34

35

36

CHAPTER V

STEAMSHIPS OF THE ATLANTIC SEAS

FRANK O. BRAYNARD

This chapter is concerned with the decorative art of the Atlantic steamship. Going from broad outline to major features to particular detail, we will endeavour to trace how the shipbuilder's artistic sensibilities have been merged with the necessity of producing a seaworthy vessel. We will note instances in which this marriage has not succeeded, and we will endeavour to show how the practical often developed into what was considered the beautiful. We will not consider the interior design of ships, as this is worth a book alone and simply cannot be included in a chapter of this limited scope.

In order to see in broad outline the artistic evolution of the Atlantic liner, the author has prepared two double-page spreads of pen-and-ink sketches (pages 68–71). The first traces the silhouette progression of the steamship through sixty-one outline drawings, approximately to scale. The second explores, on a slightly larger scale, the shapes and decorative features of the stern, the midships section and the bow of typical steamers. An examination of these two treatments will point up a number of major stylistic trends.

The Smokestack

The smokestack, probably the most easily recognized design feature on today's liner, has passed through several cycles. Strictly functional at its very beginning (note the crooked swivel stack of the *Savannah*, of 1819), the stack rose almost to mast height in order to dispel dangerous wood sparks and coal smoke. Tall stacks became a mark of the old-style steamer and, as a reaction, the small funnel came into vogue. This battle between the tall stack, for functional purposes, and the short stack, for style, has continued until this day.

The number of smokestacks is another illustration of how the decorative instincts of the designer have overpowered his practical thinking. The first two-stacked liner was the *Rising Star*, of 1821. Her two thin pipe-funnels may have been athwartships. The *Liverpool* was the first liner on the Atlantic with two smokestacks fore and aft. The only five-stacked liner ever built was the *Great Eastern*. The stacks on these pioneer steamships were all functional but, with the booming immigrant trade and the need to attract and impress passengers, the custom of adding dummy smokestacks came into being. One more illustration of the importance of exterior design to the steamship, this trend was coupled with the tendency towards very tall funnels at the turn of the century.

1 The Washington *of 1847 depicted in a highly colourful German painting of that year made in Bremerhaven. No artist's name is given, simply 'Atelier Belthagen', Bremen. The painting, a remarkably accurate study of this historic early paddle steamer, shows many early decorative trends in steamship design. The hull and tall smokestack were black. The white line with imitation gunports was strictly a decoration. The paddle box fan was white, with dark green and gold decorations. The superstructure, what there was of it, was a strong* green. *The bowsprit and masts were white. There was gilt work at the bow, but the bust head was white. The scene is the* Washington's *arrival at Bremerhaven, the first time a steamer had reached that port. She was the first subsidized American Atlantic steamship, the first ship of the line which gave birth to the Norddeutscher Lloyd and the first steamship subsidized by Germany. Her owners were the Bremen Line, a joint American-German venture which lasted only ten years*

1

It was before the day of forced draught, but the tallness of the stacks was intended to impress as much as to draw the smoke from the fire boxes. The *City of Rome* and the *Augusta Victoria* are examples of early three-stackers with relatively low stacks. The *Campania* and the magnificent *Oceanic* are examples of the era of tall smokestacks. The dummy-stack era lasted well on into the post-First World War period, as witness the second, or dummy, stack on the Spanish *Magellanes*, 1928. There were instances where virtually identical sister ships were built, several with one stack and the others with three.

Pairing and Rake

Another notable decorative aspect of the chronicle of smokestacks was the custom of pairing two and two funnels, as shown in the early German four-stacked liners (see *Kaiser Wilhelm der Grosse*). So strongly was this purely decorative design feature established that when the great new Cunard liner *Mauretania* was first being designed, one artist's conception showed her with two and then two stacks, paired. Cunard's break with this German tradition ended the custom. No more paired-stack liners have ever been built.

The rake as it was originally called for by marine designers was intended to send the smoke aft. It quickly became a decorative feature with only a slight functional basis. It was a badge of speed, and was often most extreme on slow steamers whose owners wished to make them look like record breakers. Here, as with the dummy stack, is an instance in which a decorative design feature is given a functional purpose.

Off and on throughout the last century, ship designers had periods of reaction against the tall stack, as will be seen in the outline of the first *Oceanic*, of 1870, and again in 1897 with the German immigrant carrier *Pennsylvania*. Many pages could be written on how the designer's passion to make a ship look modern overcame his common sense, with the result that the ship's stacks were too low. The perpetual problem, still a factor with oil engines, of soot falling on the decks has obliged countless shipping lines to increase the height of a ship's stacks. The *Albert Ballin*'s stacks were much too low and had to be doubled in height. The *Bremen*'s smokestacks, when first installed, were one-third lower than those in our drawing.

Stack Extensions

The smoke nuisance has brought upon us some of the most unusual stack design creations, many of which probably are chiefly decorative features and only partially smoke deflectors. Three outstanding modern ships may be cited: the *United States*, for her 'sampan type' upper-stack design; the *France*, whose wing-like ailerons do not show in our silhouette, and the flat, lid-like smoke-deflector tops of the lattice-stacked *Michelangelo*. There have been stack extensions so ugly that they destroyed the ship's outline. The Canadian Pacific Line's *Empress of Scotland* had, originally, three finely proportioned tall stacks. Rebuilt as the *Hanseatic* by Home Lines, she was given two, much lower stacks. They were too low. First one extension and then another was added, somewhat to the detriment of the general silhouette. Straight, upright pipe extensions, often fifteen or twenty feet high, have been added to freighter smokestacks whose designers could not leave the dream-land of the sleek, low-funnelled liners.

As Atlantic liners grew in size over the years, from the 300 tons of the *Savannah* to the 83,000 tons of the *Queen Elizabeth*, the stack grew proportionately, although the real smoke-pipe size requirements increased only slightly. Today's gigantic smokestacks are really huge casings around relatively tiny smoke pipes. Note particularly the bulk of the *Normandie* stacks. Her third stack was a dummy, as was the last stack on the proud pre-war *Statendam* of the Holland–America Line. The cavernous spaces within the stack housing have been put to many uses: as dog kennels, crew quarters, for odd machinery and even as smoking rooms—most appropriate.

Stack markings, of course, have long been a major decorative feature of ocean liners, even though some lines have scorned design for a plain colour. The Spanish, for example, are known, or were until very recently, for their plain black smokestacks. Certain ship lines have used the smokestack as a decorative and identifying vehicle over and beyond simple stripes and insignia carried on the stack, for example, the Blue Funnel Line, which is known in the trade by the colour of its stack. Perfectly upright smokestacks are the rule in this famous British line. Very tall stacks with no rake are as much a mark of their identity as their tradition of naming ships after characters of mythology. We need only to mention

line 1

2

3

4

5

6

7

8

9

10

2 and 3

Line 1: Savannah (*Amer.*) *1819.* Rising Star (*Br.*) *1821.* Curaçao (*Du.*) *1825.* Ferdinando (*It.*) *1830.* Royal William (*Can.*) *1833.* Sirius (*Br.*) *1838.* Great Western (*Br.*) *1838.* Liverpool (*Br.*) *1838.* British Queen (*Br.*) *1845*

Line 2: Britannia (*Br.*) *1840.* Great Britain (*Br.*) *1845.* Union (*Fr.*) *1847.* Washington (*Amer.*) *1847.* City of Glasgow (*Br.*) *1850.* Atlantic (*Amer.*) *1850.* Helena Sloman (*Ger.*) *1850.* Canadian (*Can.*) *1854*

Line 3: North Star (*Amer.*) *1855.* Hammonia (*Ger.*) *1856.* Adriatic (*Amer.*) *1857.* Bremen (*Ger.*) *1858.* Great Eastern (*Br.*) *1860.* Connaught (*Br.*) *1860.* Washington (*Fr.*) *1864*

Line 4: Oceanic (*Br.*) *1871.* Vaderland (*Bel.*) *1873.* Ohio (*Amer.*) *1873.* City of Rome (*Br.*) *1881.* Servia (*Br.*) *1881.* Alaska (*Br.*) *1881.* Regina Margherita (*It.*) *1884*

By Frank O. Braynard '64

Line 5: Augusta Victoria (Ger.) 1889. Campania (Br.) 1893. St. Louis (Amer.) 1895. Pennsylvania (Ger.) 1897. Kaiser Wilhelm der Grosse (Ger.) 1897. Oceanic (Br.) 1899

Line 6: Manchuria (Amer.) 1903. Victorian (Br.) 1905. Smolensk (Ru.) 1906. Mauretania (Br.) 1907. Imperator (Ger.) 1913

Line 7: Metagama (Br.) 1915. Albert Ballin (Ger.) 1923. Gripsholm (Swed.) 1925. American Shipper (Amer.) 1925. Magellanes (Sp.) 1928. Bremen (Ger.) 1929

Line 8: Statendam (Du.) 1929. Normandie (Fr.) 1935. Batory (Pol.) 1936. Queen Elizabeth (Br.) 1940

Line 9: Augustus (It.) 1952. United States (Amer.) 1952. Olympia (Gr.) 1953. Zion (Isr.) 1955. Gripsholm (Swed.) 1956

Line 10: Northern Star (Br.) 1962. France (Fr.) 1962. Savannah (Amer.) 1963. Michelangelo (It.) 1965

4 and 5 *Sterns, amidships and bows*
Identification is from left to right within each group.

Sterns: Savannah (*Amer.*) *1819 and*
             Edinburgh (*Br.*) *1929*
             Baltic (*Amer.*) *1850 and* Oceanic
             (*Br.*) *1899*
             California (*Amer.*) *1928 and* Queen
             Mary (*Br.*) *1936*
             Canberra (*Br.*) *1962 and* Savannah
             (*Amer.*) *1963*

Amidships: Curaçao (*Du.*) *1825 and* Barcino
             (*Sp.*) *1842*
             Fulton (*Amer.*) *1856 and* Alaska
             (*Br.*) *1881*
             Melita (*Br.*) *1918 and* Savannah
             (*Amer.*) *1963*

such famed companies as 'Blue Star' or 'Red Star' to suggest how important a decorative factor the stack insignia can be, even more so than the small house flag on which most such emblems of identity originated.

The dummy stack is still with us. The *Gripsholm* of 1925, now the Norddeutscher Lloyd's *Berlin*, is a motorship and needs no stacks. She was built with two traditionally designed funnels and, years later, when she was completely rebuilt, she was given two new, more sharply raked and more streamlined stacks, quite a bow to the importance of smokestacks in the public's impression of what a ship should look like.

Motorships were once seen as dooming the smokestack, but although a few notable small liners were built without any, the diesel passenger liners of today still have great smokestacks. The smokestack, however, is now passing into another phase, perhaps even more menacing to its tradition of dominance and grandeur than the threat of the diesel engine. All ship design is going through a period of great flux, and the smokestack is moving aft. This is not new, as will be seen in the little *Vaderland* of a century ago, but it is now so widespread that it must be considered a major development. The *Northern Star* is a case in point, as is the

Bows: Phoenix (*Amer.*) *1809 and* Savannah
(*Amer.*) *1819*
Great Eastern (*Br.*) *1860 and* Erie
(*Amer.*) *1866*
City of New York (*Br.*) *1888 and*
Deutschland (*Ger.*) *1900*
Normandie (*Fr.*) *1935 and* Galileo
Galilei (*It.*) *1963*

Canberra. Even more extreme is the probability that nuclear power will spell the end of the smokestack. The new *Savannah*, the world's first nuclear-powered passenger/cargo liner, has no stack. All sorts of design innovations are being tried on ships which still need smoke vents, such as thin pipes, combination funnel-masts, king posts (designed to look like cargo derricks but actually smokestacks) and paired smoke pipes. In some cases regular dummy stacks are also carried, and in others built-up superstructures where the stack would have been are used to give the customary balance to the design.

Sterns, Superstructures and Bows

The second double-page spread shows sketches of eight representative sterns, six interesting midsections and eight bows. The following comments apply chiefly to this set of sketches.

The stern was at one time the major area for decoration on a ship. The old *Savannah*'s stern, however, was remarkably free of any trim or colour. A plain square stern it was, typical of the modest ship of her day. In most early steamships, the often overdone extravagance of gold leaf and carving remained only briefly as evidence of the inheritance of the

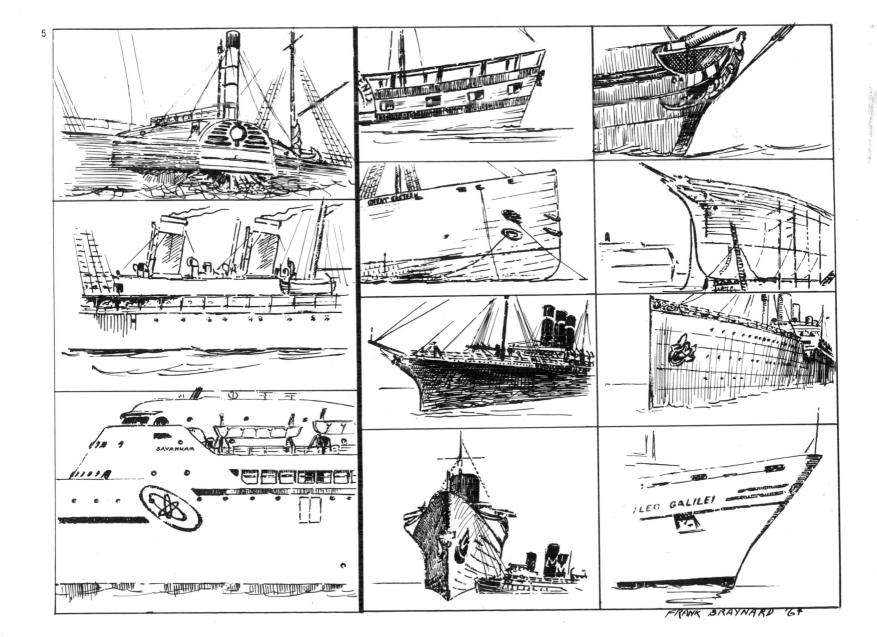

FRANK BRAYNARD '64

sailing ship. A little may be seen on the *Edinburgh* of 1829, the second stern drawing. The simplified counter-stern, highly practical and devoid of all but the most ordinary turns of the ship's carver or the ironwork artist, remained the basic design pattern up until the First World War. The *Baltic*'s stern is typical of the mid-century American steamship. The sleeker, more finely moulded stern of the *Oceanic* of 1899, shows one of the last illustrations of a true rudder above the waterline. One of the earliest cruiser sterns may be seen in that of the little *Metagama*, on the first double-page spread, while its development is seen in the Moore-

McCormack Line's first *California*. The commodious spoon stern is represented by the great Cunarder *Queen Mary*.

The perpendicular stern, which slowly evolved first into the cruiser and then the spoon stern, owed part of its origin to a need to camouflage the ship's direction. It was popularized by a large class of American troopships built in the First World War. Its application to these ships (see *American Shipper*, originally a troopship) was designed to confuse German U-boat skippers, for if they did not know which was bow and which was stern they could not properly direct their attack.

The curious stern of the *Canberra* is a special case; the
low open decks aft are known as tonnage openings, and
have a bearing on the tonnage charge in the Suez Canal.
The new *Savannah*'s turtle-back spoon stern is almost a
reversal to the counter-stern. Today's underwater hull lines
are largely the result of highly specialized towing tank ex-
periments, but the hull structure above water remains largely
subject to the decorative traditions of the company or
shipyard involved, or both.

Superstructures and vessel midsections have evolved with
somewhat less weight being paid to decoration than stacks,
sterns or bows. As will be seen on the sixty-one-ship silhouette
spread, there was virtually nothing beyond the single deck
above the hull as long as a need for sails existed. Sails remained a vital necessity until the twin-propeller ship. The
basic design feature of the earliest steamship midsection was
the colourful paddle box, as shown in the drawings of the
Curaçao, the *Barcino* and the *Fulton*. The real ratlines in the
Alaska sketch show the importance of sails to steamships as
late as 1881. Once sails became unnecessary, the modern
superstructure, with its tier on tier of decks, became possible.
At this point the opportunity for variety in decorative

7

superstructure design came into force. A multitude of special circumstances dictated bridge and deck-house design. The superabundance of lifeboats on the *Melita* was due to the sinking of the *Titanic*, which happened while the *Melita* was on the drawing-boards.

Countless interesting variations of porthole sequence, covered promenade decks, lifeboat locations, island bridge and split superstructures forward and aft to separate the different passenger-class areas, together with well decks and tonnage openings, could be studied. Many had decorative value and some were largely decorative. The three-tiered covered promenade deck layout on the old *Stavangerfjord*, uncommon in itself, was made unique by the designer's decision to have the upper hull plating shaped in a series of flat curves between each supporting stanchion, creating a crinolated or scalloped effect.

One of the most interesting superstructure designs is that of the new *Savannah*, the motive seeming to be to make her exterior as new and daring as her atomic power within. The oval symbol of the atom is an added touch on either side, which serves as a colourful break in the thick blue line around most of her hull.

Bow design has been subject to many decorative considerations. The false bow of the old *Savannah* had its practical basis in the need for bowsprit support. Although bowsprits became vestigial remnants soon thereafter they remained as decorative stalwarts until the 1880s, as witness the *City of Rome*. This vessel, incidentally, has often been described as the most beautiful Atlantic liner of all time.

Our eight drawings of bow development begin with the *Phoenix*, built as a river boat by Col. John Stevens, but forced by circumstances beyond her control to make the first excursion out into the Atlantic Ocean. Her voyage from New York to Philadelphia in 1809 is generally credited as being the first ocean passage by steam-powered craft. She was under the command of Moses Rogers, who was later the designer, master and chief engineer of the *Savannah*, whose bow is shown next. The *Great Eastern*'s bow which follows is ultra-functional. Then the bow of the *Erie* of 1866, a ship that was far behind her time, as her graceful clipper bow suggests. The *City of New York*, also with a clipper stem, was far ahead in other major details, being the first major liner with twin screws. The *Deutschland*, 1900, shows the beginning of Germany's lust for gold leaf on the stem. The *Normandie*, the giant French liner whose overall bow complex was the finest ever designed for a modern liner, is shown next. The combination of clipper prow, with ultra-fine lines and sharp overhead, plus her magnificent sweep of uncluttered deck up to the concave wave break, are features of thrilling beauty. Finally the new Lloyd Triestino liner *Galileo Galilei* combines the convex bow of the old *Savannah* and the concave clipper stem in a single two-curve stem.

The bow has been a favourite spot for decorative scrollwork, bust heads, figureheads and other company or nationalistic heraldic identification. The great German eagle on the *Imperator* (see Figs. 61, 62), is perhaps the most ornate example. Figureheads as such have not been abandoned as decorative devices on modern cargo liners, as photographs below will illustrate.

Within the sphere of the bow there are other functional appurtenances which have substantial decorative value: the way the name is lettered, the anchors and their hawse-pipe hull outlets, especially in some recent vessels, and, in most recent ships, the anchor pockets or hull casements. The hull waterline and boot-topping, not to mention colour strips along the hull, are other decorative features which are illustrated in the accompanying photographs. Our story will be continued in the picture captions of the following pages.

8 and 9 *Decorative paddle wheel boxes show the development of the bridge.* 8 *The* Sirius, *with a man standing on her paddle box, waving. It was 1838 and regular trans-Atlantic service by steamship began with this British liner.* 9 *The Cunard pioneer* Britannia, *with a clearly shown bridge connecting the two decorated paddle wheel boxes*

Norddeutscher Lloyd
BREMEN

New-York

Baltimore - Süd-Amerika

Ost-Asien

Australien

10

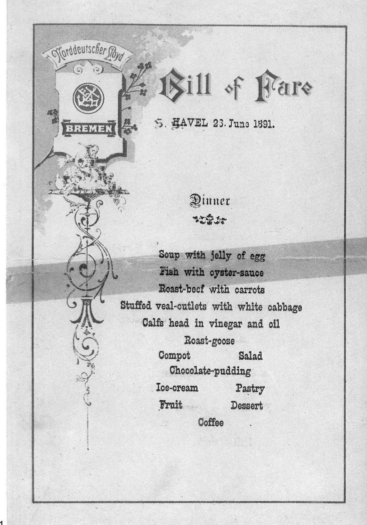

Bill of Fare

S. HAVEL 23. June 1891.

Dinner

Soup with jelly of egg

Fish with oyster-sauce

Roast-beef with carrots

Stuffed veal-cutlets with white cabbage

Calfs head in vinegar and oil

Roast-goose

Compot　　　　　Salad

Chocolate-pudding

Ice-cream　　　　Pastry

Fruit　　　　　　Dessert

Coffee

11

12

Speise-Karte

Dampf Havel 30. Juni 1891

Mittageſſen

Ochſenſchweif-Suppe

Würzfleiſch in Muſcheln

Rehbraten mit Perlbohnen

Lendenſchnitte mit Stangenſpargel

Midder in Sulze mit ſcharfer Tunke

Kükenbraten

Eingem. Obſt　　　　Salat

Apfelſinen-Pudding

Erleuchtetes Eis　　Mandelkuchen-Aufſatz

Nachtiſch

Kaffee

Bill of Fare

S. HAVEL 30. June 1891.

Dinner

Oxtail-soup

Ragout in shells

Roast-venison with string beans

Fillet-slices with asparagus

Sweet-bread in aspic with sauce remoulade

Roast-chicken

Compot　　　　　Salad

Orange-pudding

Tranrp. ice　　　Almond-tart

Fruit　　　　　　Dessert

Coffee

76

10, 11 and 12 *Priceless relics of the past—menus from the Norddeutscher Lloyd's express liner (with sails)* Havel. *Note the many decorative features in the upper left menu cover with its deck scene—the German-type air funnel in particular—and the interesting trim above and around the portholes on the deck house. The delicately coloured silhouettes at the foot of the lower menu are also interesting. The* Havel *is shown leading, of course. Next is the Inman Line's* City of Paris *(a competitor), a New York pilot boat and another Norddeutscher Lloyd steamer*

13

14

13 *The American steamer* Baltic, *of 1850, still with no bridge*

14 *The wheel house of the* Great Eastern, *from an old print*

15 *The* Washington, *French Line, whose bridge is still just a walk between the two paddle boxes*

16 *The French Line's first* France, *of 1865, with people walking on the bridge*

15

16

77

The bridge develops

17 *The* Campania, *with a real bridge and little wheel house, and* (18) *the* Oceanic, *of White Star Line*

19 *The* France, *1912, with a modern-style bridge, and two great ex-German ships, the* Majestic (*ex* Bismarck) (20) *and the* Leviathan (*ex* Vaderland), *whose bridge structures and pilot houses were major decorative features*

21 and 22 *The Cunard flagship* Queen Elizabeth *and* (opposite) *the French Line's new* France, *both of whose bridge ensembles represent the culmination of a century of decorative evolution*

1906 and 1910 German items

23 A Hamburg-American Line folder cover, in colour—quite something for that day. 24 A menu cover for the Kaiser Wilhelm II, Norddeutscher Lloyd line, dated 1910

25, 26 and 27 German lines carried more passengers than any other companies in the days just before World War I. Their ships were widely employed on cruises as well. Three folder covers are shown below in their original colours. German liner posters, like the scene on the right, were known and admired the world over for their colour and beauty

23

Hamburg-American Line

Pleasure and Health Cruises

June 1906 to September 1906

24

NORDDEUTSCHER LLOYD
BREMEN

S. D. KAISER WILHELM II. auf offener See.

PLYMOUTH.

25

NORDDEUTSCHER LLOYD
BREMEN

Express Steamer Services
BREMEN—NEW YORK

26

LLOYDREISEN
1914
Vergnügungsfahrten zur See

NORDDEUTSCHER
LLOYD BREMEN

27

To the
Mediterranean
HAMBURG-AMERICAN LINE

Before World War I the *France* was the last word in luxury. These highly decorative examples of company literature show the mood of the era. 28 The cover of a menu. 29, 30 The back and front of a passenger list. 31 The cover of a sailing schedule. 32 The picture side of a souvenir log for the voyage from Le Havre to New York that began on 20 September 1913. The artist was Albert Sébille, one of France's most noted marine painters

COMPAGNIE GÉNÉRALE
TRANSATLANTIQUE

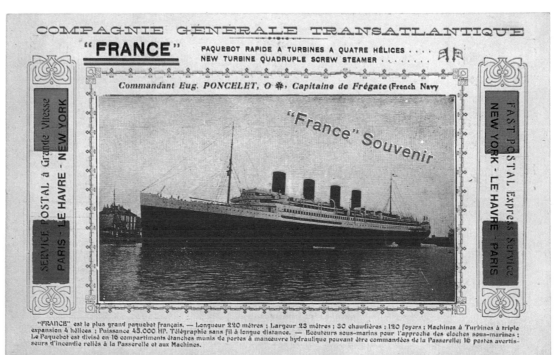

Styles on deck

33 *A prayer meeting on the deck of an early steamship in New York harbour.* 34 *An old print entitled 'Belle of the Voyage'.* 35 *Deck view on the Great Eastern, 1860, with only two of her five smokestacks appearing.* 36 *A drawing of the Great Eastern's elaborate deck compass with John Gray of Liverpool, its creator, standing beside it.* 37 *The cluttered deck of an American cable ship, the* Burnside, *during the Spanish-American war*

38

39

38, 39 *More deck scenes. In the period following the loss of the* Titanic *in 1912, lifeboats and lifeboat drill became a most important part of the public's thinking, as will be seen in the two top pictures.* 40 *Deck space on this 1924 crossing was at a premium—the* Saxonia's *lifeboats were swung out over her side to make room for deck chairs in this before-departure scene at New York.* 41 *The upper decks of the* Baltic, *White Star Line, after the rescue in 1909 of passengers from the sinking* Republic. 42 *A sports area on one of the Delta Line's passenger ships.* 43 *The massive structure at the right is an air view of the new P & O-Orient Line's* Oriana, *offering a variety of deck areas undreamed of in the past*

40

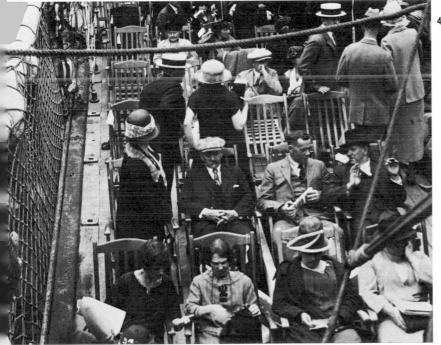

42

43

41

SS "FRANCE" Longitudinal Section

COMPAGNIE GÉ
FR

1ᵉʳ Class Passengers 534
2ᵉ " 442
3ᵉ " Whole 226
3ᵉ " 724
Crew 600
Total number
of persons on board 2526

1. Terrace Café.
2. Smoking Room.
3. Art Gallery.
4. Lounge Room.
5. Gallery.
6. Entrance to Grand stairway 1st Class.
7. Elevator.
8. Gallery.
9. Drawing Room.
10. Library.
11. Children's playroom.
12. Gymnasium.
13. Captain's Room.
14. Chart Room.
15. Wheel House.
16. Officers' Rooms.
17. Officers' Dining Room.
18. Promenade for Second Class.
19. Elevator and stairway for Second Class.
20. Sheltered Promenade 1st Class.
21. First Class Cabins.
22. Suite.
23. Entrance fort 1st Class and Grand stairway.
24. Florist.
25. Laundry.
26. Cabine de Luxe.
27. Glass enclosed promenade.
28. Promenade for Emigrants.
29. Promenade for the Crew.
30. Second Class Cabins.
31. Smoking Room Second Class.
32. Information Bureau.
33. First Class Din
34. Ladies' Hairdre
35. Office Second C
36. Post Office.
37. Bar for Third C
38. Promenade for
39. Crew Quarters
40. Check Room 1s

COMPAGNIE GÉNÉ

NOR

PASSENGERS 1ˢᵗ CLASS 848
TOURIST-CLASS 665
3ʳᵈ CLASS 458
OFFICERS AND CREW 1.355
TOTAL SOULS ON BOARD 3.326

UPPER SUNDECK
1 PROMENADE DECK OF ENGINEER OFFICERS
AND JUNIOR ENGINEERS
2 FOG PROMENADE

SUNDECK
3 PRIVATE DINING ROOM OF THE GRAND LUXE
4 MAIN APARTMENT DE LUXE
5 MAIN WIRELESS ROOM
6 VENTILATION ROOM
7 ROOMS OF CHIEF ENGINEERS
8 ROOMS OF SECOND ENGINEER
9 OFFICE OF CHIEF ENGINEER
10 APARTMENT OF CHIEF ENGINEER
11 DECK TENNIS AND DECK GOLDS
12 CHILDREN'S PLAYROOM
13 LIFEBOAT'S WORKROOM
14 FIRST-CLASS MAIN STAIRCASE
15 COMMANDER'S QUARTERS
16 BRIDGE WIRELESS STATION
17 CHART ROOM
18 WHEELHOUSE AND ENCLOSED BRIDGE
19 BRIDGE

LIFEBOAT DECK
20 FIRST-CLASS PROMENADE DECK
21 MAIN BALLROOM BAY AND GRILL ROOM
22 PRIVATE DINING ROOM OF THE CHEF
23 FIRST-CLASS LIFT AND AFT STAIRCASE
24 OFFICERS' ROOMS
25 SEARCHLIGHT
26 STARBOARD NAVIGATION LIGHT
27 FORWARD PROMENADE DECK

PROMENADE DECK
28 TOURIST-CLASS OPEN PROMENADE DECK
29 TOUR OF CLASS COVERED IN PROMENADE DECK
30 TOURIST-CLASS DINING ROOM
31 STAIRCASE AND LIFT, TOURIST CLASS
32 DECK PANTRY OF THE 1ST CLASS
33 CABIN DE LUXE WITH PRIVATE TERRACE
34 FIRST CLASS ENCLOSED PROMENADE DECK
35 SMOKING-ROOM MAIN SALOONS
36 FIRST-CLASS SMOKING-ROOM
37 MAIN LOUNGE
38 MAIN GALLERY
39 MAIN HALL AND LIFTS
40 THEATRE
41 STAGE
42 DRESSING ROOM
43 PROJECTION-ROOM
44 READING ROOM
45 WINTER GARDEN
46 ELECTRIC CRANES AND BATHHOUSE
47 CREW STAIRCASE
48 BREAK-STAIR

MAIN DECK
49 TOURIST-CLASS SWIMMING POOL
50 LOWER, TOURIST-CLASS COVERED-IN PROMENADE DECK
51 TOURIST-CLASS GYMNASIUM
52 SOAP BOOTH
53 TOURIST-CLASS CABINS
54 AUTOROGRAPHS READING-ROOM
55 MAIN LOUNGE OF TOURISTS
56 FIRST-CLASS CABINS
57 DECK PANTRY
58 STEP GREENING
59 FIRST-CLASS STATEROOMS
60 MANICURE

41 VICTUALLING STOREROOM
42 FIRST-CLASS BATHROOMS
43 TELEPHONE EXCHANGE
44 OFFICE OF THE RADIO OPERATOR
45 RADIO-TELEPHONE CABIN
46 JAIL-DEPORT
47 FIRST-CLASS INFORMATION BUREAU
48 MALL
49 FLORIST AND SHOP
50 HAIRDRESSING AND MANICURE
51 APARTMENT DE LUXE
52 COMPANION FOR FIRE-FIGHTING EQUIPMENT
53 SHIP'S CLERK'S ROOM
54 PRINTING ROOM
55 CHIEF PROVEER
56 CHIEF HAIRDRESSER
57 FIRE PATROLMEN'S QUARTERS
58 AUXILIARY PATROLMEN'S QUARTERS
59 PETTY OFFICERS' CABINS
60 CARPENTER'S WORKSHOP

61 THIRD-CLASS OPEN PROMENADE DECK
62 THIRD-CLASS COVERED-IN PROMENADE DECK
63 THIRD-CLASS SMOKING ROOM
64 THIRD-CLASS STAIRCASE
65 THIRD-CLASS BAR
66 TOURIST-CLASS PURSER
67 TOURISTS' INFORMATION BUREAU
68 TOURIST-CLASS HAIRDRESSING SALONS
69 TOURIST-CLASS CABINS
70 FIRST-CLASS BATHROOMS
71 AUXILIARY PANTRY
72 FIRST-CLASS AFT STAIRCASE
73 CENTRAL FIRE-CONTROL AND SAFETY STATION

A. DECK

44, 45 *A half-century of modern liner design. The* France *of 1812 and the* Normandie *of 1935. These two cut-away drawings show well the great changes in exteriors as well as interiors that took place within only a quarter of a century. The great* Normandie *is almost as up-to-date today as when she was built. Her clipper bow set a trend in styles which is still being followed. Her spoon stern has been virtually copied on the nuclear-powered* Savannah *(see p. 70). The tremendous dining-room in the* Normandie *is the largest room ever built in a passenger ship*

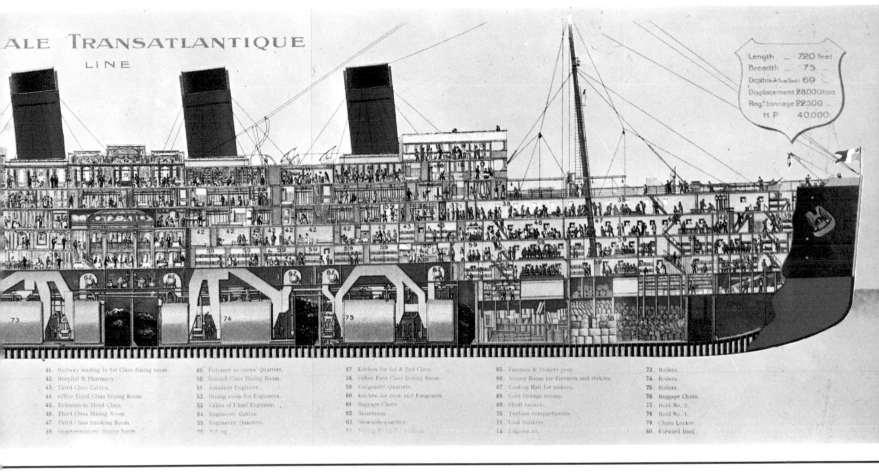

Length ____ 720 feet
Breadth ____ 75
Depth to Shelter Deck 69
Displacement 28,000 tons
Reg^d tonnage 22,500
H.P. ____ 40,000

41. Railway leading to 1st Class dining room.
42. Hospital & Pharmacy.
43. Third Class Cabins.
44. Office Third Class Dining room.
45. Entrance to Third Class.
46. Third Class Dining Room.
47. Third Class Smoking Room.
48. Quartermasters' Dining Room.
49. Entrance to crews' Quarters.
50. Second Class Dining Room.
51. Assistant Engineer.
52. Dining room for Engineers.
53. Cabin of Chief Engineer.
54. Engineers' Cabins.
55. Engineers' Quarters.
56. Galley.
57. Kitchen for 1st & 2nd Class.
58. Office First Class Dining Room.
59. Emigrants' Quarters.
60. Kitchen for crew and Emigrants.
61. Baggage Chute.
62. Storeroom.
63. Stewards quarters.
64. Dining Room for Firemen.
65. Firemen & Stokers pool.
66. Dining Room for Firemen and stokers.
67. Cooling Hall for stokers.
68. Cold Storage rooms.
69. Shaft tunnels.
70. Turbine compartments.
71. Coal bunkers.
72. Engine air.
73. Boilers.
74. Boilers.
75. Boilers.
76. Baggage Chute.
77. Hold No. 2.
78. Hold No. 1.
79. Chain Locker.
80. Forward deck.

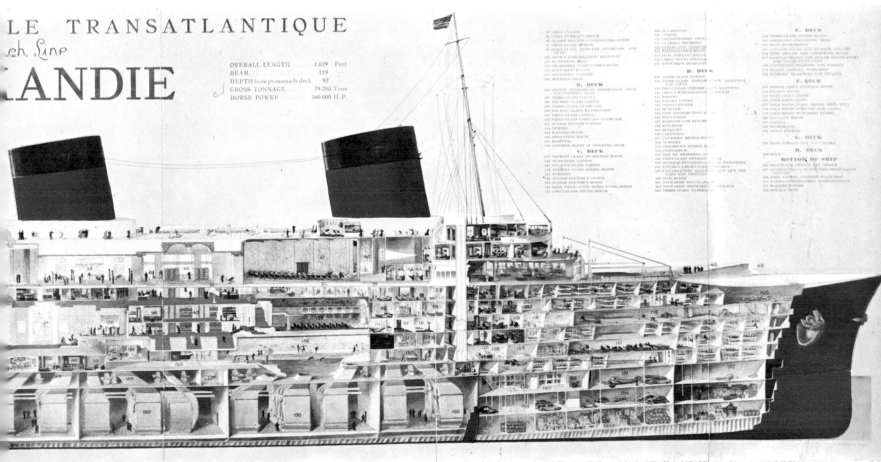

LE TRANSATLANTIQUE
ch. Line
ANDIE

OVERALL LENGTH ____ 1,029 Feet
BEAM ____ 119
DEPTH from promenade deck ____ 92
GROSS TONNAGE ____ 79,280 Tons
HORSE POWER ____ 160,000 H.P.

46 *Camouflage as a form of hull decoration was a well-developed science in World War II. It was not so firmly established in the Great War. Below is an American merchant ship, the* Berdan, *in 1918 colours*

STR. BERDAN
" #906
9-7-18

#88

47

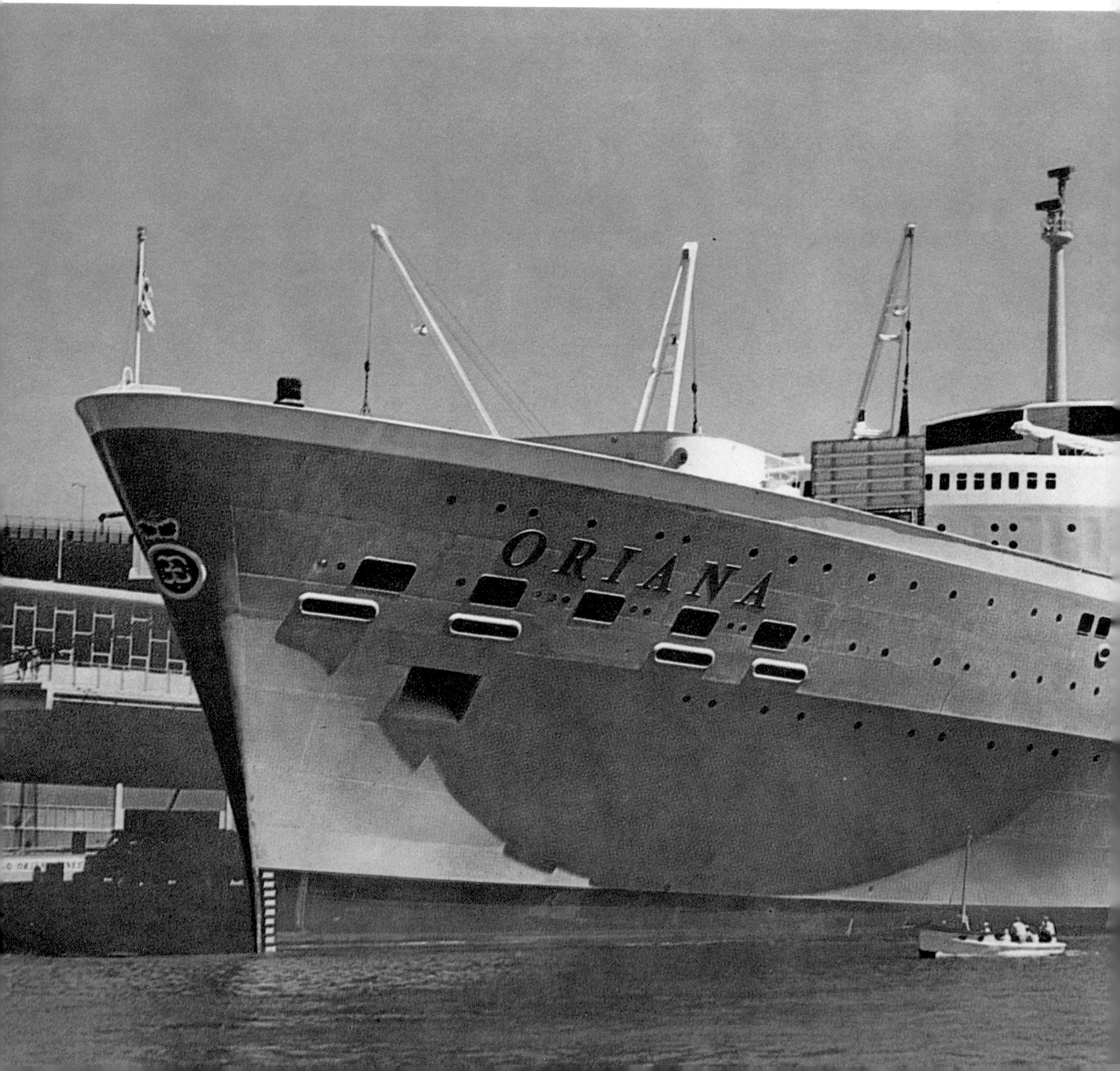
ORIANA

48 *The Oriana, 42,000-ton liner built in 1962 for P & O-Orient Lines, is certainly one of the strangest looking of all modern liners, setting new trends in many ways. Note the position of her lifeboats.* 49 *This picture, from an original watercolour by the American marine artist Fred J. Hoertz, shows the camouflage of World War II —just plain grey*

50

51

52

53

54

55

59

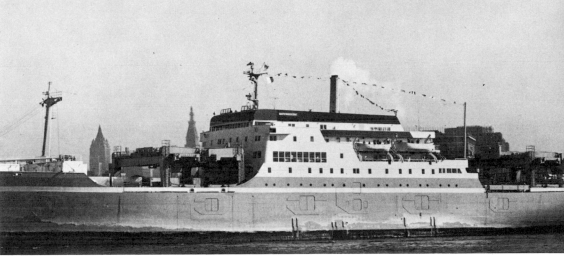

61, 62 *The Kaiser's Pride and Joy.*
The German eagle, with claws on the globe and mounting the imperial crown on its feathered head, made for one of the most grotesque ship ornaments of all time. The motto on the globe is the old German slogan 'My Field is the World'. Behind the globe is a sunburst design. The entire device was made of cast iron. It is said to have been installed to make the Imperator longer than Britain's Aquitania, but this story is probably apocryphal since the Hamburg-American Line vessel was eighteen feet longer than the Cunard liner even without the eagle. The eagle was knocked off in a storm on the ship's third voyage and was replaced by a large but much more modest decoration on either side of the prow showing the seal of the Port of Hamburg, the same three-turreted tower as on the house flag of the Hamburg-American Line

61

62

Prow Emblems Today

Prow Emblems Today

63 *A three-masted square rigger, the* Tusitala, *is shown on the prow of the* African Comet, *of Farrell Lines*

64 *Cunard's* Sylvania *boasts the Cunard lion on her bow*

65 *The familiar three gold crowns grace the bow of the* Gripsholm, *Swedish American Line*

66 *The Texaco Oil Company's star is on the bow of the tanker* National Defender

67 *The* Elin Haven, *of Kjode Line*

68 *The* Pleasantville, *of Klaveness Lines*

69 *The* Heidelberg, *of Hamburg-American*

70 *The Furness-Bermuda Lines luxury liner* Ocean Monarch, *with Neptune on her prow*

71 *The* Black Eagle, *of the Herlofson Company*

72 *The* Effie Maersk, *of the famed Maersk Line, all of whose ships have sky-blue hulls*

73 *The* Ciudad de Medellin, *of Gran-Colombiana Lines, with an unusual dip to her grey hull paint line at the bow*

74 *The* Queen of Bermuda, *whose bow scroll reads* Que Fata Ferunt— *Whither the Fates Lead. The seal shows, of all things, a shipwreck*

75 *The* Blidum, *owned by Zerssen and boasting a 'Z' at the bow and on the stack*

63

64

65

66

67

68
69

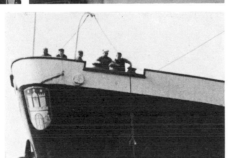

73
74
75

70
71
72

93

Today's figureheads

76 *While the old-style figurehead is treated in a later chapter there are modern cargo liners with figureheads. The Fred Olsen Line, Norway, has used full-length figurehead bow ornaments since 1936. Thirty of these are shown here.* 77 *A more recent one, on the bow of the* Burrard, *is shown on the right.*

M.S. «BAYARD» 1936
EMIL LIE

M.S. «BAGHDAD» 1936
ØRNULF BAST

M.S. «BRETAGNE» 1937
EMIL LIE

M.S. «BAALBEK» 1937
ØRNULF BAST

M.S. «BLACK PRINCE» 1938
EMIL LIE

M.S. «BOMMA» 193
PER HURUM

M.S. «BOLIVAR» 1946
EMIL LIE

M.S. «BENGAZI» 1947
PER HURUM

M.S. «BATAAN» 1947
ØRNULF BAST

M.S. «BALDRIAN» 1947
RAGNHILD BUTENSCHÖN

M.S. «BYSANZ» 1947
ALFRED SELAND

S.S. «BAMSE» 19
ØRNULF BAST

76   M.S. «BOLT» 1950
KJELL RASMUSSEN

M.S. «BAROK» 1950
J. GRIMELAND

M.S. «BOMMA» 1950
ØRNULF BAST

M.S. «BENCOMO» 1950
ØRNULF BAST

S.S. «BERBY» 1950
ØRNULF BAST

M.S. «BISMILLAH»
J. GRIMELAND

78 *The full-page illustration overleaf shows a still more recent bow decoration, on the Fred Olsen Line's Borgny. It is a 25,000-piece glass mosaic in the brightest of colours. The 'figurehead', as the Olsen people call it, was made on a curved steel sheet with raised edges which was welded to the bow. A special glue cemented the glass pieces into place. This glue passed a six-months' immersion test on the prow of a ship, exposed to the waves of winter, tearing winds, snow, sleet and ice. Unfortunately the company which chartered the ship from Olsen asked for the mosaic to be painted over; however, the welded colour demarcation seams will permit the bow to be restored to the original colours when the* Borgny *is back under the Fred Olsen house flag*

M.S. «BRAGA» 1938
EMIL LIE

M.S. «BLACK WATCH» 1939
ØRNULF BAST

M.S. «BALKIS» 1939
EMIL LIE

M.S. «BESS» 1939
EMIL LIE

S. «BOREALIS» 1948
GUNNAR JANSON

M.S. «BRUNO» 1948
PER HURUM

M.S. «BALBLOM» 1948
PER PALLE STORM

M.S. «BORRE» 1949
PER HURUM

S. «BOHEMUND» 1950
PER HURUM

M.T. «BOLETTE» OG «BOLLSTA» 1951
ØRNULF BAST

M.S. «BAYARD» 1951
SIGURD NOME

M.S. «BLENHEIM» 1951
ØRNULF BAST

77

CHAPTER VI

STATE BARGES

PHILIP COWBURN

In nautical language the term 'barge' implies a rowing vessel with more than eight oars, something larger than a pinnace. These barges vary considerably in size, appearance and ornamentation as well as function, but here we shall only consider those used for ceremonial occasions. Also, because almost every country has lavished craftsmanship and decorative skill on such vessels throughout history and a complete survey is impossible, we shall limit ourselves to the English State barges. One exception, however, will be made to remind us of the others, and this is perhaps the most famous of all, the State barge of the Venetian Republic.

In 1863 Nathaniel Hawthorne deplored the fact that the River Thames, 'the high street of the metropolis', had degenerated into 'a multitude of smoke-begrimed steamers'. His description of the earlier function of the river is accurate, and it must have provided an approach of great beauty, a pleasant alternative to noisome alleys and jostling streets. Since progress was quicker by water, the Thames was used for special processions to welcome distinguished visitors, for pageants and many other functions. There were the civic occasions such as the swearing-in of the new sheriffs and, most important of all, the occasion 'on the morrow of St Simon and St Jude' when the Lord Mayor-elect of London took his oath before the Barons of the Exchequer. The account books of the Drapers' Company show that twice in 1496 the barge which the Drapers shared with the Merchant Taylors was hired for a deputation to go to Sheen 'to speak with the King', costing the two Companies £3 13s. 4d. 'in vytils, supplicacion and learned counsell', though we are not told what the business actually was. Less officially, Fraser Honywood, a Warden of the Merchant Taylors' Company, took some friends by river to Brentwood in 1749 to support his candidature for Parliament.

Towards the end of the seventeenth century, the Cloth-workers seem to have used barges more often and the Livery-men and their ladies 'went abroad' as far as Putney, returning to Chelsea to dine and see the sights. Perhaps these occasions became too convivial, for 'the distribution of wine' was thought to be attended with 'considerable inconvenience'—a nice euphemism—and each Liveryman was later restricted to a pint of Lisbon. When Sir Thomas Lane, a Clothworker, became Lord Mayor in 1694, his Company planned the water ceremonial, which included four floating pageants illustrating the Seat of Sovereignty, the Garden of Plenty, the Chariot of Apollo and the Pageant of Trade. The texts of these pageants are an interesting, though often pedestrian, aspect of the literature of the period. Middleton, Webster, Dekker and Heywood all wrote pageants, and in 1660 John Tatham's *The Royal Oak* seems to have been particularly outstanding. Sir Richard Brown, Lord Mayor that year, was confronted by a stage with a mock-up of a ship at one end, 'floating, rigged and manned', and, at the other, a rock on which figures reclined or stood—Oceanus with 'several fishes' playing at his feet, tritons in attitudes of conventional abandon, and four virgins loosely clothed, their brows decked with sage. But there were few opportunities for variation, so it is hardly surprising that the Vintners' pageant of as long ago as 1702 was the last.

Let us recall some of the times when the English State barges were seen at their best, as integral parts of great occasions, gracefully gliding over the river 'with', in Leland's phrase, 'swift but gentle course'. At her coronation, Henry VII's queen was attended by the mayor, sheriffs, aldermen and 'divers and worshipful commoners chosen out of every craft in their liveries'. These were conveyed 'in barges freshly furnished with banners and streamers of silk, richly beaten with the arms and badges of their crafts' and there was an additional barge called the bachelors' barge 'garnished and apparelled', surpassing the rest and bearing 'a great red dragon . . . which spouted flames of fire into the Thames'. At Anne Boleyn's coronation in 1533 some fifty barges, all required to have 'mynstrelsie', attended the queen on her journey upstream from Greenwich, and Stow tells us more about the bachelors' barge, how her decks, sail-yards and top-castles were 'hanged with rich cloth of gold and silk' and her sides 'adorned with three dozen metal escutcheons on buckram squares bearing the royal arms'. There were also banners with the devices of the Haberdashers and Merchant Adventurers, and the 'lasserers, or cords, were hanged with innumerable pensels having little bells at the ends which make a goodly noise and was a goodly sight wavering in the wind'. Another memorable occasion was when Charles II brought Catherine of Braganza to London on 23 August 1662. This was the Queen's first visit and Evelyn

thought it 'the most magnificent triumph that ever floated on the Thames', far exceeding 'all the Venetian Bucentoras . . . when they go to espouse the Adriatic'. He records how the King and Queen came in an 'antique-shaped, open vessel covered with a state, or canopy, of cloth of gold made in form of a cupola and supported with high Corinthian pillars wreathed with flowers, festoons and garlands'. All this can be seen in the Stoop engraving, which also conveys some idea of the throng of craft that apparently 'hid the very water'.

When did the Lord Mayor's water procession to Westminster actually begin? John Norman, Lord Mayor in 1454, is often given the credit for it, and most authorities agree that he had a barge built at his own expense and that thereafter the procession was retained till 1857. Stow thought it a novelty, yet in 1422, when William Warderne became Lord Mayor, he went to Westminster 'in barges', though without minstrels, and in 1435, according to the Grocers' Company accounts, the sheriffs travelled by water, and decorated barges complete with musicians were hired. The answer may be that Norman formalized an occasional practice that was for the next four hundred years to become traditional.

Up to the end of the sixteenth century, barges were usually hired by the City Companies, and these practical vessels, deriving from wherries, were elaborately decorated with flags, pennants and awnings and often the whole superstructure was covered with blue plunket or, on royal occasions, murrey-coloured cloth. In the seventeenth century the Companies began to purchase their own craft. Thenceforward they were built on more decorative lines with ornate stern-pieces often embellished with armorial escutcheons and figures of water-sprites with conches or trumpets. Cleopatra's barge, immortalized by Shakespeare, is probably the picture of a State barge most of us carry in our minds, but there is little doubt that for about two hundred years Livery Company barges ran her very close.

The Merchant Taylors acquired their first barge in 1640. She was 'for passing of their livery to and from Westminster on the Lord Mayor's Day and other their necessary occasions' and was in general 'for the Company's decent and convenient passage by water'. The contract was given to Abraham Tue, a shipwright of Southwark, and the cost, including the gilding

2

3

and painting, was £120 4s. od. The vessel was probably not particularly ornate, but the Company's account books tell us that she was regularly repainted and that the seventeen watermen's uniforms, which included caps of 'sky-coloured thread plush faced and lined with calico' were frequently replaced. By 1668 the bargemaster considered the craft to be 'so rotten' that he dared not 'adventure the Company therein', so a new barge was built at nearly twice the cost, though she only lasted eighteen years. The third barge must have been larger, as the boathouse had to be lengthened. The barge of 1718, incorporating carvings from her predecessor, lasted till 1762, but by that time the Master and Wardens doubted her condition and asked to be excused attendance on the Lord Mayor. The 1764 barge lasted till 1800 and we know a good deal about her from the Articles of Agreement. She was to be built in seven months 'in a good substantial and workmanlike manner' by Thomas Searle of Lambeth and painted and gilded by Nathaniel Clarkson, a member of the Livery. She was an eighteen-oared vessel and her scantlings were 'all to be of white English oak free from Redness, Rot, Sap and Prejudicial Knotts' while the floorboards were to be made of yellow Christiania deal and the thirty-five-foot 'house' was to have sash-windows between fluted columns. There were to be two carved trailboards abaft and the royal arms carved over the Master's seat. Clarkson wished to paint 'the historical facts relating to the Company', as he put it, instead of the more conventional gods and goddesses. For example, the two doors at the front of the 'house' were to portray 'emblematical representation of the four quarters of the world'. The panel for Europe was to show a crowned figure holding a temple seated beside a cornucopia, while Asia's included a kneeling camel and sprigs of tea to show 'the rich Traffic and Produce of that Quarter of the World'. Elsewhere Henry VI was to be depicted granting the Company its charter of re-incorporation, and the 'dignity and opulence' of the City were to be a woman crowned with a tower, holding a praetorian wand and flanked by youths, one of whom was embracing a stork symbolizing the unity of the City of London. All this was duly executed 'in a genteel, workmanlike and reasonable manner'.

The barge, built in 1800, seventy-nine feet long by fourteen feet wide with a 'house' thirty-seven feet long and six feet high, was the last word in comfort with such refinements as a pantry and a water-closet, but by the 1840s she was costing about £250 a year to maintain, so she was sold to the Oxford University Boat Club whence she passed to University College and was broken up in the late 1870s. Her armorial sternboard, handsomely gilded and coloured, is displayed above the Grand Staircase of the Company's Hall.

Early in the seventeenth century, the Clothworkers abandoned the practice of hiring barges and decided to have their own. William Foster, a Brother of the Company and a lighterman by trade, offered to build 'a decent and convenient barge' for the carriage of sixty men, and it was agreed that this vessel with her five pairs of oars should be ready 'upon a day's warning for any service . . . upon any occasion'. She was to be kept at Vauxhall on land shared with the Mercers and Fishmongers, and the sum of five pounds a day was fixed to pay the watermen's food and wages. There was also to be 'a western azure woollen cloth to make a convenient and comely covering'. Eight years after the Company took delivery, we find the Clothmakers attending Catherine of Braganza's first visit to London in some style. Fortified against thirst with three dozen bottles of Lambeth ale 'for their better accommodation', they had five trumpeters in attendance and a consort of strings, and the barge was adorned with gaily fluttering standards, streamers, colours and 'other usual ornaments' such as the hooks and teasel of their profession.

The surviving English barges must be mentioned. In the National Maritime Museum the Queen's Shallop, the Prince Frederick Barge and the Admiralty Barge are preserved. The first of these was built in 1689 on Dutch lines for Mary II and was last used by George V at the peace celebrations in 1919. Though really a large rowing-boat, she was a heavy vessel, was forty-one and a half feet long and six and a half feet in the beam, and instead of a 'house' had a green and gold canopy, now replaced by a red one.

The barge designed for Prince Frederick of Wales in 1732 by William Kent and built by John Hall was over twenty feet longer and a foot wider, but the 'house' was comparatively small. She was originally twelve-oared but was adapted for twenty-one later. She was elaborately decorated by the woodcarver John Richards and gilded and painted by Paul

3 *The Queen's shallop, built 1689*

4 *The coat of arms at the stern of the Queen's shallop*

Pettit, though the royal arms on the ceiling of the 'house' are a later addition. She cost £1,000 8s. 7d., and even Prince Frederick thought her too elaborate, though he was soon persuaded that it was 'good-natured to entertain people' and that when the public took so much trouble to gratify their Prince, the latter should oblige them in his turn. For nearly a hundred years after Frederick's death in 1751 the barge was used for State purposes.

The Admiralty Commissioners' barge was built in the seventeenth century and was used by their Lordships for official visits to the Victualling Yard, but also by the Brethren of Trinity House on their annual visits to Deptford. She was used for the last time when the Coal Exchange was opened in 1849.

Another historic barge is preserved in the HMS *Victory* Museum at Portsmouth. Originally built for Charles II, she was used to convey Nelson's body on its last journey from Greenwich in January 1806. This sombre occasion may have been one of the most impressive of all river ceremonies and it was the last great pageant on the Thames; for although the Prince Consort was rowed down to the City in Prince Frederick's barge forty-three years later, the days of river pageantry were numbered, and when in the mid-1850s the Lord Mayor's procession abandoned the water route to Westminster, a colourful chapter in the history of State occasions came to an end.

The State barge that might claim to be the best known of all was the vessel in which each Ascension Day the Doge of Venice performed the ceremony known as *sposalizio del mare*, the wedding between the Doge and the sea. Originating about the year 1000 to commemorate Doge Orseolo II's conquest of Dalmatia, this ceremony was gradually elaborated, especially after 1177, the year in which Pope Alexander III gave Doge Sebastiano Ziani a ring to be thrown into the sea. At first a small barge draped in crimson conveyed the clergy towards the Lido to meet the Doge. On arrival at S. Nicolo the bishop sprinkled the Doge and his attendants with ceremonial water. Later the procedure became more elaborate, but it never lost its original significance.

The Doge's barge is usually known as *Bucentaur* from *Bucintoro*, an adaptation of *buzino d'oro*, barque of gold. A decree of 1311 mentions *Bucintoro* first, and this particular barge lasted a long time. She was seen by Henry of Valois before he became king and was still in existence in the early eighteenth century. The next barge was the last. One hundred feet long, twenty-four feet high and designed by Michele Stefano Conti, she was launched in 1728, but she came on evil days when Venice capitulated to the French: the gold was removed and melted down and she was used as a floating battery until 1824. Part of her mainmast survives in the Arsenale museum.

The earlier of these two barges must have been an impressive sight. Engravings show that the upper deck extended the whole length of the vessel and was covered with a crimson awning fringed with tassels of gold braid. Separating the two decks was a continuous band of allegorical bas-reliefs. The Doge and senior officials sat on the upper deck, the former in a highly decorated chair at the stern with a shell-like canopy supported by cherubs and flanked by gilded figures of Prudence and Strength. Four *arsenalotti*, those privileged citizens, half-artisan and half-soldier, manned each of the forty-two oars, and the barge led the procession to the island of Sant'Elena where the Doge was given a bunch of damask roses in a silver vase in return for the surprising but traditional offering of peeled chestnuts and red wine. When the procession reached the open sea and the patriarch had blessed the ring, the Doge flung it into the water with the words 'We wed thee, O Sea, in token of our perpetual dominion'. After solemn mass in the church of S. Nicolo and a decorous return to Venice, the admirals, the hundred head officers of the Arsenal, the chief magistrates and all ambassadors were entertained to dinner—the formidable menu has survived—and the city gave itself over to eight days of revelry.

5

5 *Barge of the Victualling Commissioners. From the* Navy and Army Illustrated

6 *Quarter ornament from the Fishmongers' Barge*

7 *Stern ornament from the Merchant Taylors' Barge*

6

8

9 Stern ornament from the Fishmongers' Barge

9 The Lord Mayor proceeding to Westminster Hall

10 Stationers' Barge

11 State Barge, City of London

9

14

15

16

15 *Greenwich. The return of George IV in the*
Royal George, *10 August 1822. Oil painting by*
W. Anderson

16 *The bows of Nelson's galley*

17

18 *The* Bucentaur *at Venice. Line engraving by Jan Sadeler after Stefano Scolari*

18

21 *Walnut model of the State barge of Charles II*

22 *Sultan of Turkey's barge. Coloured lithograph by Sabatier and Schranz*

CHAPTER VII

VESSELS OF THE INLAND WATERWAYS OF ENGLAND & HOLLAND

HUGH McKNIGHT

Although England and Holland are the two countries represented in this section, these are not the only parts of Europe where decorated vessels may be found inland; however, it is these countries which have the most comprehensive and interesting assortment of painted or carved canal boats, where widely differing influences have produced styles so unalike.

The Dutch waterways have long been, and still are, the greatest carriers of freight in Holland, taking an annual twelve million kilometre-tons in 1963, just thirty-five times more than British waterways. But in this atmosphere of strict commercialism few modern Dutch craft are decorated and for examples of the art we must look to relics of the eighteenth and nineteenth centuries. Ironically, it is on the sadly neglected canals of England, little changed in almost two hundred years, that the boatman's art continues to flourish.

Between 1761 and 1834, England built one of the finest systems of navigable inland waterways then existing; much of her industrial greatness was a direct result of the Canal Age. But with the coming of the railways, which frequently bought up their rivals, canal prosperity dwindled. The boatman who had formerly housed his family in a cottage ashore now brought his wife and children into the boat, which became their only home. It is probable that the decorations of today date from this period. Most of the traffic was carried by narrow boats, seventy-two feet long with a beam of seven feet, horse-drawn and with a capacity of twenty-five tons. The diminutive cabin at the stern, barely twelve feet long, was the living accommodation. Whereas in more recent times modern craft have been developed for isolated use on a few enlarged waterways, it is these narrow boats which have traditionally been given lavish decoration.

The limited living space dictates that not an inch must be wasted: the general layout of the narrow boat cabin varies little. Immediately inside, on the left, a coal-burning stove provides for cooking and for heat in winter. Facing it against the opposite side of the hull a narrow bench serves as a child's bed by night and a seat during the daytime. Beyond the stove on the same side are storage cupboards for food and utensils, at the front of which is a door folding open to serve as table. At the far end of the cabin, a folding bed to accommodate the boatman and his wife, with space by the pillow for a small child, extends from one side of the boat to the other. Coal supplies are stored in a box which is also a step into the cabin: ticket drawer and 'soap hole' are located in traditional positions near the cabin doors. Such is the basic plan. In former years an additional cabin, even smaller, was sometimes built in the bows, to house extra members of a large family.

Towards the end of the nineteenth century, steam power, and later the diesel engine, began to replace the horse as motive power, and narrow boats worked in pairs as they always do today. A diesel-powered 'motor', whose stern is rounded, but is in other respects similar to the old horse boats, tows an unpowered 'butty' or companion boat. Between them they carry about fifty tons.

So much for the design of the narrow boat, which only gets its character and individuality when painted in gorgeous colours from bow to stern. A sparkling array of castles, roses and geometrical designs vie for positions both inside the cabin and out. Cabin sides bear the owner's name in thick shaded lettering. Nowadays most narrow boats belong to the fleets of large carrying companies, but formerly very many were 'Number Ones', or craft owned by their skippers, whose family had worked the 'Cut' for generations. Joe Skinner of the *Friendship*, now living aboard in retirement at Hawkesbury Junction near Coventry, is the last 'Number One': his boat is painted in a livery of crimson and emerald, with touches of yellow and white. Company boats also had distinctive colour schemes. Before nationalization of the canals in 1948, the largest carriers, Fellows, Morton and Clayton, had their familiar black-and-white name boards throughout the country; the Grand Union Canal Company generally used white lettering on two shades of green. When most narrow boats came into the unfeeling hands of the Docks and Inland Waterways Executive, a completely untraditional and objectionable blue and yellow scheme was devised, devoid of intricate adornment. But gradually castles and hearts began to reappear on cabin door and slide, as if to indicate that government officialdom could not kill a long-established folk-art. Now that narrow boat carrying has almost completely reverted to private enterprise, the former glory of traditional decoration has returned. Leaders in the field are the Willow Wren Group, who control the majority of long-distance traffic. Their painted boats lack none of the former skills, but prove that the economics of the machine age cannot erase all that was loved in the past.

The boats are built either of wood or, more commonly these days, of steel. In each case the hull is tarred, in contrast to the brightness of the superstructure. 'Motor' and 'butty' have similar bows, bluff but attractively shaped, with a thick band of iron extending from the keel and curving over on to the foredeck. Each side of the gunwales is painted for several feet, with a cluster of roses on a coloured ground and perhaps a row of lozenges in green, yellow or red. Sometimes these diamonds are formed by iron bands terminating in a fleur-de-lis design, the spaces between painted as before. It is thought likely that carrying companies once had their own distinctive arrangement of symbols for purposes of identification, although this is no longer the practice. The fore-end of the cargo space terminates in a triangular board, called the 'cratch', raised to the same height as the cabin roof and connected to it via a number of upright 'stands' and a towing mast, by planks supporting a tent of tarpaulins to keep weather out of the hold. The outer side of the cratch is often painted with diamonds or roses, and hung with a decorated navigation lamp, although more functional electric spot-lights are more commonly in use. With typical disregard for nautical terminology, the hinged cover of the foredeck is called a 'deck-lid', and is painted with a playing-card motif—red heart or ace of clubs—surrounded by a geometrical design in contrasting colours. Down the length of the boat, the top of each 'stand' carries a cluster of diamonds, the only adornment between the bows and the stern cabin.

Although the vessel's bows are gay enough, they represent only a foretaste of the riot of colour in the stern. The cabin top, behind which the boatman spends most of his daylight hours, is frequently of yellowish-brown grained wood. A shiny black chimney from the stove below, bound with rings of polished brass, stands on the left, complete with brass chain to secure it, should a low bridge or overhanging branch knock it from its socket. Ahead of the chimney rest two or three metal watercans, representing the sum total of plumbing aboard. A mop made of felt strips, with a barber's pole handle, rests on the cans. Formerly water was stored in small wooden barrels but since 1900, if not before, the can has been *de rigueur*. It is in the watercan that the boatman's art is seen at its best: clusters of roses cover top and sides, with sometimes a castle scene on the front. Often the skipper's name or that of his boat appears on a coloured band about the middle, and a row of stripes, consisting of the colours used in the design, encircles the base. Some boat people paint their own, although it was always an ambition, especially with Company boats, to purchase an 'artist's' can produced at one of a number of centres throughout the Midlands. Most famous of these was a little shop at the top of Buckby Locks on the Grand Union Canal in Northamptonshire, where a rare woman painter, whose artistic capabilities in other directions were limited, passed a lifetime painting cans for sale.

Two little doors lead from the counter to the cabin, and above, a wooden slide in the roof opens to make access easier. Each door is decorated with matching panels of roses, in some cases with a castle above, visible from outside when they are open, while the slide usually carries a playing-card motif similar to that on the foredeck lid. More castles feature in the decoration of the cabin sides, each in its own distinctive style, but generally depicting a fairy-tale castle by the side of a lake where a hump-backed bridge—like so many on the English waterways—spans a narrow stream in the foreground.

The origin of the canal castle is as obscure as theories are varied. One school of thought finds a link between narrow-boat paintings and the gipsy caravans of eastern Europe: it is possible that gipsies worked on the construction of canals in the eighteenth century and in time progressed to operating boats which they would have painted in their native style. More likely is the notion that these castles were the idealized factory buildings of the Midland waterways, and that of a number of farm-and-country scenes popular in the last century, the castle became most popular. Ask a boatman for his views and one is generally told that 'a boat just wouldn't be the same without its castles', beyond which he is of no assistance. The subject is so poorly documented that the most detailed research is unlikely to produce positive evidence.

The rudder of a motor-boat, although ablaze with more barber's pole painting, is a strictly functional curve of metal, with a detachable polished brass tiller. Not so with the butty boat: the whole rudder is referred to as the ram's head, and carries more elaborate adornment than any other part of the boat. There seems to be no set precedent for painting designs; often one finds a circle divided into coloured sections, like a child's first efforts with his pair of compasses. Elsewhere there will be neat bunches of roses and it is not uncommon to see the two together. The greatest ingenuity is put into decorative ropework: twin bands of entwined Turk's heads encircle the top of the rudder post, with an elegant pipe-clayed plait at the back, known as the swan's neck. The long curved wooden tiller, striped in keeping with the colour scheme of the boat, is also ringed with several Turk's heads whose function is to protect the paintwork when it is detached and lying on the cabin top. A neat circular fender on the extreme stern called a 'tipcat' protects the rudder when passing through locks. Though the function of ropework is to protect paintwork, it is in itself one of the most attractive aspects of narrow-boat decoration, and is maintained in spotless condition on a well-ordered boat. Plaited 'cabin side-strings' hang from the roof on the painted cabin sides to lessen wear on lettering should the chimney fall: they may also be looped through the handle of a watercan to secure it. Very occasionally one may still see a white horse's tail attached to the ram's head, as an ever-present reminder of a dead boat-horse.

Within the cabin, where it is less subject to the ravages of rain and wear, the decoration is even more lavish. Most prominent is the table, folding open from the cupboard, on which yet another castle is surrounded by roses and daisies. The walls are of grained wood, picked out with panels of flowers and fading wedding photographs or pictures of long-dead relations. Every boatwoman takes pride in her collection of 'hanging plates', originally Victorian souvenirs of a rare visit to the seaside, showing scenes of Blackpool or lettered 'A Present from Skegness', or alternatively hand-painted in pastel colours with flowers or fruit. Pierced at the edges in a delicate lace pattern, they are threaded with coloured ribbons to be tied to brass hooks or to a twisted brass rod above the stove. Hand-worked lace curtains, some serving no functional purpose, are gathered round the cabin

1 The helmsman at the tiller of a Thomas Clayton tar boat at Wolverhampton, showing the decorated doors and watercan forward of the funnel

2–9 The stern cabins of the barges are homes to the families who crew them. Although the owning companies choose the general colour scheme there is still plenty of scope for individual painting and decorative skill.
A pair of narrow boats exactly fills a broad lock on the Grand Union Canal; 6 shows the stern cabins of the motor and butty boats

sides and the main bed, contrasting with the glitter of rows of polished brass knobs and miniature windlasses, like the real ones used for opening the paddles on canal locks. Somewhere a deep metal bowl hangs on the wall, painted in the manner of the watercans: this is the 'dipper' and is used for a variety of domestic purposes, such as for washing-up or scooping water from the canal.

In such confined quarters, there is no room for chairs or other mobile furniture, but a small painted stool is quite common. Individual boat families will often decorate items for culinary use such as tea caddies and sugar tins, although traditionally Measham ware was used. This is a dark-brown glazed pottery picked out in relief with birds or flowers, and incorporating on the *pièce de résistance*, a magnificent teapot, a motto such as 'Forget-me-not'. Measham teapots, once bought by the boat people at that town on the Ashby Canal, are now sought-after antiques, and are rarely seen on narrow boats today.

Much of the decoration described above can still be seen on the English waterways: vanished however are boat-horses, with gay harness, crocheted ear caps and rose-covered feed bowls. Gone also—but not long since—is the elaborate dress of the boat people themselves. Victorian in origin, it was a quite distinctive style, and stubbornly resisted the changes which affected the clothes of people 'on the land'.

While English canal boats are famous for their elaborate painting, the craft of Holland, when they carried any decoration at all, excelled in carved wood. The Dutch waterways of the mid-twentieth century, like those of almost every country in Europe, annually become more prosperous, with the rather unfortunate result that the vessels which work on them are almost completely functional.

Consequently, this study of boat decoration is mainly concerned with the eighteenth and nineteenth centuries, which are rich in examples, and are well documented in a number of maritime museums in different parts of the country. Basically, decorative work was undertaken on the broad wooden *boeiers* and other sailing barges used as fishing boats and cargo vessels, and in a finer, more specialized form on pleasure craft.

The top of the wide rudder of commercial craft was always surmounted by a curved block of wood named a *klikbord*,

carved on each side with identical designs. Often the horn of plenty features in the design, no doubt because it is a symbol of good fortune, in the same way that a ship's figurehead was intended to bring good luck. Scrolls of flowers are the commonest motif, painted in bright reds, greens and yellows, while geometrical designs are also seen. The fore-end of the *klikbord* sometimes terminates in three carved circles which may also be painted direct on the wood instead of being in relief. Usually the entire *klikbord* is painted, but there are those simply varnished, with a pattern picked out in one colour. Being an easily removed part of the boat, many of these objects have survived, outliving the vessels which they originally adorned.

The long, curved tiller, extending from the *klikbord*, and generally present, even if rigged for wheel-steering, echoed the colours of the rudder top. In certain instances, a carved lion—always associated with Dutch sailing vessels—replaced the *klikbord*, varying in size from six inches in length on the smallest pleasure sailing boat to several feet long on commercial craft. Without exception they were gilded. Alternatively, carved heads of royalty and noblemen and seductive females took pride of place on the rudder, wisely guiding the boat to safety. Even though these heads were made until the late nineteenth century, the style of dress is always of a hundred years earlier. As well as being placed at the stern, the carved lions sometimes featured at the main cabin entrance, where they would be visible all the time.

Larger barges, especially those which were more ornate, carried a great shield on the stern above the top of the rudder, deeply carved and painted on each side. This was the *hakkebord*, and as the design on the side facing away from the boat incorporated the arms of the town of origin, it served as an identification mark, in much the same way as the registration number of a modern coastal port. The other side, facing the bows, bore a Biblical scene, which in some instances also appeared on the *klikbord*. Thus there was an odd mixture of Christian and pagan symbols.

Similar square shields with rounded tops, also displaying a coat of arms, were made as decorative shutters to windows in the ship's stern. Though not as popular as the lion, the dolphin was another creature used on carved panels, generally gilded.

When steel barges began to replace those made of wood, there was little place for carvings, so boats on the canals of Amsterdam and Rotterdam may now be seen with painted flowers and scrolls on their rounded sterns. There is no elaborate work such as is displayed on the narrow boats of English canals, and a design of this kind is frequently in two colours only.

One feature surviving to the present day is the wrought-iron device to hold an ensign mast, this being a short rod with two rings on one side for the mast, and on the other an elaborate profusion of curled fronds. Strips of iron, coiled or in half-circles, were used on the gunwales and leeboards, especially on small pleasure boats. Originally they served the purpose of strengthening a join where two timbers came together, but often they have no functional use.

Sailing barges of the eighteenth century have left the Dutch museums a number of interesting relics, the purpose of which is in some instances obscure. *Mastwortel* is the Dutch word for a fanciful pagoda-like rod of carved wood which stood at the very top of the mast, set in a wooden sphere varying in design from something not unlike a pineapple to a cottage loaf covered with abstract patterns! They were

gilded, occasionally being picked out in a single bright colour.

Cabin sides are often adorned with painted shutters, where a number of triangles in two colours are used. Waterside cottages also have these shutters and it is not clear whether the pattern originated ashore or afloat.

Some of the finest complete craft are to be found preserved in museums in Amsterdam and at the Zuider Zee port of Enkhuizen. These are small pleasure boats, of which practically every inch is elaborately carved and painted. The number of these craft must originally have been very great, as travel by water in Holland was as convenient and obvious a mode of transport as movement by road in England, and the Dutch took as much pride in their passenger barges as the English did in their carriages. All the devices common on commercial vessels were used, with greater emphasis on carved leaves, scrolls and iron work. Borders of coloured triangles are to be found about the rudder and on the inside curve of the bluff, rounded bows. Yet these boats were far from fragile, and today, two centuries after some of them were built, they are as strong as they ever were.

14

15

16

17

18

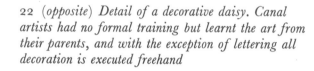

19

22 (opposite) Detail of a decorative daisy. Canal artists had no formal training but learnt the art from their parents, and with the exception of lettering all decoration is executed freehand

20

21

24

25

26

23

27
28

126

23–30 *It is always a boatman's ambition to cover every available area on his boat with decorative painting. When there were sufficient boats in private ownership, yards specialized in building and decorating narrow boats, and provided artists' patterns which a customer could choose and have copied on to his boat*

29

30

31 (opposite) This watercan, of the type produced on the Grand Union Canal until the 1930s, is a fine example of canal boat art

32 The rampant lion is Dutch—the decorated shutter of a stern window—and well illustrates the sharp contrast between the barge art of the two nations

33–38 Castles set in lakes, and roses, are popular decorations for doors, coal boxes and tables. 36 is a painting of the last surviving horse-drawn narrow boat, owned by Joe Skinner but decorated by Herbert Tooley of Banbury, whose family has practised this art for generations

32

33

34   35

36

37

38

39–60 *These pictures show the wonderful variety of design and colour which can be achieved within the formality of style which is peculiar to British barges. Everything that has a surface—horsebowl or cabin stool, watercan or navigation lamp—is covered with decoration.*

The British 'ram's head' (52) is quite different from the rudder heads of Dutch barges, which are capped with klikbords *(bottom row) whose popular motif is the horn of plenty*

44–48

49–53

54–60

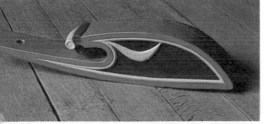

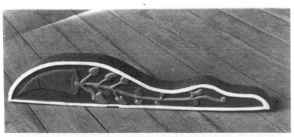

61 *Narrow-boat girl of the Upper Thames, 1875*

62–77 The Dutch delighted in carved wood on their barges, which they sometimes painted as well. Biblical scenes are frequent and 69 shows Christ walking on the water. (Matt. xiv : 22–34)

On pleasure craft, in contrast to commercial vessels, the klikbord *is often replaced by a carved and gilded lion, or a carved head. The carved and painted tiller in 72 may represent Jonah being swallowed by the big fish.*

As well as carved klikbords *the masts were topped with carved cappings (64 and 76) surmounted by a spike called a* mastwortel *(65), and wrought iron was much used, such as the ensign-staff support in 74*

64

65

66
67

71

70

72 73 74 75 76 77

IOHANNIS II.

80

81

78–79 *Probably the finest carving was to be found on the* hakkebord, *a heavy wooden shield positioned at the stern of the boat above the rudder. This one is the scene of the marriage feast at Cana (John ii : 1–11) and was carved in the first half of the eighteenth century. On the side away from the vessel are the arms of Amsterdam and Amersfoort, the towns between which the barge plied*

80–81 *This model of a Zeeland pleasure boat was built in 1763. The stern view shows a coat of arms and the rowlocks forward of the cabin indicate that it was designed for oars*

82 *This* hakkebord *is again a Biblical scene, surrounded by an ornate border of flowers. The crown above the seraph suggests a royal connection*

82

83–87 *In North Holland the horse-drawn barge served on the waterways in lieu of the carriage and was no doubt considerably more comfortable for the occupants. This barge was built in the middle of the eighteenth century and the detailed illustrations, from this and a similar vessel, show the elaborate decoration of stem and stern*

83

8

85

86

136

8

MISSISSIPPI RIVERCRAFT

WILLARD PRICE

The floating palaces of the old-time Mississippi are gone. Or nearly so. In five months' search from the river's source to its mouth, we found only twenty-six survivors.

One is the *Avalon*. She still holds together and is used for daytime excursions out from St Paul. We went aboard to the lusty strains of the calliope playing 'Cruising Down the River'.

We climbed to the top deck to see this remarkable instrument. At the keyboard was Clark Hawley, first mate and musician. Between selections, we got in a few questions.

'How old is this instrument?'

'About half a century.'

'Are there many of them left?'

'This is the last save one.'

He burst into 'Old Man River'. It was deafening, but at the same time stirring. As each key was pressed, the corresponding valve sent up a shrill shriek of steam.

'Is it like playing the organ?' my wife asked when he had finished.

'About the same, but harder. Each note requires fifty-five pounds' pressure.'

It takes strong fingers and a strong back, and cotton in the ears. But it is effective. No one within half a mile could be unaware that the *Avalon* was about to sail. People were swarming aboard.

With 1,300 passengers, the *Avalon* left the dock, her giant stern-wheel sending up clouds of spray.

We went into the pilot house. The pilot stood behind a wheel eight feet in diameter, one of three still in use on the Mississippi. Modern river-boats are steered by small levers.

The pilot was proud of the boat's whistle. To make it blow, he must put his full weight on a pedal. Today's whistles are operated by touching a button. But the result is not the same. There is no such rich, deep-throated thunder from the modern whistle.

As for the interior décor, only vestiges of the old glory remained. The halcyon days of the steamboat age were famous for crystal chandeliers, murals, mirrors, hand-carved woodwork, lush carpets, fine furniture, marble statues and oil paintings. Dining saloon service was epicurean. The menu was two feet long and offered thirteen desserts.

One vessel, the *Eclipse*, eclipsed her competitors by providing forty-eight bridal chambers, a grand piano, complete orchestra and sumptuous quarters for the wealthy planter who chose to take along a full retinue of servants.

'The steamboats were finer than anything on shore,' wrote Mark Twain. 'When a citizen stepped on board a big fine steamboat he entered a new and marvellous world.'

The boat was as fine outside as within. Her great stern-wheel or two immense side wheels, flinging up rainbows, were a sight to behold. Her tall twin stacks were surmounted by iron feathers. Her name was lettered in gold leaf. She was adorned from stem to stern by flags, burgees and pennants. If she won the annual speed contest, she wore a pair of gilded horns on the forehead of her pilot house.

All that is history. Yet there are some notable veterans.

At St Louis we boarded the side-wheeler *Admiral* for an afternoon excursion. Built in the late nineteenth century as a railroad ferry, she was remodelled as an excursion boat in 1941. She is truly fabulous—the world's largest river excursion boat, 387 feet long, six decks high. Her huge ballroom accommodates 2,000 dancers at a time.

The main deck is a floating carnival, a water-borne Coney Island or Southend, with all manner of amusements, games, rifle ranges, peep-shows, side-shows, painted horses, grizzly bears, fortune-tellers, snack bars, spread over a deck so large it could accommodate a freight train, and formerly did. This amusement park afloat has been featured in *Cinerama*. The capacity of the boat is 4,000, and she is always sold out. Two great paddle-wheels churn her three hours down river and back.

Moored close to the *Admiral* at the St Louis waterfront was one of the last of the showboats, the *Goldenrod*. On the night of our visit the production in the floating theatre was an old-time melodrama involving an innocent maiden, a scheming villain and of course an indomitable hero. A strong-armed musician ripped the intestines out of an ancient upright.

1

138

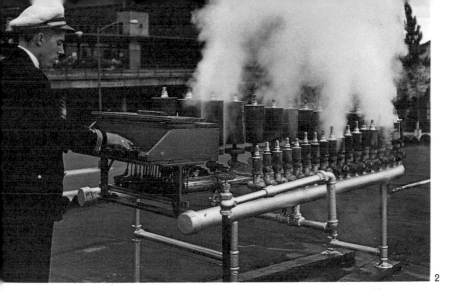

Another showboat, the *Mississippi Melodie*, carrying seventy actors and a band, puts on regular productions during the summer months. And the ancient giant, *Sprague*, entertains Vicksburg audiences with 'Gold in the Hills'. This vessel is notable for her steering-wheel *fourteen feet* in diameter. Eight men were needed to turn it. It is turned no longer, for the decrepit *Sprague* is now permanently moored to the shore.

The last of the steamboats to take overnight passengers is the *Delta Queen*. This venerable sternwheeler still makes regular cruises from Cincinnati to New Orleans and from Cincinnati to St Paul. We sailed her south. We found her a floating hotel in the old tradition of deep comfort and fine food, but there was one agreeably modern feature, air-conditioning.

The steamboat era has passed, but the Mississippi is not dead. Quite the contrary. The million-dollar towboat with her quarter-mile of barges can move more cargo than could be carried in a fully loaded train four miles long.

In the best days of the steamboat age a thousand packets sailed the Mississippi, carrying 250,000 tons. Now it takes not a thousand, but only ten diesel towboats to handle that tonnage.

The river swarms with these monsters. They do an inestimably important job. But they are quite devoid of chandeliers and murals, calliopes and grand pianos, iron plumes and gilded horns. The glamour is gone.

1 *The twin-stacked sternwheeler* Avalon *taking on excursion passengers at St Paul*

2 *The calliope of the* Avalon

3 *The* Admiral, *old-time railroad ferry. Remodelled, it is the world's largest river excursion boat*

4 *Some old-time steamboats such as the* Mississippi *have been taken over by the U.S. engineers who maintain the waterway*

5

5 *Murals such as this one, copied from the original in a long-gone riverboat, represented fine Southern homes seen along the lower reaches of the Mississippi*

6 *The old showboat* Goldenrod

6

7 *The* Mississippi Melodie, *new boat on an old model, carries seventy actors and a band and puts on nightly productions during the summer months*

8 *Mural such as those used in the old-time river boats*

9 Delta Queen, *last of the Mississippi riverboats still carrying overnight passengers*

10 *The great sternwheel of the* Delta Queen

8

9

11 *The double-faced* Pelican, *a pilot house at each end, transports railroad cars back and forth across the Mississippi*

CHAPTER IX

Charts & Maps

CHRISTOPHER LLOYD

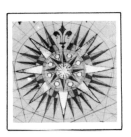

It was said of Thomas Hobbes the philosopher that 'when at Oxford he used to love to visit the booksellers' shops, there to lie gaping on maps'. Those who have looked at the old sea charts and atlases which are now, on account of their rarity, chiefly in libraries and museums will readily sympathize with him. Apart from their historical interest, their chief attraction lies in their decorative fantasies and the brilliant colouring with which so many are embellished: as aids to navigation, few were trustworthy even in their own day. What Swift wrote of land maps is even more true of sea charts, because the oceans provided plenty of convenient blank spaces for the cartographer to enliven his art:

> So geographers, in Afric-maps,
> With savage-pictures fill their gaps;
> And o'er unhabitable downs
> Place elephants for want of towns.

Art played as important a part as science in the minds of the early cartographers, because imagination was needed to supplement the meagre geographical knowledge available to them. Without precision instruments for survey and in the absence of any substantial body of recorded observations, large areas could not be delineated with any accuracy; and for shorter distances most seamen, feeling their way around the coasts with log, lead and line, had little use for the new-fangled methods of navigation. They groped their way like blind men, complained William Bourne, the Gravesend inn-keeper who wrote the first English textbook on navigation, and 'derided and mocked them that have occupied their cards and plats, saying they care not for their sheep's skins, for they could keep a better account upon a board'.

Early charts were therefore more often made for the delec-tation of the shipowner and the curious-minded patron than for the use of the skipper who, if he owned such a thing, kept it as a secret part of his 'mystery' or trade. The more practical information came from sailing directions or itineraries which precede the chart proper, though when charts began to be printed these were usually bound up with them in a sea atlas. Thus the *portolano, routier, rutter* or *leescaert* antedate the *portulan, pascaart* or *card*—hence chart. These manuscripts were usually done on vellum, though sometimes on cardboard or wood. They are very rare, very lovely and for short distances astonishingly accurate. They are seldom gridded for latitude

Placidus Caloiro et Oliua fecit in nobili urbe Messane
ano 1656

and longitude, since ascertaining the latter accurately was an unsolved problem until the invention of the chronometer in the eighteenth century, but are essentially plain charts or guides for short distances, showing in varying colours the towns, rivers, capes and headlands.

The mariner needs to know at which country he has arrived, so heraldic banners are planted along the coasts, and there is a symbolic representation of an important port. The Mediterranean coastline is invariably thus beflagged. In the land of Prester John, the Emperor of Ethiopia is seated upon his throne. Arab chieftains cluster in tents along the shores of Barbary. Natives run naked and strange animals prowl in unknown hinterlands. The Red Sea is always coloured red. A taste for monsters is inherited from medieval maps, because the oceans are wide and the unexplored parts of the world offered a sinister blank. Such fabulous additions to the map range from the anthropophagi and the men whose heads do grow beneath their shoulders to lobsters catching mariners in their claws, or (a tale told of St Brandan) whales on which ships anchored, mistaking them for islands.

Not all such decoration is useless or incredible, because a galleon ploughing a lonely ocean often suggests a trade route or the direction of a prevailing wind. To show sailing routes rhumb lines, or lines of constant bearing, radiate like spiders' webs from compasses or wind-roses placed at convenient points. Sometimes there is a mile or league scale, every country having its own sea mile and most of them their own meridian.

It was a Mediterranean art based on Venice, Genoa, Lisbon and Majorca, where the great Catalan school of portulan makers flourished in the fifteenth and sixteenth centuries. Their names—Grazioso Benincasa, Vesconte Maggiolo, Battista Agnese—indicate their origin. It was never a northern art, though Henry VIII would have liked to have founded a school of cartography (as he did Trinity House) recruited from the pilots of Dieppe. One of these, Jean Rotz, executed for him a wonderful collection of maps: the Royal Atlas of 1542, which he called 'the boke of Ydrographie made by me John Rotz, sarvant to the King's mooste excellent Majeste. Gode save his Majeste'. In this the borders are gilded half an inch broad, the land covered

with brightly coloured animals and vegetation, but the sea left blank except for ornate compass roses and a lonely galleon crossing the Atlantic from 'the new fonde lande quhar men goeth a fishing'. A more prolific cartographer of Tudor times was Diogo Homem, who worked in London during the reign of Mary after being involved in a murder at Lisbon.

These beautiful manuscripts were gradually superseded by printed charts after the invention of copperplate engraving by the Italians about 1540. Wood engraving was a more clumsy technique and only one notable chart was so engraved, the huge Carta Marina done by Olaus Magnus, a Swedish archbishop living at Venice in 1539. To judge from the monsters then inhabiting the North Sea, it must have been a fearsome place.

Printed charts, like printed books, enjoyed a wider circulation and lasted longer than the portulans. Improved calligraphy made them more legible than those done with the old Gothic script, but since engraving was expensive, plates continued in use long after the rapid expansion of geographical knowledge had exposed their errors. Italic cursive lettering was popularized by Abraham Ortelius in the earliest comprehensive collection of maps, the *Theatrum Orbis Terrarum* of 1570, and by his partner Gerhard Mercator, who introduced the word 'atlas' for such collections in his title-page in 1585, which shows a titan with the globe upon his shoulders and the inscription 'Atlas, or the meditations of a cosmographer upon the shape of the world'. Now that explorers had opened up the ocean routes, these large-scale maps were useful to seamen for 'running down' a latitude, because Mercator's projection (invented in 1569) gave true bearings between any two points.

The practical application of this projection to oceanic maps was demonstrated by Edward Wright of Cambridge in 1599, when he published his world map in the second edition of Hakluyt's *Principal Navigations*. The first marine atlas to be drawn on it is Sir Robert Dudley's *Arcano del Mare*, printed in Florence in 1646. In this 'mighty work attempting to set forth into pages all the secrets of the sea', the calligraphic arabesques are so convoluted that they are sometimes difficult to read.

A plainer, smaller, cheaper marine atlas was *The Mariners'*

2 *The medieval fear of the sea is illustrated in this section from the huge* Carta Marina *done by the Swedish archbishop Olaus Magnus at Venice in 1539. It is more useful for its information about the land (e.g. the hot springs of Iceland) than the sea. Marine information was derived from seamen of the Hanseatic League and from medieval legends, such as the tale of St Brandan, in which a ship is sunk by a whale after anchoring to it by mistake.*

The area depicted is from Greenland (Gruntland) south to Iceland (Islandia), the Faroes, Shetland (Hetlandia), the Orkneys (Orcades) and Iona (Hebrides). 'Tile' is Magnus's version of the legendary Thule. South of Iceland the crew of a Hanseatic vessel try to placate a monster by throwing beer barrels overboard and charming it with music from the poop. Farther west a Hamburg ship is engaging one from Scotland with gunfire

Mirrour by Lucas Janszoon Waghenaer, published (as were the fourteen editions of Ortelius) by the famous Antwerp printer Christopher Plantin in 1584. This was translated into English in the year of the Armada and proved so popular that the word 'wagoner' came to denote any collection of charts. An innovation was the delineation of the coastline in low angle oblique and in elevation profile at the top of the chart, forming a silhouette of the land as seen from the sea, which still features in modern charts. This, the first sea atlas, marks the shift from Italian cartography to new centres in Antwerp and Amsterdam. The rise of Dutch sea power was accompanied by a virtual monopoly in the map and chart trade. Ortelius and Mercator were the Flemish fathers of the sea atlases of the Dutchmen, Waghenaer, Hondius and the great firm of Blaeu. In the seventeenth century their huge and finely ornamented atlases were sold everywhere and translated into all languages, so that it is difficult to recognize Jan Jansson as 'John Johnson, bookseller, dwelling upon the water side by the old bridge at the sign of the sea mappe' until we see 'Amsterdam 1620' printed below. Jansson corrected the maps of predecessors like Waghenaer, Barents and Van Linschoten, who published the first itinerary to the Spice Islands in 1596, thereby laying the foundation of the great East India navigation. Publishers bought, borrowed and stole each other's plates, but in the numerous take-over bids the firm of Blaeu triumphed.

All these atlases have the same characteristics: elaborate title-pages illustrating the use of marine and survey instruments, beautiful cartouches or town plans which provide valuable information for the historian. Coastal elevations are usually printed in the text of the sailing instructions. Charts could be purchased coloured or uncoloured (Ortelius started life as a 'painter of maps') but most existing examples have been coloured by later collectors. To add to the variety of titles—*Sea Mirrour, Treasure of the Sea, Light of Navigation, Sea Beacon, Torch of the Sea*—one publisher, Arnold Colom, used his name as a pun in *The Upright Fiery Colomme*.

Perhaps the most splendid of them is Johannes van Keulen's *New Great Shining Torch of the Sea* (1682), in which the art of the cartouche reaches its zenith. The Italians had introduced the framed title of a map, using plain, elegant strapwork designs for the borders. But in the age of the baroque the Dutchmen preferred swags of fruit, garlanded nymphs and pink-cheeked cherubs, pendants of birds and swash lettering. Blaeu introduced figure supporters to illustrate the costumes and customs of the area delineated. In his *Atlas Major* (1648–65) he added plans of cities and battles in the margins, but such vignettes seldom appear in sea charts, however ornamented the framework of the cartouches or the mile scale. To meet the demand for such ornamentation, William Folkingham says in his *Feudigraphia: the synopsis or epitome of Surveying Methodized* (1610) that 'the tricking of Plots [i.e. decoration of maps] consists in Complements and Compartiments. Compliments comprehend the Flie or Flies [compass roses], Scale and Compasse [i.e. dividers], Kalendar Characters, Colours, etc. . . . Compartiments are Blankes or Figures bordered with Antique Boscage or Croteska-worke, wherein Evidences or other Memorables may be abreviated'. Here, adds Henry Peachum in his *Art of Drawing and Limming* (1612) 'you may, if you list, draw naked boys riding . . . with a thousand more such idle toys, so that herein you cannot be too fantastical. The late Dutch peeces in this kinde excell all others.'

The Italians continued to publish good charts until the end of the century, especially those by Fra Vincenzo Coronelli, Cosmographer of the Republic of Venice, whose *Mediterraneo* (1688) and *Specchio del Mare* (1698) are of the highest standard of engraving, with finely executed views of seaports. The French were now in the field with their highly decorated and comparatively accurate series called *Le Neptune François*, which began to be issued in 1693 by Alexis Hubert Jaillot in collaboration with the famous surveyor Cassini. This covered most of the known world and was much used by their rivals, for instance by Nelson at the Battle of the Nile.

The English were slow to make a reputation for cartography. In the Tudor period there is nothing save a few charts of the Thames estuary and for a long time they relied on the Dutch. Even in their first sea atlas—*The English Pilot*, published by John Seller in 1671—old worn Dutch plates were used, as Pepys complained, for a mere business venture. Such a state of affairs could no longer be tolerated in a nation which, by the defeat of their Dutch rivals, was now the premier maritime power. Nor was it acceptable to a

GRVNTLANDIÆ
PARS

HVITSARK

ISLANDIA

GEOGRAPHIAE STVDIOSO
TYPOGRAPHVS.

MARE,
DEVCALIDONICVM

149

3 *A typical portulan of the Mediterranean in which the coastline is depicted with remarkable accuracy, but legendary lands are not far off in the interior. South of Cairo is the land of Prester John, seen enthroned in his tent. Beyond the Red Sea (shown in red) are unicorns and camelopards, and elephants in Turkey. At the top are the kings of Muscovy (left) and Grand Tartary (right). The signature, not shown here because it is on the extreme left of the chart which extends to Iceland, states that it was done by Vesconte de Maggiolo at Genoa in 1548. The chart, covering a whole sheepskin, measures 46 by 31 inches*

4 *Western Europe by Jean Rotz of Dieppe, whose collection of charts on vellum is often called the Royal Atlas because it was dedicated to Henry VIII in 1542. It is a sumptuous example of the portulan type. Since such manuscript charts were not orientated in the modern manner, this is reproduced here as the lettering suggests. The northern part (at the bottom) shows the old Ptolemaic idea that Scotland was somehow divided from England. The compass roses are brilliantly coloured*

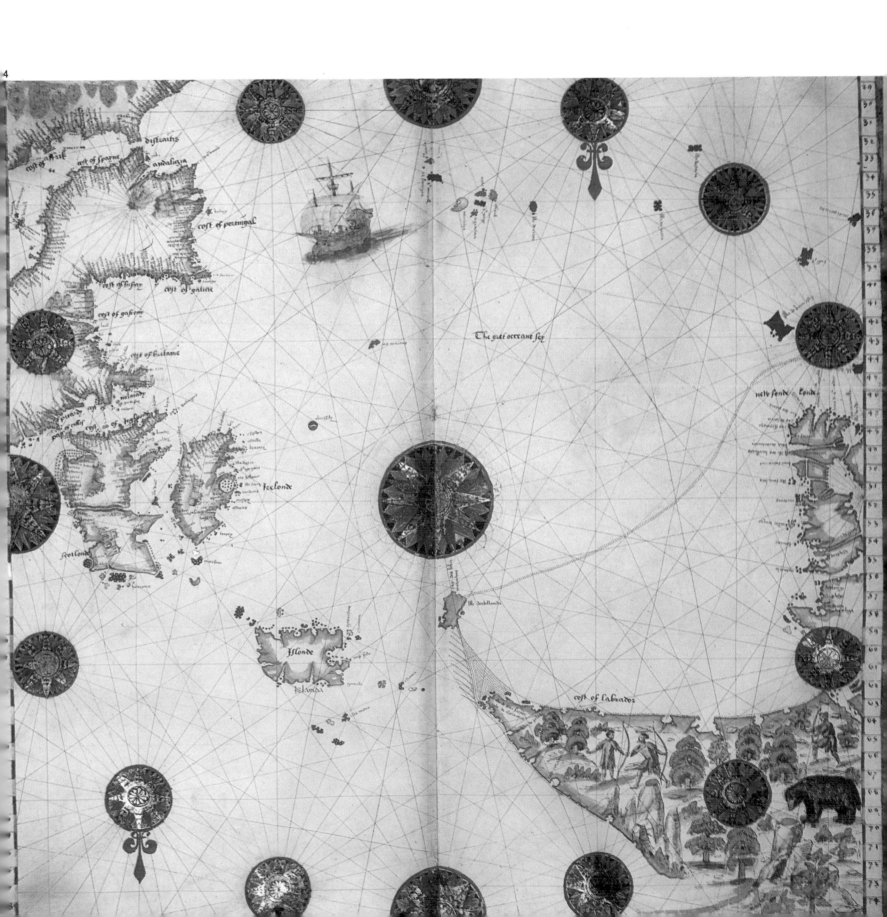

man like Samuel Pepys, Secretary of the Admiralty, Master of Trinity House, President of the Royal Society and a great collector of maps. At his suggestion Captain Greenvile Collins was chosen 'to make a survey of the sea coasts of the kingdom by measuring all the sea coasts with a chain and taking all the bearings of the headlands with their exact latitude'. The fruits of this immense task were embodied in *Great Britain's Coasting Pilot*, which was re-issued for a century after 1693.

By that date there was considerable trade in charts centred in the Ratcliffe Highway in London. The copyists dealt chiefly in portulans, which were still used by masters of coasting vessels and often embellished with pretty devices. One notable copyist was William Hack of Wapping, a friend of the buccaneer Bartholomew Sharp, who, when he returned from a cruise in the Pacific with some captured Spanish charts, bought himself off from a charge of piracy by getting Hack to do three copies of these secret documents for the King. The rich colouring of this *Wagoner of the Great South Sea* is not matched by a very high standard of draughtsmanship.

New standards of cartographical work were set by the British in the next century. The first steps were taken by Murdoch Mackenzie in his use of the theodolite and the principle of triangulation when charting the western coasts of Britain. He began the tendency towards scientific accuracy at the expense of purely decorative elements in charts, though both are present in the huge series composing *The Atlantic Neptune* by J. F. W. DesBarres, subsidized for the purposes of the American War of Independence by the Admiralty from 1774. DesBarres, a Swiss by birth, was an engineer-surveyor in the Royal American Regiment and a friend of General Wolfe at the capture of Quebec in 1759. In the years that followed he turned to marine survey and taught two of the most notable cartographers their trade—Captain James Cook and Captain Thomas Hurd, who became head of the Hydrographic Department of the Admiralty. As part of his surveys of the North American coastline, DesBarres executed in watercolour a beautiful series of vignettes and views which give a lively picture of Nova Scotia, where he spent his old age, dying at the age of a hundred and two as Governor of Prince Edward Island.

The original impetus towards a higher standard of accuracy was given by the Royal Society in London and the Académie Française in Paris. Disasters attributed to bad charts, such as the shipwreck of Sir Cloudesley Shovell on the Isles of Scilly in 1707, shocked the public into an awareness of such dangers. These defects were partly due to a continued failure to find the means of ascertaining the longitude, until the problem was solved by John Harrison with the chronometer, the fourth model of which Cook carried with him on his second voyage in 1772–5. This made feasible the construction of accurate large-scale charts, which now became utilitarian instruments of navigation, tools for the seaman to do his job in safety, rather than artistic exercises for the delectation of rich patrons. Colour and ornament disappear in the interests of accuracy and convenience, and the chart becomes part of the equipment of the ship rather than an ornament for the closet or library.

The man who symbolizes this scientific revolution is Captain James Cook, the finest seaman England has ever produced. He made his reputation as a Master, that is to say a navigating officer, in the Royal Navy when charting the St Lawrence and the coasts of Newfoundland under the tutelage of DesBarres. When, as a lieutenant, he was appointed to the command of the *Endeavour* in 1768 for his first voyage in the Pacific, he criticized those publishers who passed off 'rude sketches of the navigator as accurate surveys', and he blamed seamen for laying down a coast they had never even seen, or marking soundings where they had never sailed. 'These things must in time be attended with bad consequences and cannot fail of bringing the whole of their works into disrepute.' It was his work to make the chart a scientific instrument of navigation and therefore to dispense with all the delightful nonsense which intrigues us in earlier work of this sort.

The transformation of cartography from an art to a science was secured by the establishment of the Hydrographic Department of the Admiralty in 1795, four years after the Ordnance Survey was founded to map the land of Britain. It was the high reputation for the accuracy, not the beauty, of the charts issued by this office which enabled seamen of all nations in the nineteenth century to overcome their fears of unknown seas and to sail with confidence to every part of the world 'By God and the Admiralty Chart'.

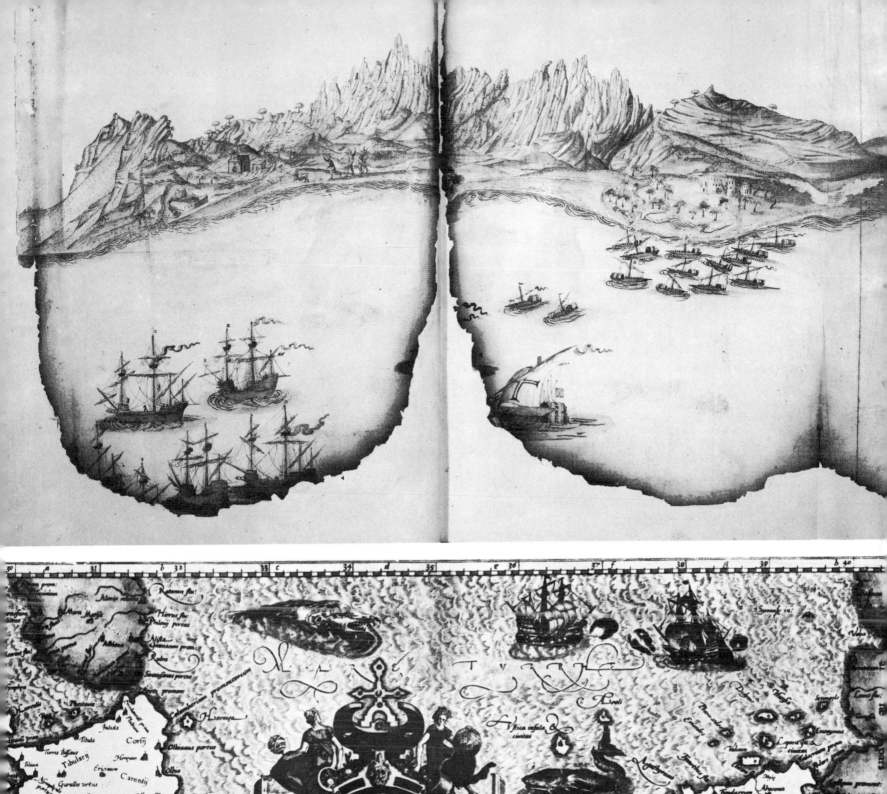

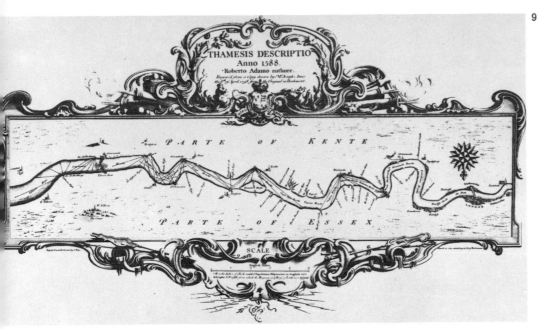

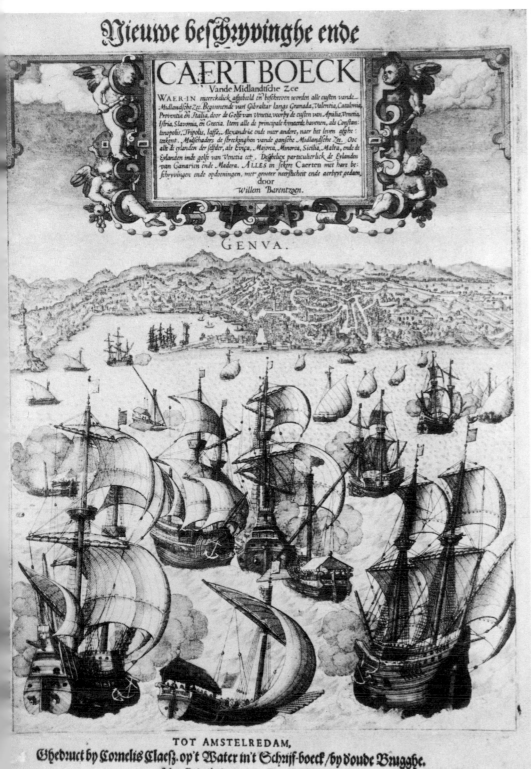

7 *A chart of the South Atlantic called* Oceanus Aethiopicus *by Jan Huyghen van Lintschoten (or Linschoten) whose* Itinerario *was printed at Amsterdam in 1596 to provide the first public description of the route to the Indies. It was much used by the East India companies of all nations which were founded shortly after it appeared. In the strapwork cartouche are views of two of the watering bases on the way, Ascension and St Helena. In some copies the central cartouche is coloured a brilliant red. The book includes sailing directions, pictures of oriental shipping (including the first European representation of a Chinese junk), and views of the Dutch and Portuguese factories in the East*

8 *Hudson's ships discovering Hudson Bay in 1608, from a chart by Hessel Gerritsz published in 1612. Most of the names given by earlier explorers such as Davis and Frobisher remain to this day, but the Ilha de Bacalhoa (Isle of Cod) at the bottom is now Newfoundland. The island of Good Fortune is now Resolution Island and Hold-with-Hope has become Cape Hope's Advance. Yslandt is, of course, Iceland, and Queen Elizabeth's Foreland should have been identified with Cape Elizabeth farther west*

9 *The Thames from Westminster (right) to the camp and defences at Tilbury (left) drawn by Robert Adam as part of his series of battle plans done to celebrate the victory over the Spanish Armada in 1588. These were engraved by Augustine Ryther and originally published in Saxton's* County Atlas of England, *dedicated to Howard of Effingham, the Lord Admiral. Howard had the plans copied in a magnificent set of tapestries for the House of Lords and these in turn were reproduced by the eighteenth-century engraver John Pine in 1739: hence the rococo frame to the original drawing. The boom defences at Gravesend and Lee Nesse (Blackwall Point) are shown, with the palace at Greenwich where Queen Elizabeth resided during the crisis. Greenwich Observatory, with the line of the prime meridian, was then only a fort on the hill above the palace*

10 *The title-page of Willem Barents' book of charts printed at Amsterdam in 1595, showing the harbour and town of Genoa in the background. Various types of Mediterranean shipping—lateen-rigged galleys and square-rigged galleons—are beautifully delineated. Barents is better known as a polar explorer who gave his name to the sea north of Russia. He died of scurvy on the last of his three voyages in 1596, and his hut and journals were found on the Kola peninsula in 1871*

11 *The American coast from Cape Hatteras to Cape James on the Delaware, from Sir Robert Dudley's* Dell'Arcano del Mare, *printed at Florence in 1646. This huge collection of charts was the first to use Mercator's projection throughout. The standard of engraving is very high, but the italic lettering is sometimes too elaborate to be easily read and charts such as these could never have been used at sea. The outline of the coast is derived from Captain John Smith, the founder of Virginia*

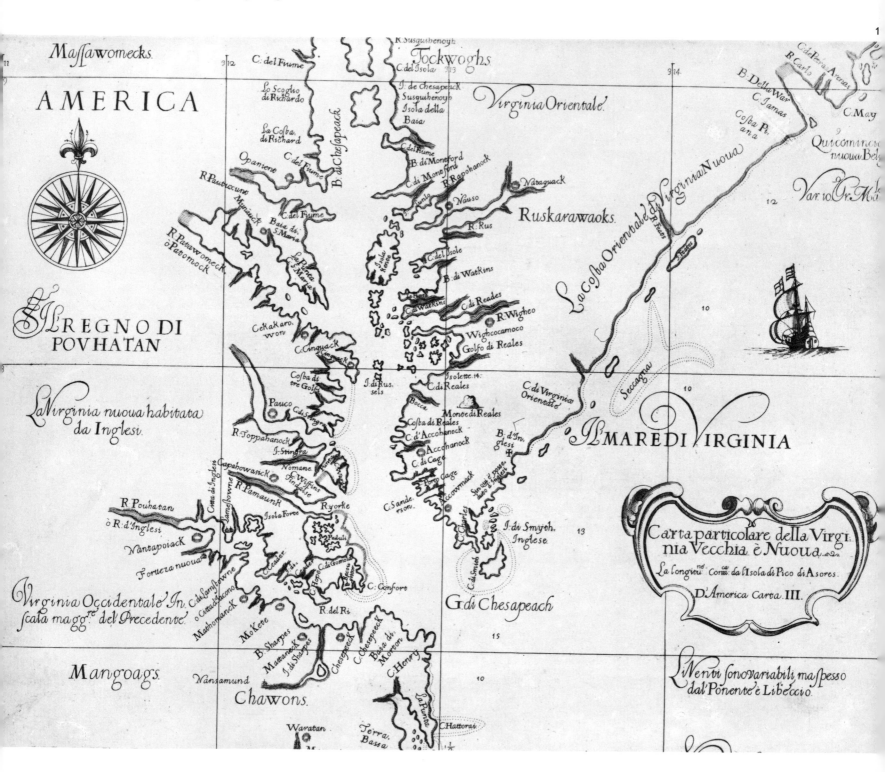

12 *The frontispiece of* The Light of Navigation, *wherein are declared and lively pourtrayed all the Coasts and Havens of the West, North and East Seas; collected out of the books of the Principall Authors which have written of Navigation (as Lucas Johnson Waghenaer and divers others), partly out of manie expert Seafaring men's writings and verball declarations, originally published by Blaeu at Amsterdam in 1620. A pirated English edition appeared by Jansson, calling himself* John Johnson, *dwelling upon the Waterside by the Old Bridge at the Signe of the Sea-Mappes.*

Below the Dutch fleet at sea is a semicircle of cartographers and seamen (to be distinguished by their conical caps) with their instruments. A sentence in the preface reads: 'What great good and profit (gentle reader) is procured unto all seafaring men by books of seacards which heretofore have been made by L. J. Waghenaer, W. Barents and others, wherein they with great diligence have written the situation of the streams, havens and channels of the seas in diverse countries, it is impossible to declare.'

13 *A cartouche from the chart of the seas north of Russia by Frederick De Wit in his* Sea Atlas *of 1675. There were three generations of cartographers of the same name and their firm bought Blaeu's plates after a fire had destroyed the premises of the older firm in 1672*

14 The Mariner's Mirrour *by Lucas Jan
Waghenaer, published in 1588, included the work of
several distinguished engravers, such as Theodore
De Bry, Ryther and Hondius. Originally printed
by the great Antwerp printer Christopher Plantin in
1584, this was the first collection of charts of
northern waters. The sheet here reproduced shows
the coast between Whitby and Tynemouth. The
fleur-de-lis on the compass rose shows the north
(septentrio) pointing to the scales of English,
Spanish and Dutch leagues. In all these charts ships
were well depicted, and here the Dogger Bank
fishing vessels are hauling in their trawls, with
the herring positively waiting to be caught.
Waghenaer adds 'In these coasts and specially at
Newcastle is merveillous great traffique for sea coles,
which are transported thence to other countries.'*

*The silhouette at the top repeats the oblique
perspective representation of the coastline, so that
landmarks and seamarks may be easily distinguished
and suitable anchorages are shown in each estuary*

15 *The title-page of a splendidly coloured Spanish
edition of Joannes Van Keulen's* Torch of the Sea,
*which began publication in 1681. This Spanish
edition of 1700 was printed, as were those in
English and French, at Amsterdam. Under the signs
of the zodiac and various tutelary deities, geographers
are shown at work on a globe, assisted by seamen
and others holding the tools of their trade—dividers,
cross-staff, compass and mariner's astrolabe*

14

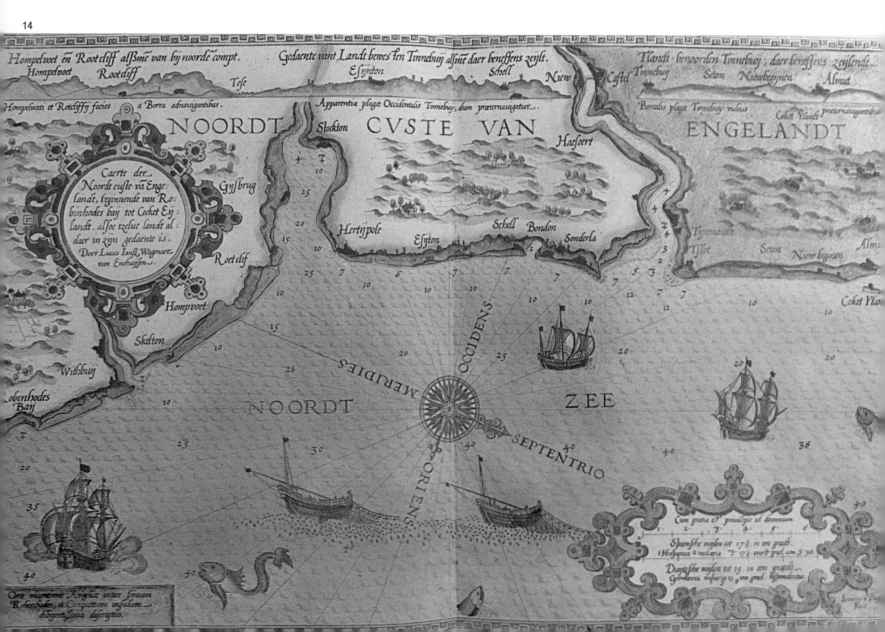

La Nueva y Grande Relumbrante

NTORCHA DE LA MAR,

QUE CONTIENE

efcription de las coftas Maritimas Meredionales de la *Mar* del *Nord*, de la Mancha, Inglaterra, Efcocia

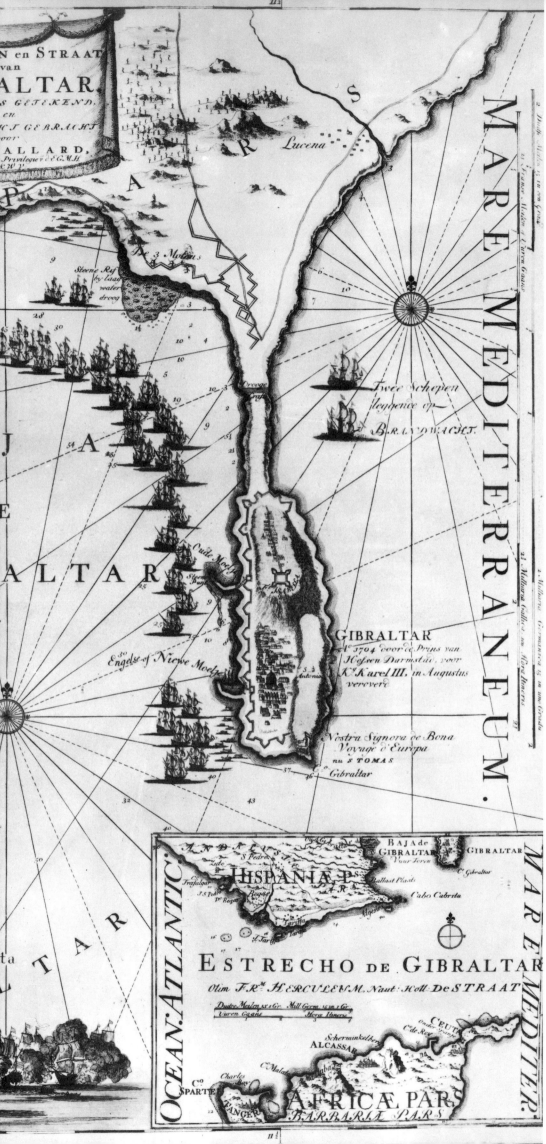

The capture of Gibraltar as depicted in Schenk's Atlas Contractus, *Amsterdam, 1713. This rare and splendid collection of maps of sea and land also contains brilliantly coloured plans of the victories in the War of the Spanish Succession, together with views of royal palaces and cities. In this plan Rooke's fleet is shown to the left where the landing was made. In the legend on the right all credit is given to the Prince of Hesse Darmstadt, who led the landing of the maritime regiments. Schenk was originally an employee of Jansson, whose plates he bought when he set up in business on his own account after 1660. The engraver of this plan was his partner, Carel Allard*

17 Another cartouche from Joannes Van Keulen's Torch of the Sea *showing Holland with its typical dried fish and familiar round Dutch cheeses*

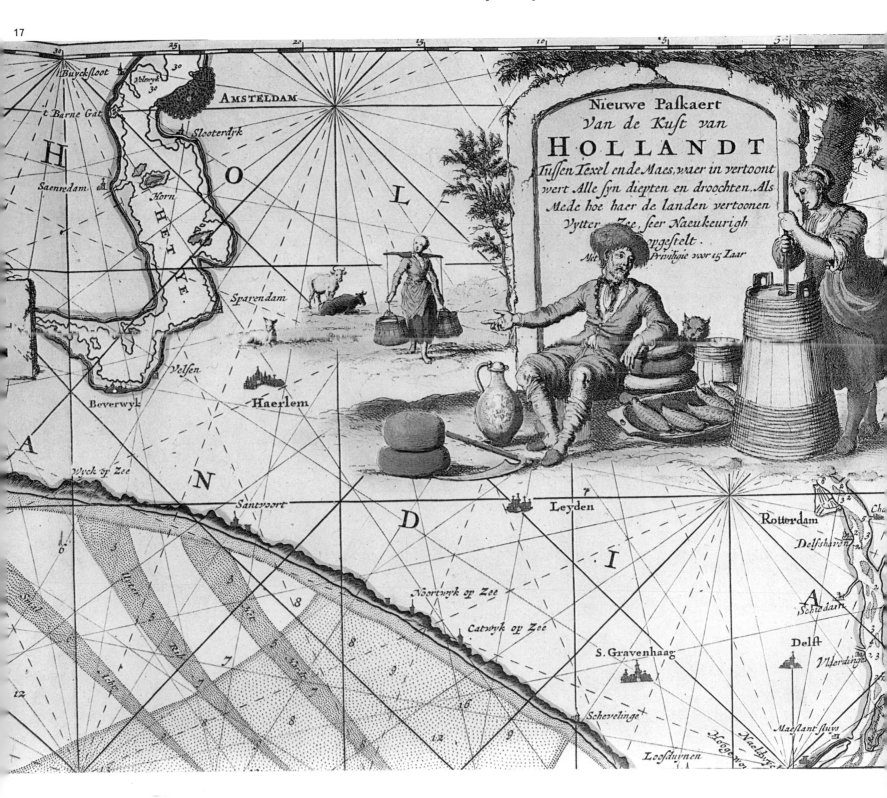

18 *A vignette with a rococo frame of the Greek island and city of Negroponte in the Aegean from the collection of views and charts entitled* Il Mediterraneo, *published in 1688 by Vincenzo Coronelli, cosmographer of the Republic of Venice. He was the last of the great Italian engravers on copper, more restrained in his style than the Dutch and more oldfashioned in the way he retains the use of the rhumb lines instead of a grid*

19 *The title-page of* Great Britain's Coasting Pilot *by Captain Greenvile Collins, hydrographer to Their Majesties William and Mary, 1693. This first survey of the coasts of Britain was inspired by Samuel Pepys and ordered, as Collins says in a prefatory letter to Trinity House, in 1681 so that henceforward all charts must be approved by the Elder Brethren of that body and 'the common scandal of their badness be removed, that God may prosper all your generous and charitable undertakings'.*

*The motto of William III is shown under the royal coat of arms—*Je Maintiendray. *The miniature chart at the bottom shows the British Isles lying on their sides, as it were, and the Dogger Bank fishing area is heavily shaded*

18

NEGROPONTE

19

HONI SOIT QVI MALY PENSE

IE MAIN= TIENDRAY

Great Britains
Coasting Pylot
BEING
A NEW SURVEY
OF THE
Sea Coast
By Capt.
GREENVILE COLLINS
HYDROGRAPHER
to their
MAJESTYS
1693

20 *A view of the forest and dockyard at Annapolis Royal in Nova Scotia on the Bay of Fundy in 1779; from* The Atlantic Neptune *by J. F. W. DesBarres, who embellished his charts of the North American coastline with watercolour vignettes of this sort. The artist-surveyor may be seen on the left and the type of boat used for making sounding records is on the right. A midshipman was usually in charge of such arduous boatwork, which could prove dangerous and unhealthy in certain parts of the world*

20

CHAPTER X

Navigational Instruments and Timekeepers

Lt.-Cdr. D. W. WATERS, R.N.

The art of navigation is the art of conducting a ship in a safe and timely manner between assigned places. Although the art is as ancient as civilization, the use of instrumental navigational aids is, with the exception of the sounding lead and line, relatively recent—900 years old in China, 800 in Europe. The first of the modern aids was the needle magnetized by a piece of lodestone and then floated in a shallow bowl of water and used to give a sense of direction to the mariner sailing under overcast skies out of sight of land, for he relied upon the winds, sun and stars for direction.

By the mid-thirteenth century this had been developed in the Mediterranean into the sea-compass which continually indicated to the mariner the direction of north and divided the whole of his horizon or compass into 128 directional points or winds based upon eight (later four) cardinal points. It was the start of the science of navigation, for the sea-compass enabled the mariner for the first time to measure continually the direction in which he was going.

The advance of navigation depends upon providing the mariner with improved means of measuring and calculating his position and progress at sea. This is reflected in the instruments of navigation developed since the thirteenth century. As time has passed these have increased in variety and become more precise instruments of measurement and calculation. They have become also (with rare exceptions) more austere, more economical, in design. It may seem, since navigational instruments are essentially scientific instruments, inconsistent to include them amongst examples of the decorative art of the mariner. But they are legitimately so included because for sheer artistry of design and rightness of choice of material for function many navigational instruments are masterpieces, the work of the hands of master craftsmen.

Certain traditional motifs constantly recur in the design and decoration of navigational instruments—the eight-rayed star and fleur-de-lis of the compass rose, the dolphin, the crown and the circle. Almost all instruments of measurement of navigation are based upon the circle, and one of the satisfactions to be derived from studying them is that of discerning the variations of design, based on the circular theme, which each displays. Often the beauty of a navigational instrument, whether it be for observation or calculation, lies in the exquisite workmanship displayed in some unobtrusive detail. What can only be fully appreciated by personal handling is the rightness of *feel* of a well-designed, well-made navigational instrument; while this may appear to be outside the scheme of decorative art it is actually often a vital factor in determining the decorative pattern and the material used to shape and to adorn an instrument. The over-riding consideration of the designer and of the craftsmen was rightly to provide a seaman with an instrument which he could use efficiently with his hands on board a ship at sea.

After the lead and line and compass, the sand-glass and dividers are the oldest navigational instruments. They were needed for estimating distance sailed and pricking off the ship's track on a bearing and distance chart. A bell, struck at each turning of the half-hour glass during the watch, told the crew of the passage of time. No medieval and very few sixteenth-century navigational instruments survive. Fortunately the early publishers of navigational books were on occasion lavish with their woodcut or copperplate engravings, adorning the title-pages, frontispieces, text and even charts with illustrations of navigational instruments currently in use. In the early eighteenth century the engraved title-page decorated with navigational aids went out of fashion but, fortunately, from that period a sufficiency of navigational instruments survives to enable representative collections to be preserved; furthermore, the science of engineering drawing was developing at this time and many perspective and sectional engravings of great beauty as well as of detailed accuracy are to be found in the encyclopaedias and manuals of navigation of the later eighteenth and early nineteenth centuries.

A ship's position is determined precisely when her latitude (angular distance north or south of the equator) and longitude (angular distance east or west of a prime or zero meridian) are known. From about 1470, when Portuguese mariners first crossed the equator, the Portuguese navigators must have observed the sun's noon altitude (angular height above the horizon) in order to determine their latitude. When they were south of the equator, to facilitate these observations from on board ship an astronomical instrument used for celestial observations on land and astronomical calculations, the planispheric astrolabe, was modified by Portuguese or Spanish scholars, probably in the 1490s, into a

nautical astronomical instrument—the sea or mariner's astrolabe. Originally it was made of sheet brass. By the 1540s, as a navigational manuscript by Jean Rotz shows, it had become an instrument of cast-brass of massive beauty designed to hang plumb on the heaving deck of a small ship sailing in mid-ocean before a stiff breeze. The mariner's astrolabe went out of use in the seventeenth century after Captain John Davis invented (about 1590) his backstaff or quadrant, but the mariner's astrolabe continued to be represented as a decorative *motif* until the eighteenth century.

The Davis quadrant never entirely superseded the cross-staff or fore-staff. Surviving examples of both are rare and probably the oldest cross-staff and Davis quadrant preserved are of ivory and were made by the English instrument-maker Tuttell, at the close of the seventeenth century. The scales are beautifully engraved and adorned with finely chased scrollwork.

Planispheric astrolabe-quadrants were still used by seamen, in the first half of the seventeenth century, as mechanical almanacs and sun-dials. Edmund Gunter's astronomical quadrant, which he designed about 1615, was long popular.

The sand-glass remained the standard timekeeper at sea well into the nineteenth century and, as a log-glass for timing the ship's speed through the water, it is still used amongst small craft today. But early in the sixteenth century an instrument—the nocturnal—for finding the time at night by the stars, came into use and many beautifully designed and constructed examples survive. The earliest examples are predominantly of Italian and German manufacture but from the 1550s English craftsmen began to acquire the skill necessary to make instruments of measurement. On the back of many nocturnals will be found a tide-calculator and lunar dial. This latter was invaluable in indicating when nights would be moonlit—a matter of much practical importance when a candle was the strongest light at hand. The nocturnal remained in popular use amongst seamen up to the nineteenth century. The Rule of the North Star often engraved on a nocturnal corrected a Pole Star observation so as to give the latitude more precisely.

When the English and Dutch took to oceanic navigation in the latter half of the sixteenth century they adapted the nocturnal for use with the more conspicuous constellation

the Great Bear. The greater distance from the Pole of the 'Guards' of the Great Bear, *Dubhe* and *Merak*, enabled more accurate observations to be made.

From about the middle of the sixteenth century into the first quarter of the seventeenth century astronomical compendia were popular amongst well-to-do voyagers, and many of these display high artistic sense combined with great mechanical ingenuity. These compendia were mechanical almanacs. They included a nocturnal, sun-dial, tide-computer, compass and surveying instrument, a table of latitudes of places, tide-tables, tables of movable feast days and so on.

Gemma Frisius, the brilliant astronomer of the Emperor, designed an Astronomical Ring Dial in the 1530s which first met the seaman's need to find time by the sun in any latitude and on any day with an inexpensive instrument. The original design comprised three folding rings. About 1600 the English mathematician, William Oughtred, modified it into the form which it retained until the middle of the nineteenth century when it ceased to be manufactured. These dials are often of great delicacy of design, with a finely chased bridge and scales of latitude of silver inlaid in the brass. Around one or more of the rings will often be found a table of latitudes. On one side of the meridian ring a quadrantal scale enabled the instrument to be used to observe the altitude of the sun at midday in order to determine the latitude of the place of observation.

Sometimes a portrait of a sea-captain contains an admirable representation of some much-prized instrument. Amongst such is the portrait of Queen Elizabeth's Lord High Admiral until his death in 1585, Lord Clinton and Saye. In his left hand he holds a sea-compass, the fleur-de-lis of the north point, the cross of the east point and the eight-rayed star of the card being clearly visible. Until the nineteenth century the compass card was more often than not brilliantly coloured in red, green, white and black. In the nineteenth century the black-and-white printed card supplanted the coloured engraved card introduced in the sixteenth century. About the 1850s the marking of the east point finally disappeared too, but the fleur-de-lis and the eight-rayed star continue to decorate the seaman's compass.

The carved, coloured and gilded crown or hanging cabin compass, beloved of sea-captains of the seventeenth and eighteenth centuries, has given place to the austere design of the machine-turned bowl of brass, usually blackened externally to avoid distracting reflections of light at night.

From the earliest time, compasses have been housed in binnacles to protect them from damage and to permit their illumination at night. Until the nineteenth century the binnacle was a box-like casing but, with the increasing use of iron and steel for ship-building, it developed into a pillar-like structure in order to accommodate the various magnetic correctors necessary to free the steering compass from the effects of the iron ship's magnetism. Of these the most decorative must surely have been those fitted to the steam yachts of royalty in the nineteenth century.

The development of nautical astronomy gave rise to a demand for models of the universe for instruction in astronomy, to facilitate identification of constellations and individual stars and for finding the declination of the sun. The need was met to begin with by the production of celestial globes, on which the constellations were depicted in traditional patterns on engraved, and often hand-coloured, paper gores, mounted in a highly decorated horizon ring with a pattern comprising a calendar, the signs of the zodiac and various nautical wind systems. One of the most popular of such globes was published by Gerhard Mercator, in 1551, as a companion to his terrestrial globe of ten years earlier.

The globe-makers throughout the seventeenth century were the Dutch, notably the Van Langeren, Hondius, Blaeu and Greuter families. However, by the middle of that century mariners had in general ceased to take globes to sea for navigational purposes. Compared with the engraved planisphere they were bulky, fragile and expensive. From the middle of the sixteenth century engraved celestial planispheres had become increasingly available. Outstanding for brilliance of design and execution is the sphere by the Elizabethan mathematician, Thomas Hood. At the end of the century this development of the celestial planisphere was paralleled by the discovery and publication of the mathematical construction of the Mercator chart by Edward Wright. This spelt the doom of the terrestrial globe also as a navigational instrument.

In the seventeenth century, improvements in the methods

A SHORT
TREATISE
of Magneticall
Bodies, and
Motions.

By
Marke Ridley Dr in phisicke
and Philosophie.
Latly
Physition to the Emperour
of Russia, and one of y̍ eight
principals or Elects of the
Colledge of Physitions
in London.

LONDON.
Printed by Nicholas Okes.
1613.

R. Elstrak
Sculpsit

of calculation resulted in the invention of several mathematical instruments of great utility to the mariner, notably Gunter's sector and his equally popular logarithmical scale. The aesthetic satisfaction of such instruments, whether they be in boxwood, brass, silver or ivory, lies in their proportions, in the precision of the graduations, the spacing of the lines and the scale of the figures and letters, all of which were still engraved by hand, for mechanical engraving was not developed until late in the eighteenth century.

The effect of mechanical engraving is noticeable in the increased severity and economy of design of the instrument of the nineteenth century. This contrasts noticeably with the rather florid taste of the Victorians and is an early and interesting reflection of the consequences of mechanization upon décor. Particularly good examples of austere design in precision instruments are the sextant and the repeating circle. They were developed from John Hadley's reflecting quadrant of 1731 which supplanted Davis's backstaff. The vernier scale now replaced the less precise diagonal scale, and in the latest instruments the vernier has been superseded by the micrometer. Out of the bulky telescope of the seventeenth century has been developed the slender star telescope of the modern sextant.

Longitude is difference of time, therefore the mariner's problem of finding longitude is that of finding and keeping time accurately on board a ship at sea. The earth turns through 360° in the course of one twenty-four-hour day. On the equator this is equivalent to fifteen miles in one minute. Clearly, to fix a ship's position in longitude necessitates extreme instrumental precision in astronomical observation and in timekeeping. A decisive step was taken towards this when King Charles II built the Royal Observatory at Greenwich 'to find out the so-much desired longitude of places for perfecting the art of navigation'. The positions of the stars and motions of the heavenly bodies were observed and recorded with unprecedented precision. In 1731 Hadley published his description of the reflecting quadrant, which made accurate celestial observations on board ship practicable for finding local time, and in 1736 John Harrison completed his first marine timekeeper. This spring-driven, temperature-compensated clock was the first timekeeper to keep time accurately at sea, but Harrison won the great award for inventing a means of finding longitude at sea with his exquisitely wrought fourth marine timekeeper, a watch.

In England a craftsman capable of even finer workmanship was Thomas Mudge who competed for a new prize offered in 1774. In France brilliant craftsmen were at work at the same problem and probably the chronometers of Breuget have never been surpassed for the deceptive simplicity and elegance of their designs. In England the commercial production of chronometers was developed by John Arnold and Thomas Earnshaw whose productions were simple, reliable and strikingly modern in appearance. Their tradition of high craftsmanship is inherited and maintained by the only chronometer-makers now in business in England —Mercer's of St Albans.

To enable shipmasters to check their chronometers against observatory time a time-ball was installed on the Royal Observatory in 1833. When released daily at 1 p.m. it indicated Greenwich mean time.

Although the stick barometer had been developed out of Torricelli's tube by the end of the seventeenth century, these barometers were not carried by many ships until the early nineteenth century. The case was still traditionally of wood and, until the severely practical Meteorological Office standard pattern barometer was issued in the latter half of the century, this was often heavily carved, convoluted or fluted—a rare example of the landsman's taste of the times being imposed on the seaman.

The early surveyor used a simple type of theodolite, primarily for taking and plotting the bearings of objects. Some of the earliest were made by Englishmen, such as Humphry Cole who made instruments for Sir Martin Frobisher.

In the seventeenth century the French surveying instruments were notable for their elegance of design and high standard of workmanship, but in the eighteenth century it was the English instrument-makers who excelled in craftsmanship and in the quantity and variety of design of their levels, theodolites and surveyors' compasses. Their instruments were the means of effecting the great improvements in charts that began in the mid-eighteenth century. Of outstanding importance was the station-pointer, probably invented by the Scots hydrographer Murdoch Mackenzie in

4 *A pilot's lodestone, seventeenth century. The lodestone and needle were probably first used by European seamen to indicate north in the Mediterranean in the twelfth century. This was developed into the mariner's compass in the thirteenth century. The compass-needle was of soft iron and, in consequence, after being magnetized by a lodestone, it gradually lost its magnetism. The pilot therefore carried a lodestone such as this seventeenth-century example in order to refresh the needle periodically. The large stone is sheathed in a brass filigree case with an iron bar attached to it by brass chains held in the mouths of two lions. When steel needles, which retain magnetism permanently, were introduced, lodestones went out of use*

the 1770s, for plotting the position of the offshore soundings fixed by horizontal sextant angles between conspicuous objects on shore. Scarcely less useful, to the navigator in particular, were the parallel rulers which came into general use for plotting a ship's position in terms of latitude and of longitude, now found with the sextant, chronometer and mechanical rotary log.

5 *The Ptolemaic System, 1559. In the fifteenth century, seamen began to use nautical astronomy to assist them to find their position at sea. One of the first books in English to describe and illustrate the most generally accepted theory of the universe, known as the Ptolemaic, was William Cuningham's* The Cosmographical Glasse, *published in London in 1559 by John Daye. This fine woodcut shows Atlas supporting the universe, of which the earth was believed to be at the centre.*

Enclosing the four interpenetrating elements— Earth, Water, Air and Fire—were believed to be eleven concentric spheres, each solid yet transparent. They were the Moon, Mercury, Venus, the Sun, Mars, Jupiter and Saturn, the Firmament wherein were embedded the fixed stars (all here shown symbolically), the Christaline Heaven or Second Mover and the Primum Mobile, or First Mover; beyond lay the Imperial Heaven where God and his Angels were said to dwell. This was immovable. The First Mover gave the daily east–west impetus to the movable spheres, the Second Mover gave the Firmament of the Stars the additional movement known as the Precession of the Equinoxes, which makes them continually shift their positions relative to the poles and celestial equator in a cycle of 26,000 years

PRIMVM MOBILE ·
CRISTALLINE ☆
FIRMAMENT ☆

FIER
AER
YEARTH

CŒLIFER ATLAS

Hic canet errantē Lunam, Solifq; labores
Arcturūq; pluuiafq; hyad.gēinofq; triōes

ID.

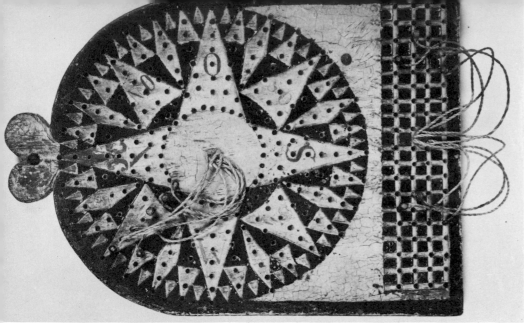

6 *The traverse board was in use amongst seamen of north-west Europe from the early sixteenth to the late nineteenth centuries. This example, perhaps late eighteenth century and from the Baltic, is of wood, painted in white and black with the traditional compass dial fleur-de-lis and arrow indicating North to the mariner.*

The base to the circular portion was probably not provided before the first quarter of the seventeenth century, when knotted log-lines and half-minute glasses began to come into use. The speed was pegged each half-hour of the watch though the log was usually cast every hour or two hours

7 *This fine portrait of Edward Fiennes, Lord Clinton and Saye, Lord High Admiral 1550–4 and 1558–85 (under Queen Elizabeth I) shows him wearing his badge of office, a bo'sun's call (whistle) and proudly holding a sea-compass in his left hand. This is the earliest known perspective illustration of a sea-compass and clearly shows the traditional pattern of the compass fly or card. The fleur-de-lis of the north point is conspicuous*

8 *Instruments of navigation, 1583.*
The first part of Lucas Janszoon Waghenaer's great sea-atlas, Spieghel der Zeevaerdt was published in Leyden in 1584 by Christopher Plantin and is a superb example of the work of that famous publishing house. The title-page was engraved by Joannes a Doetecum (Jan van Doetechum). The book contained, in addition to charts, a compendium of navigation, sailing directions, a nautical almanac and celestial planisphere, instructions for making and using nautical astronomical instruments and illustrations of them. It set a fashion in nautical literature that lasted for over a century and a quarter

Teerste Deel vande

Spieghel der Zeevaerdt, vande navigatie
der Westersche Zee, Innehoudende alle de Custe
va Vranckryck Spaignen en t'principaelste
deel van Engelandt, in diuersche Zee Caertē
begrepē, met den gebruycke van dien, nu met
grooter naersticheyt by ēē vergadert en ghe-
practizeert, Door Lucas Iansz. Waghenaer
Piloot ofte Stuyrman Residerende Inde
vermaerde Zeesta dt Enchuysen.

Cum Priuilegio ad decennium.

Reg.i 5 8 3 Ma.ris.
et Cancellarie Brabantie.

Ioannes à Doetecum Fecit.

Ghedruct tot Leyden/ by Christoffel Plantijn/
voor Lucas Janssz Waghenaer van Enckhuysen.

Anno M. D. LXXXIIII.

9 *Mariner's astrolabe* c. *1588.*
This plain but handsome instrument is typical of
what was one of the most popular navigational
instruments from about 1485 to 1635 for taking the
height of the sun at midday to determine the ship's
latitude. It was evolved in the late fifteenth century
for Portuguese navigators pushing their way south
and west into the Atlantic.

This instrument is probably Spanish, having been
recovered in 1845 from under a rock on the island of
Valencia, Ireland, the scene of the wrecking of three
of the ships of the Spanish Armada in 1588.
Nowadays mariners' astrolabes are remarkably rare;
fewer than a score are known to survive and not
all of these are complete. This one, for instance, never
had the numbering of the degree scale finished

10 *Victorian marine barometer.*
With growth of meteorological knowledge and the
formulation of the laws of storms came the develop-
ment of various instruments to help seamen to
determine scientifically the state of the weather and
to anticipate its changes in good time. This hand-
some ship's barometer, probably from a passenger
liner of the mid-Victorian era, incorporates a
thermometer and sympiesometer in a glazed central
panel. The sympiesometer, invented by Adie in 1818,
was designed to give early warning of changes in
barometric pressure. The shell and acanthus motif
echoes the décor of the classical fountains of Roman
times and their emblems of the sea and shore

10

11 *Horizontal planisphere made in 1574 by Humphry Cole*

12 *Cross-staff and Gunter's scales c. 1695. The cross-staff is first mentioned in a Portuguese manuscript of 1514, and it was most probably developed from an Arabian navigating instrument called the Kamal. This instrument, by Thomas Tuttell of Charing Cross, London, is typical in size and proportion. Usually, however, the staves were made of lignum vitae or pear wood, with boxwood crosses. Each side has a different scale appropriate to one of the four crosses, of which only one was used when taking a sight. The crosses are enriched in this instrument with scrollwork based on an English rose motif.*

Edmund Gunter, a professor at Gresham's College, London, devised his rulers or scales to enable the navigator to make logarithmic calculations instrumentally. He projected the various tables on to the rulers in the form of straight-line scales which could be used with the aid of a pair of compasses to perform multiplication, division, etc., without mental effort

11

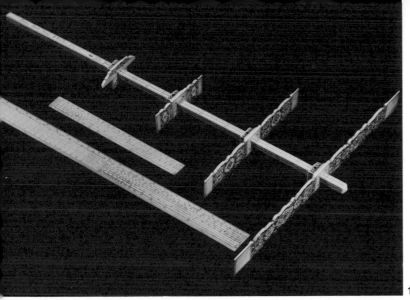

13 *Planisphere of the southern skies by Thomas Hood, 1590.*
Thomas Hood was the first public lecturer on mathematics in the City of London, where he started teaching navigation and other mathematical subjects in 1588. He engraved planispheres of the northern and southern skies according to Gerhard Mercator's celestial globe of 1551. For this reason the newly discovered stars and constellations such as the Southern Cross and Triangle are not shown

14 *The compass card or fly, by E. Williams, 1724.*
A page from a navigator's manuscript notebook.
The 2 by 12 hours around the edge of the compass
card are for converting time, expressed in terms of
the compass points in tide tables, into hours and
minutes

15 *A royal yacht's binnacle, 1899.*
Sea compasses have been stowed in binnacles to
protect them from damage since medieval times. Until
the advent of the iron ship the binnacle was a box-
like structure, but the necessity of surrounding a
steering compass in an iron ship with bars, magnets

and soft iron spheres to neutralize the influence of
the ship's magnetism led to the development of the
modern pillar-type binnacle. The white-painted and
gilded carved binnacle here shown is a splendid
example of the shipwright's decorative carving. It
was fitted in the royal yacht Victoria and Albert

16 *Brass sextant by Nairne & Blunt* c. *1775.*
The sextant was developed from Hadley's quadrant
to enable angular observations to be made up to 120°
and came into use from 1758. This splendid
example, though devoid of decoration, is visually
most satisfying because of its beautifully balanced
functional design and precision of finish

14

15

17 H.1, John Harrison's first marine timekeeper, 1735.
John Harrison, the maker of this, the first timekeeper accurate enough to be of use in discovering longitude at sea, was a carpenter, born at Foulby, Yorkshire, in 1693. With his younger brother, James, he made several clocks of great accuracy incorporating a number of inventions including a virtually frictionless escapement known as the 'grasshopper' and a temperature-compensated pendulum. The Longitude Act of Parliament of 1714 offered awards of up to £20,000 (an immense sum in those days) to anyone discovering a means to find longitude at sea. John Harrison decided to win the award. In 1729 he adapted his horological inventions to a portable spring-driven clock, which he completed in 1735 and tested successfully on a voyage to Lisbon and back in 1736. He spent the next twenty years perfecting it.

The machine is a clock whose movement is controlled by two balances inter-connected by wires and whose balance springs are adjusted to changes of temperature by a bi-metallic grid-iron temperature control of brass and steel rods. The clock runs for thirty-six hours, incorporates a 'maintaining power' to keep it going during rewinding and is fitted with anti-friction wheels wherever practicable. The dial shows days, hours, minutes and seconds

18 H.2, Harrison's second marine timekeeper, 1737.
A marvellous piece of mechanical ingenuity which was never tested at sea for fear of capture by the French or Spaniards in the wars of 1739–48

19 Backplate of H.4, Harrison's fourth marine timekeeper, 1759.
A large silver watch, made by John Harrison and his son William, probably with the assistance of other craftsmen. It was tested on a voyage to the West Indies in 1761–2 and on arrival at Jamaica was found, after allowing for its rate of going, to have lost only 5·1 seconds, an error equal to just over one mile. At this time it was the common experience of the most skilled navigators to be hundreds of miles in error after such a voyage.

It was later tested on a voyage to Barbados and at the Royal Observatory at Greenwich. Harrison was eventually awarded the longitude prize for its performance but only by obtaining the support of the King, George III, and by petitioning Parliament. He was eighty when, in 1773, the final instalment of the £20,000 prize was paid to him.

The machine is of the most exquisite workmanship throughout

18

17

9

1762

Larcum Kendall LONDON

20 *Backplate of K.1, the first marine timekeeper by Larcum Kendall, 1769.*
In 1767 Kendall was engaged by the Board of Longitude to copy H.4 in order to find out whether timekeepers on Harrison's principles could be made satisfactorily by other makers. K.1, completed in 1769, corresponds in all essential circumstances with H.4. It was tried at the Royal Observatory at Greenwich and was then sent to sea with Captain James Cook on his second (1772–5) and third (1776–80) voyages. During these protracted voyages it performed reliably under rigorous conditions. It was later lent to Captain George Vancouver for his voyage to the north-west coast of America, 1791–5.

Kendall thought Harrison's design over-complicated and made two later timekeepers in which he attempted to simplify it. One of these was used by Captain Bligh of the Bounty

21 *Backplate of the* Bounty *watch, K.2, 1771.*
This marine timekeeper, Larcum Kendall's second, was made in an attempt to simplify the mechanism of H.4 and so make timekeepers cheaper and easier to produce. It was used in the Arctic in 1773 and afterwards on the North American station. In 1787 it was issued by the Board of Longitude to Captain Bligh for his voyage to the Pacific in the Bounty. *When the mutineers set Bligh and the loyal members of the crew adrift in 1789 they kept K.2. It subsequently passed through many hands. Finally Admiral Sir Thomas Herbert bought it in 1840 from the British Consul in Concepción, Chile, and after taking it to China he brought it back to England.*

Kendall's workmanship was of the finest and, true to his object, he simplified the design externally as well as internally. Decoration is severely practical yet the result is most pleasing to the eye

21a *The dial of the* Bounty *watch, K.2, 1771. The elegance of simplicity*

185

21a

22 *Mudge's No. 1 marine timekeeper, 1774.*
The eight-day timekeeper for which Mudge was
awarded £3,000 by the Board of Longitude.
Modern tests have shown that it is not only more
accurate than Harrison's prize-winning No. 4, but
that its accuracy was not surpassed until 1873.
Mudge's craftsmanship was superlative

23 *'The Little Midshipman', c. 1800.*
Nautical instrument-makers of the eighteenth and
nineteenth centuries customarily hung such a sign
over their shop fronts. A few still survive today.
Charles Dickens described just such a sign in
Dombey and Son

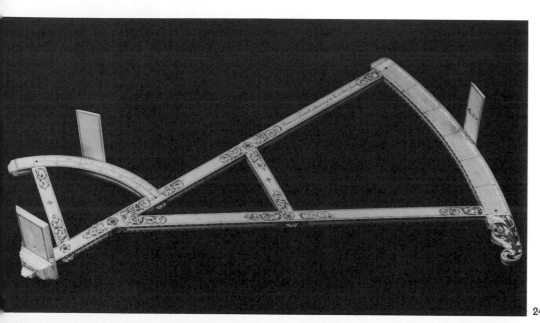

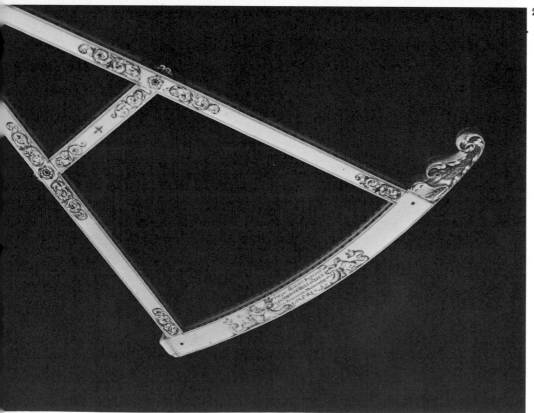

24 and 24a *Detail of ivory backstaff, c. 1695*

25 *Brass quadrant by 'Magnie a Dunkerque',*
c. 1786.
A beautiful instrument dedicated to His Majesty
Louis XVI by the maker. An unusual feature is the
magnetic compass which is incorporated in the
frame and hinged so that it lies in the horizontal
plane when the quadrant is held in the vertical
plane

24

24a

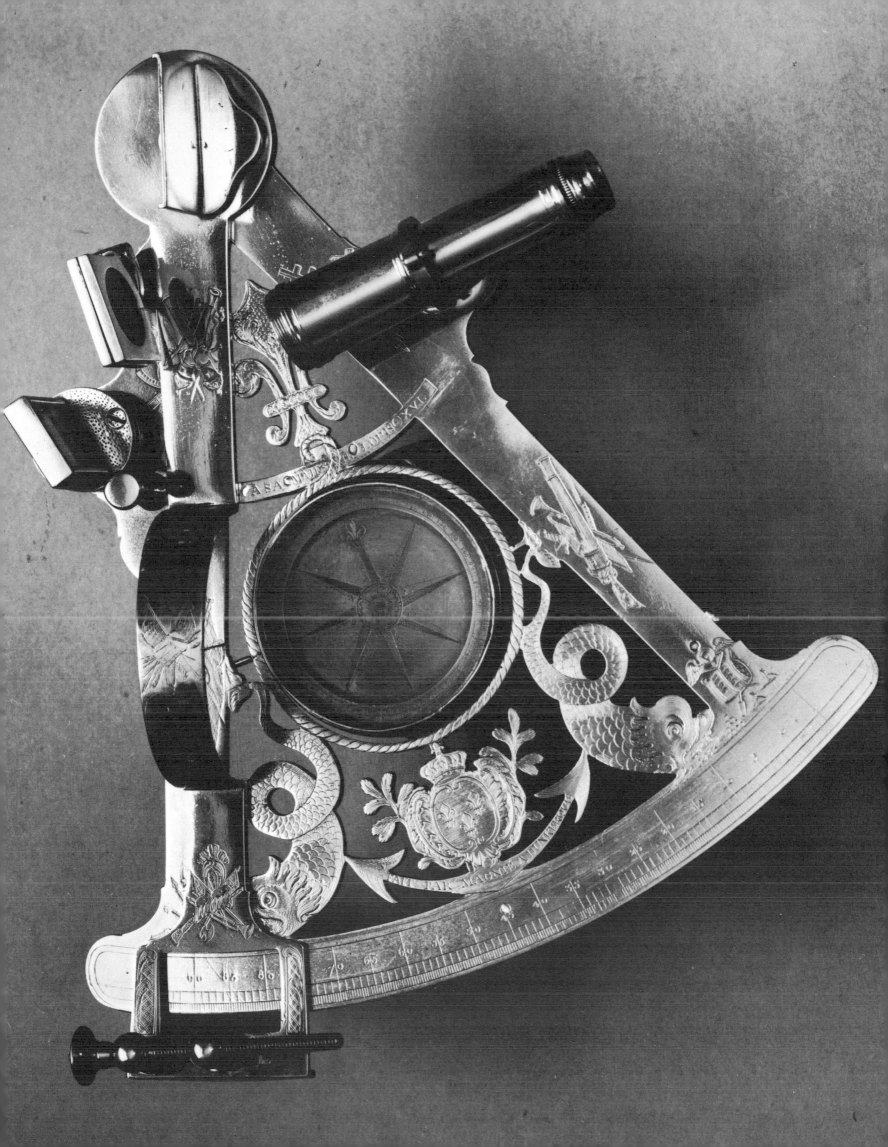

26 *A royal quintant, c. 1855.*
This fine silver quintant with the Prince of Wales's plumes was made for the Prince by, or through the agency of, Mrs Janet Taylor, a remarkable Victorian lady who took over her husband's business on his death in 1845 and continued it until 1858. She taught navigation and ran a nautical instrument shop at 104, Minories, London. Many an American clipper captain bought his sextant from Mrs Janet Taylor's shop

26

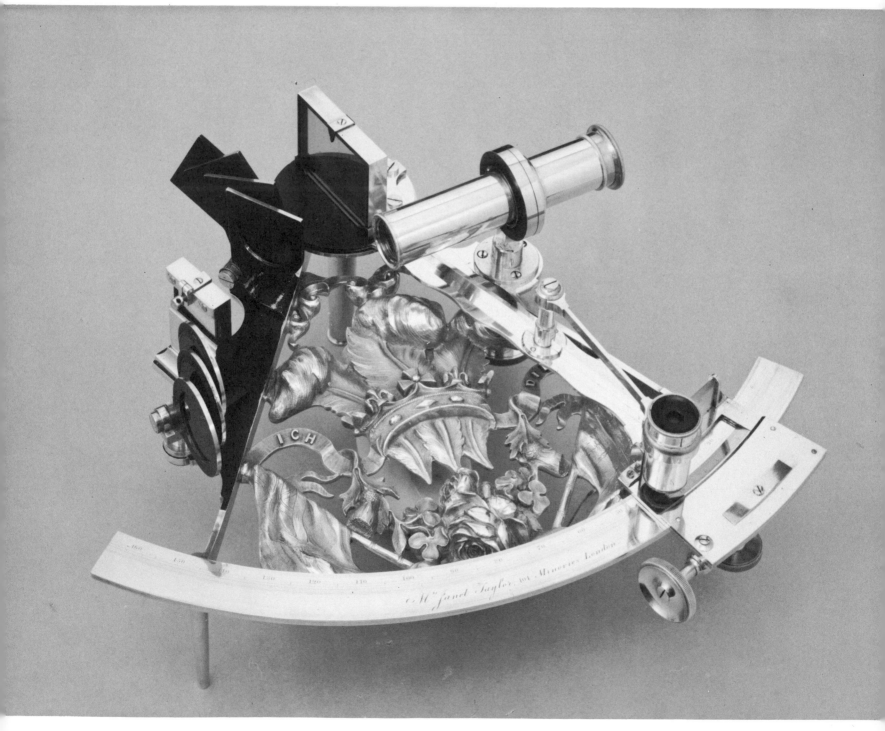

27 *Dutchman's log-timer, 1729.*
This is a brass tobacco box on the lid of which is engraved a representation of Julius Caesar and '45 before Christ', and Pope Gregory and '1582'. These commemorate the institution of the Julian and of the reformed Gregorian Calendars. Between is a perpetual calendar and the surmised date of the box.

On the bottom is the engraved head of Amerigo Vespucci(?) and '1497' and a speed table by means of which a chip of wood tossed over the side of the vessel was timed by counting rhythmically as the chip travelled the distance between the two marks of known distance apart on the ship's side. It was designed by Pieter Holm, who ran a navigation school in Amsterdam

28 *(overleaf) Armillary sphere, 1586.*
This splendid armillary sphere, made in Louvain in 1586 by Gualterius Arsenius, one of the great sixteenth-century craftsmen, was used to demonstrate the theory of the movements of the celestial sphere.

Armillary spheres such as this were frequently illustrated in the navigation manuals of the sixteenth century

27

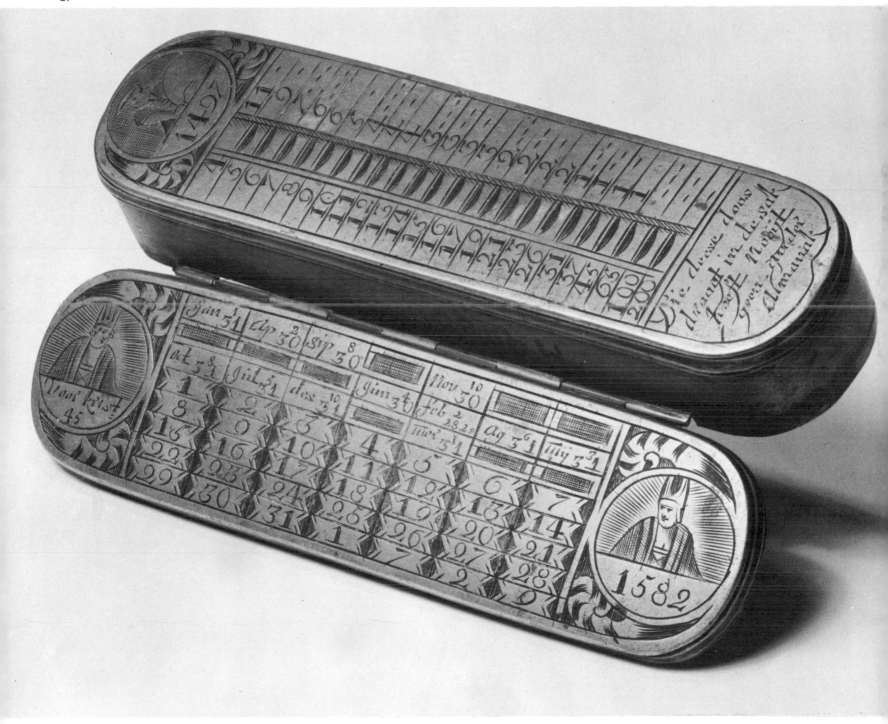

CHAPTER XI

FIGUREHEADS

A. E. WEIGHTMAN

The art of the mariner is in no way better expressed than in the ship's figurehead and of course in the wealth of other decoration which adorned the ships of bygone days. The origin of the figurehead is perhaps bound up in man's desire for a means of stalking his animal food (by using the skin and head of an animal on his craft as a decoy); purely for decoration, showing his skill in the arts by using his hands and tools; for the purposes of identification; prestige; to overawe his enemies and to indicate personal or tribal ownership. From these there developed the ceremonial or mystic rites connected with ships and there we find some connection with ceremonies performed in modern times.

Although evidence of decoration on ships goes back more than two thousand years, nearly all the knowledge we have of ship decoration on early vessels has come from MSS, drawings and paintings, models, coins, mosaics, tapestries and ceramics.

The vessels of the Romans had a graceful swan at the stern and a fan-shaped decoration at the bow. Some of them had martial figures in the form of busts and also finely executed bronze panels. The Phoenician traders gave their vessels a most virile horse as a symbolic figurehead. The Athenians had bronze animals and gods and the Carthaginians carried the statue of Ammon. War vessels carried decorated rams which were usually of an animal figure and the *oculus* was prevalent on all kinds of vessel.

By the Middle Ages the figurehead was missing, being more or less crowded out by the building of platforms or 'castles' for fighting purposes. Decoration on the castles was not much used at first but later on took arch Gothic forms, diaper, heraldic work and painted portions. By the beginning of the fifteenth century, decoration had taken the form of carved badges or some kind of sculptured figure which may have been a saintly subject, and then a flood of decoration was added in the form of flags and banners.

A small head on the end of a post at the extreme end of the platform structure, and a terminal decoration of an animal, projecting forward, with shield decoration round the forward and after platforms, was the next form of general adornment.

It was the sixteenth century which heralded the greatest developments in the production of ship decoration.

The rams with bronze figures of animals, which I think were the first real form of figurehead, had come in and then faded into history, as did the round bow with its small device or shield in the centre. Vessels appeared with beaks extending forward from the stem taking a small animal shape, such as the *Golden Hind* of Drake fame. The beak took platforms, rails, headbands, cheeks and trailboards. Stems were built farther forward and then shaped to form a sharper bow. On these the figureheads changed still further and appeared with all kinds of supporting decoration. Tiers of it rose above the general deck level and stern decoration grew very lavish indeed. The lion head dominated the scene for more than a hundred years. Equestrian statues came and went, so did twin heads.

All the trading nations of the world sported adornment in keeping with their national spirit, and although the Americans when they became a powerful seafaring nation tended at first to follow the British line in their design, they nevertheless developed and established a native style of their own. There was a period in the early part of the eighteenth century when an Eastern influence, in the form of Chinese figures, seemed to be making itself felt. This perhaps came about when ships were being built in Eastern waters for trading or naval service, or decoration of an Oriental nature was placed on ships in order to impress the people in the countries where trade was being developed.

By now the stem was approaching the shape most familiar to ourselves. All the countries kept pretty much in step with one another, though at times the carving, for the sake of prestige, became a bit too rich and over-developed. When the powers that be found that more importance was being placed on the reputation and skill of the carver than on the safety of the vessel a halt to excessive work was called by both the French and British authorities.

Decoration again went into a decline and in most cases only a simple form of bust or figurehead was considered necessary; some ships took on the billet or scroll head. Carving, however, continued into the steam age with figures and an occasional trailboard. Tradition and superstition about figureheads were difficult to get rid of where the seaman was concerned. With a change of bow to the straight stem the figurehead was seen no more except on the occasional sailing vessel struggling to keep its end up in the ocean trades where time was not so important in landing its cargoes.

New ideas changed the construction of the bow shapes once again, to the modern, soft-nosed raked stem we have today. This gives a fine open space on which to set off the shape with some form of decoration. Some shipowners have taken advantage of this and have reintroduced the figurehead. Not carved out of wood as before, but cast in bronze and welded to the bows on plates. One company in particular should be given credit for having revived the practice, Messrs Fred Olsen of Norway, not only for their magnificent bronze figures but also for their bold excursions into other art forms for ship adornment. One of their vessels, the *Borgny*, has a most striking figurehead made up of a large number of pieces of Ravenna glass in the form of mosaics. Some of their very latest ships have modern designs in multi-coloured futuristic shapes. Many modern vessels have shields and other devices in relief or painted with lines at the side giving a streamlined wing effect.

Modern bow decoration is on the increase and almost every ship launched today sports some form of decoration on bow or bridge. Many of the craft on the Rhine and other rivers, and on the European lakes have decoration in the form of shields or flags painted on bridge and bow.

1

2 *Unknown subject, eighteenth century, Sweden*

3 *Typical scroll or billet-head. Formerly at the Lookout, Gravesend, now with the* Cutty Sark *Preservation Society*

4 *Figurehead from Captain Scott's exploration vessel,* Terra Nova, *at Cardiff*

3

4

5 *Prow of Marie Antoinette's skiff*

6

7

8

6 *Figurehead of the* Sirius, *the first steam vessel to cross the Atlantic under her own power*

7 *Figurehead of USS* Delaware *at the US Naval Academy, Annapolis*

8 *Russian figurehead from the* Katarina II

9 *HMS* Wellesley *at Chatham RN Dockyard*

10 *TS* Arethusa *at Lower Upnor*

11 *HMS* Diana *at Chatham RN Dockyard*

12 *HMS* Columbine *at Chatham RN Dockyard*

13 *HMS* Amazon *at Chatham RN Dockyard*

14 *HMS* Britomart *at Chatham RN Dockyard*

10

12

14

11

13

15 *Figurehead from the frigate* La Bellone. *Naval Museum, Toulon*

16 *HMS* Pylades. *Flinders Naval Depot, Australia*

17 *HMS* Eurydice. *The telescope was found by divers slung on the figurehead in the same position in which it is now placed*

15   16   17

18 *HMS* Ganges, *at Shotley*

19 *Lion figurehead of the sailing vessel* Cimba

20 *Johan Tornstrom's figureheads at the Naval Dockyard Museum, Karlskrona, Sweden*

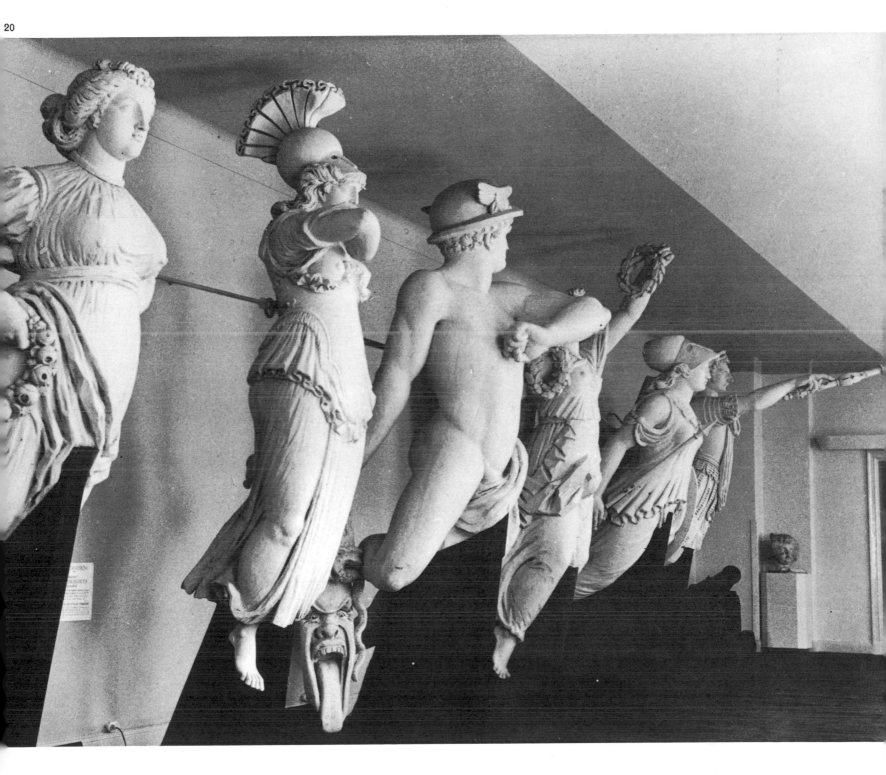

21

22

21 *The Fred Olsen Line vessel* Botticelli

22 *The Fred Olsen Line vessel* Bosphorus

CHAPTER XII

Decorative Rope and Canvaswork

P. W. BLANDFORD

Decorative ropework reached a very high standard at the turn of this century, yet its development was probably due as much to the need for an answer to boredom as to any intention of creating a work of art. Particularly in the heyday of the large sailing ships, periods of intense activity alternated with days when there was little or nothing to do. When becalmed, the point must have often been reached when the needs of the ship were taken care of and the seaman was left idle. To occupy his time he turned to the only materials readily to hand—usually rope and, to a lesser extent, canvas. It was the reverse of a modern production schedule. Quick results were not wanted. Instead, the worker was looking for something to pass the time and maintain his interest for the longest possible period. With time of little consequence, considerable care was lavished on the work and many examples which have survived represent hundreds of hours of painstaking and patient work. As an indication of the time involved, an experienced modern worker found that he took twenty-seven hours to make the lanyard (Fig. 4).

Until recent years all cordage was made of natural fibres, which are not durable, so that much ropework has rotted away and we have lost most examples of fancywork made in the last century. Common working ropes were hemp, flax, coir and, latterly, sisal. All of these tend to be rough and unattractive. A better rope for decorative work was cotton. It is a pity that the smooth durable synthetic fibre ropes, such as nylon and terylene (dacron), were not available in the great days of sail.

Some of the fancywork was a development of utilitarian knots—a simple stopper knot to prevent a rope pulling through an eye would be expanded into an ornamental button (Fig. 8) or a boat's yoke lines would be made with intricate sennits and knots (Fig. 5). Chest handles (Figs. 12, 13) were a matter of personal pride—his chest usually being the only piece of substantial property owned by the ordinary seaman. Where his skill was exercised on something purely decorative, the worker tended to over-elaborate. Complicated knotting in a picture frame may have been on a par with other fanciful Victorian art, but it would not be considered beautiful today. Fancywork which was also functional usually produced the most satisfying results. The bell rope (Fig. 11) was the pride of the ship.

1

Ropework has the advantage of needing few tools. A knife with a spike does almost everything. A fid (large wooden spike) is needed for large ropes and a few nails may be driven into a board or spar when working the more complicated woven-pattern mats and rings (Fig. 14). The man with an interest in finer work used his skill to make very similar knots in the drawn threads of canvas, so as to produce borders, fringes and tassels (Fig. 21).

Decorative ropework is based on the everyday knots used at sea. The best worker was already skilled at the practical knots of his calling and he adapted and embellished them to produce artistic effects. In doing this many experimenters must have arrived at similar results on different craft, at different times and without knowledge of each other's work. Books on seamanship from the eighteenth century have mentioned decorative ropework and given varying names based on the authors' restricted knowledge. The result has been a confusion of names, which persists today.

Although there are neither the opportunities for decorative ropework nor the time to practise it on modern ships, a few enthusiasts continue the craft and reach advanced stages, while a greater number can manage the basic Turk's heads, stopper knots and similar things. A modern ship may have its intricately plaited bell rope, decorative touches on the manropes and odd bits of fancywork about its other ropes, provided by traditionally minded seamen.

Rope fenders are practical applications of fancywork which still persist, despite the supply of rubber and plastic alternatives. The inland waterways of Britain still have their traditional type of narrow boats, which travel in pairs; a power boat towing its 'butty' boat. The tiny cabins of the pair of boats formed the homes of the families making up the crews. They took an immense pride in their boats and decorated them with fancy ropework. Although the number of families living aboard their boats in this way has greatly diminished, there are still a few, and the other crews who live ashore continue using ropework decorations, so fancy ropework no longer seen at sea can often be found on British canals.

Fortunately, some exponents of fancy ropework made knot boards—mounted collections of specimens—which may have been intended for instruction, but also serve as records of the better-known decorative, as well as practical, examples of knotting (Figs. 22, 23). Other enthusiasts have committed the descriptions to paper; although getting the instructions for making an intricate knot into print, with drawings or photographs, so that any reader can understand it, is a very difficult undertaking. The most comprehensive book of instruction on decorative ropework is believed to be *Encyclopedia of Knots and Fancy Rope Work*, by Raoul Graumont and John Hensel (Cornell Maritime Press, New York).

A British book with considerable information on the subject is *Knots, Splices and Fancy Work* by Charles L. Spencer (Brown, Son & Ferguson, Glasgow). The book containing instructions on the largest number of knots of all kinds is *The Ashley Book of Knots* by Clifford W. Ashley (Doubleday, Doran & Co., New York).

2 *If the boatswain's plait is made with granny knots instead of reef knots it automatically forms a twist*

3 *The simplest plait is made with three parts—in this case used as a decoration beside a staircase. The mat is a simple coil, with the turns sewn together*

2

3

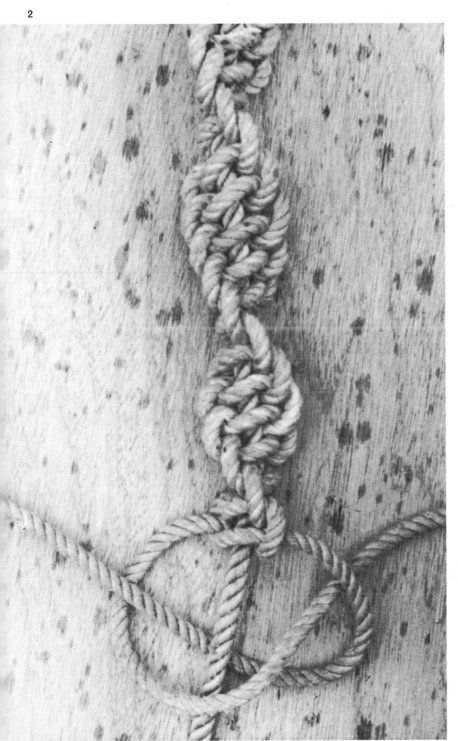

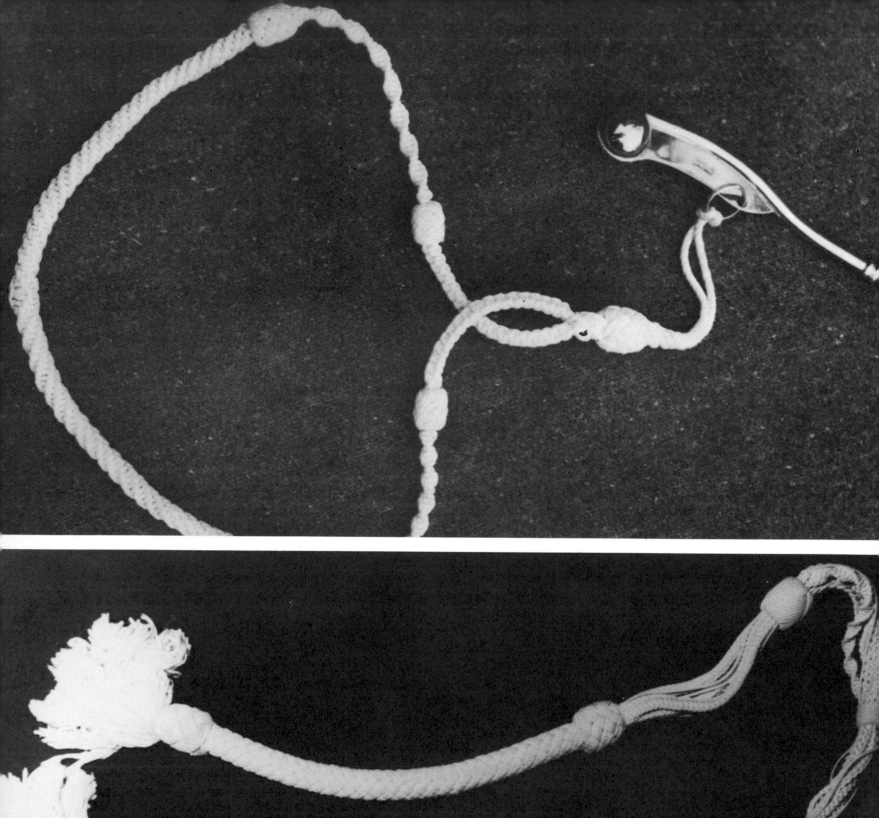

4 A lanyard for a boatswain's call, made from white cotton cord, with round sennit and twisted boatswain's plaits divided by Turk's heads and pineapple knots

5 The ends of intricately plaited yoke lines for a ship's boat. The hand grips have tight round sennits, with pineapple knots, then the strands are divided to make thinner examples of various kinds of flexible plait

6 A collection of plaits making flexible decorative thongs with Turk's heads worked at intervals

7 An example of the sort of thing done mainly to relieve monotony. These specimens were worked in galvanized wire by seamen on the Royal Navy research ship Discovery during an Antarctic expedition. The continuous round sennit encircles a seven-strand wire rope laid back on itself around a thimble, with the ends worked into a version of the pineapple knot. The lower wires are worked into a wrought or paunch mat plait

8 *A basic Turk's head knot. This is a 'three-part four-turn' version, with the end followed round twice. Innumerable variations are developed from this. These are probably used more in fancy ropework than any other knot*

9 *Variations on the Turk's head, from the knot board (22). The carrick mat at the top is a form of Turk's head flattened, where it bears a resemblance to the carrick bend, hence its name. In the centre is a seven-part, and below it three, five and four-part Turk's heads, all followed round twice. A many-part Turk's head has a similar appearance to a pineapple knot, which differs in its method of construction*

10 *Pineapple knots worked on the ends of fids, using cords of two colours, protected by varnishing. The result is both decorative and functional, as the knots form handles*

9

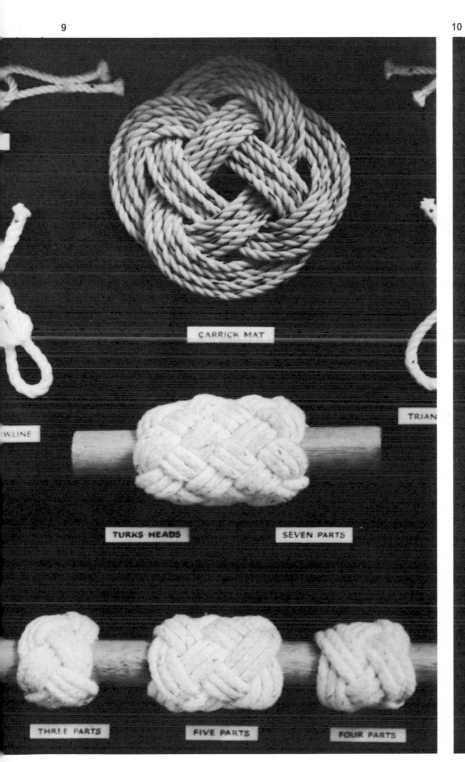

CARRICK MAT

WLINE

TRIAN

TURKS HEADS

SEVEN PARTS

THREE PARTS

FIVE PARTS

FOUR PARTS

10

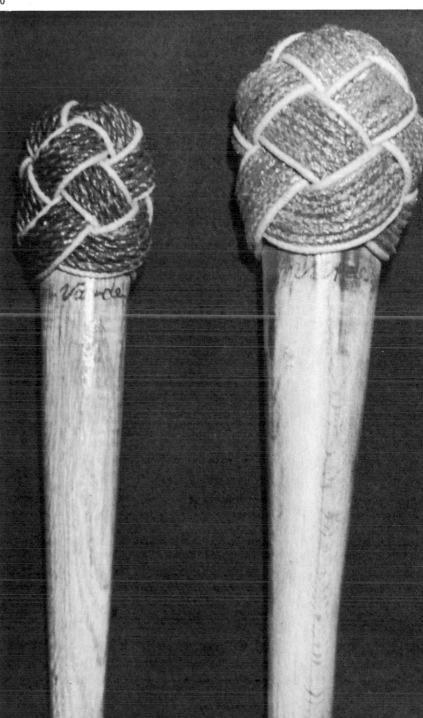

12

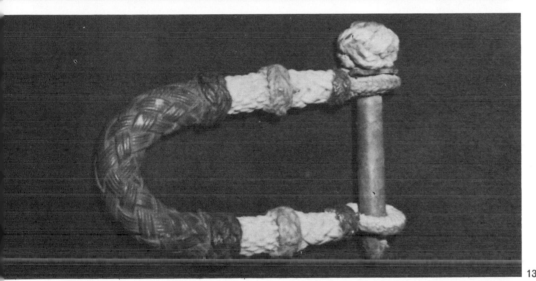

13

11 *A typical bell rope, with variations on the Turk's head worked over a hard core. The loop is covered with cockscombing—half hitches in alternate directions*

12 *A pair of well-used chest handles. The 'pins' are of rope covered with leather and finished with manrope knots. The handles are spliced rope covered with serving of light line worked as a round sennit*

13 *Chest handle. The basic spliced rope has been thickened, probably with rags, and this is served over with a three-strand woven pattern for the part gripped, then Turk's heads separate portions of round sennit. The rope has been painted*

14 *An ocean mat, formed by following round in an over-and-under weaving pattern and capable of several variations. Besides being made in large rope for use as a floor mat, the same design may be used as a decoration on a lanyard or other article made of light line*

15 *Crown or wall knots are used to make round objects from the strands of a rope—in this case a 'mast dropper', used purely as a decoration on the short mast of a canal boat, but also often used in the same way to make fenders. A rope is doubled back to form a loop, then the strands separated to give six parts, which are made into wall knots to the required length, then, in this case, a Turk's head completes the job*

BACK SPLICE

OCEAN MAT

14

15

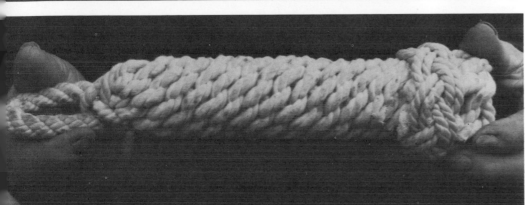

213

16 *The rudder of a canal 'butty' boat. The upper part is known as the 'ram's head'. This is surmounted by a horse's tail (shown here) or a plaited rope called a 'swan's neck'. Around the tiller are four Turk's heads. Around the ram's head are two three-part multi-turn Turk's heads, and another around the top of the blade. Forward of the rudder is a plaited 'jumping rope', used to retain the rudder if it strikes the bottom and is lifted off its hangings*

17 *Plaiting a swan's neck, for use as a canal boat rudder decoration instead of a horse's tail*

16

17

18 *A five-strand tingle fender, which is chained to the rudder blade of a canal boat to protect it when the boat surges with the inrush of water in a lock. A knot of similar form was used in the end of a heaving line at sea*

19 *A set of canal boat 'back fenders' in position. These are worked around chains or ropes, padded to shape with waste rope and covered with interwoven strands. Their object is to provide considerable resilience when the boat surges against lock gates*

20 *A 'side string' hanging over the traditionally painted cabin of a canal boat. This is a grab rope and the thickened grip is provided in a decorative way by working the separated strands back over the main part of the rope in a series of crown knots*

21 *A sampler of drawn thread work in stout canvas. Crosswise threads are removed and the lengthwise threads knotted together to form patterns and tassels*

18

20

19

21

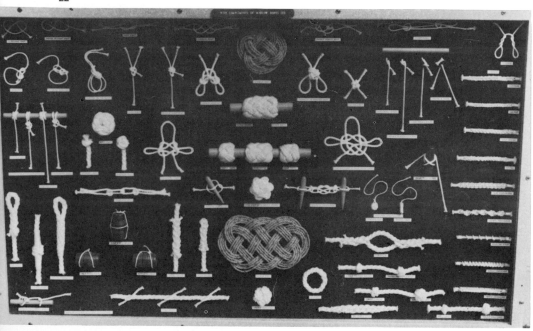

22 *A modern knot board made for exhibition, showing fancy and utility knots, by H. J. Dawe and J. J. Hill of the Trinity House vessel* Stella

23 *A knot board made in the form of a book, substantially constructed and brass-bound so as to close for transport, used for instructing apprentices. Each 'page' covers a particular aspect of knotting*

23

CHAPTER XIII

SHIP MODELS

Lt.-Cdr. GEORGE NAISH, R.N.R.

Models of Nile boats, dating back to *c.* 2500 B.C., have been found in Egyptian and other tombs, and votive models, representing different types of early Mediterranean shipping, have been found by archaeologists. These models have come from the islands of Crete and Cyprus and the site of Carthage. The earliest ship models usually seem to have had a religious significance, but there is no reason to suppose children were less fond of sailing their model boats in ancient times although models used in this way do not get preserved.

Votive models continued into the seventeenth and eighteenth centuries and to the present day. In Holland, well-known examples hang from a beam over the nave in the great church of St Bavo at Haarlem, commemorating the breaking of the boom at Damietta in 1219 during the Fifth Crusade, represented by delightful models of Dutch ships of the early seventeenth century. Many charming models of different dates will be found in the chapels of Breton fishing villages, commemorating escapes from shipwrecks and other perils.

From early times, architects have made models of important buildings to show their clients and the same has probably been done by shipbuilders. There is plenty of evidence that this was a common practice by the seventeenth century and the English were particularly keen on producing fine models in advance of new construction. Phineas Pett, one of a great family of shipbuilders, tells us how in 1607 he made with his own hands a model for Prince Henry 'most fairly garnished with carving and painting'. This little ship was taken to Richmond where it was examined by King James, attended by Prince Henry and the same Lord High Admiral who had defeated the Spanish Armada in 1588. Pett reports 'His Majesty was exceedingly delighted with the sight of the model, and spent some time in questioning me divers material things concerning the same, and demanding whether I would build the great ship in all points like to the same, for I will (says His Majesty) compare them together when they shall be finished'. The great ship, the *Prince Royal*, was launched in 1610 and while she was still on the stocks the king 'spent almost two hours in great content in surveying the ship both within and without'.

In 1634 the model of a 'great new ship' to be called the *Sovereign of the Seas* was carried to Hampton Court to be

examined by King Charles I. The loquacious traveller Peter Mundy examined this model with Peter Pett, son of Phineas, at Woolwich in 1636. The model was 'of exquisite workmanship, curiously painted and gilt with azure and gold. So contrived that every timber in her might be seen, left open and unplanked for that purpose, very neat and delightsome.' Pett had 'models of divers others ships lately built'. When the Dutch came up the Medway in 1667, Pett was blamed for saving his ship models at the (supposed) expense of the royal dockyard. These fair copies of the ships' lines were considered of value to the enemy. Shipwrights in those days were usually illiterate and the models made it easier for them to explain their art to the king and his admirals and other officers. For example, there was 'old Shish', 'a plain honest carpenter . . . hardly capable of reading, yet of great ability in his calling'. It was most necessary to examine the model before contracting for an expensive new ship, and reference to the model would show whether the finished product was made more expensive by excessive ornamentation beyond that agreed upon.

Models were demanded officially in 1649 when the Admiralty Committee to the Navy Council minuted: 'But before the said builders proceed in building this Committee desire you to order the builders to present models of the frigotts they severally undertake, according to the direction aforesaid.' Thus in England we are lucky to have a number of scale models of warships sometimes identifiable with ships actually built. These models are very beautiful because the fine decorations have been carefully reproduced in miniature, including elaborate figureheads and stern ornaments, wreathed gunports and frieze of trophies of arms along the sides.

Not surprisingly these ship models were collected as ornaments and Lord Sandwich had a model in 1660 which his servant Samuel Pepys coveted. Pepys soon had a fully rigged ship model hanging in his office 'which', he wrote, 'pleases me more and more'. Mr Cooper, late Master of the *Royal Charles*, made use of it when he lectured Pepys on navigation, shipbuilding and seamanship. In September 1662 Pepys's shipwright friend Anthony Deane gave him a model. Unhappily Pepys's 'most considerable' collection of ship models, which he willed to his friend William Hewer, has disappeared.

Early pictures of ships often appear to have been drawn from models and we know that the elder Van de Velde 'had a Model of the Mast and Tackle of a Ship always before him, to that nicety and exactness that nothing was wanting in it, nor nothing unproportionable'.

Scale model ships continued to be made during the eighteenth century for the navies of Europe and the survivors will be found displayed in numerous maritime museums. More were apparently made in this country than in any other. An interesting example is a large rigged model of the *Victory* now at Greenwich. Of 100 guns, she was launched at Portsmouth in 1737 and lost off the Casquets in October 1744. The model is built to a scale of about three feet to the inch and the model was used for the instruction of naval cadets at the Academy opened at Portsmouth in 1733. It was quite inadequate as the scholars petitioned in 1742 'the model of the *Victory* is so small, her rigging so slight, that we cannot learn anything from it, neither do we know anything of rigging or stowage, of anchors or cables, we are quite ignorant of everything that belongeth to sails'. So their lordships provided them with an old yacht instead.

The draughts of almost all ships built, bought or captured for the Royal Navy since 1700 have been preserved and, up to 1920, are in the National Maritime Museum. As well as the plans, the museum has a generous selection of scale models of the type usually called 'Navy Board', some rigged, mostly unrigged. As well as the built models there is a large collection of block models and by the end of the century these have

1 *Beakhead of a first rate of about 1670*

2 *A 90-gun ship of about 1675*

3

4

been replaced by half-block models. The block models have details of gunports and decoration painted on the hulls. It is thus possible to compare, in the solid, two such interesting ships as the French *Magnanime*, of seventy guns, built in 1744, and the English *Hampton Court*, of the same force and year of launching. The Frenchman, captured four years later, became a popular ship in the Royal Navy and was commanded by Lord Howe in 1759 at the battle of Quiberon Bay. Although of the same force, the French-built ship is 173 ft. 8 in. on the gun deck compared with the English-built ship's 154 ft., and has a beam of 49 ft. 6 in. compared with 44 ft. Put the two models together and the French-built ship is much larger, and the larger ship generally sailed faster and made a better gun platform in action. The English naval constructors were often accused of crowding too many guns into too small a hull, of which this is an example.

Few scale models of merchant ships were made. Fortunately a number of plans of storeships and other merchant-ship hulls survive in the Admiralty collection, but merchant-ship models are rare earlier than the nineteenth century. The few good ones are generally of ships in the service of the East India Company.

Very popular in the years when the long-drawn-out Napoleonic wars were ending were the models made by French prisoners-of-war in bone, ivory or boxwood. These men, crowded into prison hulks and old castles or prisons up and down the country, relieved their boredom and supplemented their rations and gaming money by selling model ships, most delicately made. Very French-looking ships were generally given English names and flags. These models fetch big prices today and are most ornamental.

Official models, other than blocks, became rare during

the wars but returned to favour at the peace. The brilliant Controllers, Sir Robert Seppings and Sir William Symonds, collected the models together at Somerset House and in 1864 these were transferred to the care of the School of Naval Architecture at South Kensington. They later followed the school to Greenwich. Thus fine models illustrate the last days of the sailing navy. All Symonds' best ships are represented, such as the *Queen*, the *Vanguard* and the *Pique*. In the middle of the century the tea clippers raced home from China with the first of the new crop and the race was followed with popular enthusiasm, yet few fine contemporary models of the tea clippers exist.

Whereas the old Navy Board models were both useful records and beautiful ornaments, the models used today for tank trials and plate bending are purely for utility. Shipbuilders turn out splendid ship-models as advertisements, which are too big for private houses but must grace shipping offices and museums, and well-polished half-block models decorate the walls of the boardrooms of the firms who built or owned the ships represented. There are, however, attractive mementoes in the sailor-made models of four-masted barques pushing their way through seas of putty and cotton wool, with wooden sails bellying, or sheet-metal sails which are not quite so realistic.

The author well remembers his pleasure at watching black children on a strip of beach by a village in the mangrove swamps behind Mombasa island. They were playing with their model dug-outs and dhows and outriggers, splashing happily after a motley collection of model boats which gathered together would have stocked a museum and kept the curator puzzling over appropriate labels for years to come.

3 *Stern of the* Magnanime, *70 guns, built in France in 1744 and captured in 1748; added to the Royal Navy and commanded by Captain Lord Howe at the Battle of Quiberon Bay, 1759*

4 *Stern of the* Royal George. *One hundred guns, built 1756. Hawke's flagship at Quiberon Bay in 1759; sank at Spithead in 1782*

5 *Fifty-gun ship of c. 1720*

221

6 *Stern of the* Boyne, *80 guns, of 1682*

7 *Broadside of the* Boyne

8 and 8a *Model of the galley built in
Amsterdam for Tsar Peter the Great; to be used on
the Volga and the Caspian Sea. Rowed with
thirty-four oars*

9 *The* Hawke *cutter of 1777*

10 *Paddle steamer of c. 1830*

11 *Screw frigate of 51 guns, c. 1857, probably the same class as HMS* Shannon

12 *Bone model from Royal Thames Yacht Club*

9

10

13 *Modern shipbuilder's model of HM destroyers*
Matabele *and* Punjabi, *Tribal Class fleet*
destroyers built by Scott's of Greenock in 1937

13

scrimshaw

EDOUARD A. STACKPOLE

The word 'scrimshaw' is of doubtful origin and in the nineteenth century usually denoted both the working of an art form and the object so created. Scrimshaw, developed early in that century by American whalemen, concerns the etching or incising of designs on the ivory teeth of the sperm whale or on whalebone and the use of both the ivory and bone for various implements used aboard ship and in the home. To pass away the time during long hours at sea, whalemen of New England created a variety of scrimshaw items. While the derivation of the name itself is obscure, the terms 'skrimshander', 'scrimshonter' and 'scrimshorn' are found in early logbooks, such as the *By Chance* of Dartmouth, and reported in Cheever's *The Whale and His Captors* and Melville's *Moby Dick*. Some believe it originated from a Dutch expression meaning a lazy fellow and was thus easily transferred to work done in a shipboard lazy period such as a 'dog watch'.

While many consider scrimshaw strictly as an American whaleman's invention, it is probably better described as the whaleman's adaptation of an old art form. Carving in ivory elephant and walrus tusks was known as early as the eleventh century, and so it may be said that scrimshaw was the American whalemen's contribution to an ancient folk art—an adaptation of the older form which became peculiarly American. It is probable that when the Nantucket whalemen used Dunkirk in France as a whaling port in 1785 they had contact with the French ivory workers of Normandy who for over two centuries had worked on elephant tusks brought from the African coast. Even before that the tusks of the 'morse' or walrus were brought into Europe for carving, and many examples of this art exist.

In his long voyages (often three years in duration), the whaleman had plenty of time to indulge his fancy by engraving or etching varied designs or pictures on the ivory teeth of the sperm whale or the whalebone from both right and sperm whales. For years the whaler's jack-knife had been used to carve in wood many practical keepsakes for the sweethearts, wives, mothers and sisters at home. As early as 1782, Hector St John de Crèvecœur had noted the Nantucket whaleman's proclivity towards fashioning ditty-boxes, bowls, 'and a variety of boxes and pretty toys, in wood . . . executed cooper-wise, with the greatest neatness and elegance'. Inlay

1 Coconut shell dipper with oak and ivory handle

2 Bird cage of whalebone with ivory rings and minarets, showing how strips of whalebone were steamed into position for the bars and how the floor may be pulled out for cleaning

with mother-of-pearl and tortoiseshell was followed by the use of bits of ivory. Finally the sperm whale's teeth were used for etching familiar scenes of ships and whales. One of the earliest known dated pieces of scrimshaw is a sperm whale's tooth done on board the *Susan* of Nantucket in 1828, but earlier pieces are dated 1821 and 1827, the later with a slave girl and slave ship. The whaleman incised flags, eagles and whaling scenes, as well as figures of ladies and gentlemen. Sometimes the designs were transferred by pricking the outline of a picture pasted on the tooth or bone.

The techniques of scrimshaw found the whaleman developing his own tools. First, no doubt, was the omnipotent jack-knife, ground to a fine point on the whetstone, but the most versatile tools were the sailor's needles for pricking and scraping out the design. Herman Melville remarked: 'Some of them have little boxes of dentistical-looking implements, specially intended for the skrimshandering business. But, in general, they toil with their jack-knives alone.' Files, awls and gimlets were used in boring holes and piercing bone. Many of the handles for these tools were whalebone or wood tipped with ivory and the skill of the cooper was often borrowed. As the log of the *Abigail* reported: 'Times are dull. . . The cooper is going ahead making tools for scrimshon. . . .'

Perhaps two of the most common types of scrimshaw are the busk and jagging or crimping wheel. The busk, made of whalebone, was the bodice stay in the corsets of the ladies of the time, and many a whaler etched elaborate patterns and designs on his gift for his lady-love. Jagging or crimping wheels were of various patterns; some had plain handles for the little wheel intended for laying a design along the edge of a pie; others had a fork at one end and the wheel on the other; still others with serpents' or horses' heads or whales provided further designs.

Among the extensive variety of scrimshaw articles were the 'swifts' of whalebone, used to wind yarn; workboxes, ranging from those entirely of bone to wooden boxes with ivory inlay; rolling-pins, often with only the handles of sperm ivory; coconut dippers with bone handles; napkin rings and spool holders; canes of great variety; wick-pickers for whale-oil lamps and bodkins for sewing; knitting needles, clothes-pins and coat racks. The ingenuity of the whaleman-artisan

was amazing. Whether he was fashioning a bird cage or workbasket of whalebone, or a jagging wheel of pure ivory, his work did not have to be hurried as time was an expendable commodity.

It was in his choice of design as well as of object that the whaleman evolved an art peculiar to his trade and thus developed scrimshaw as a special folk art. His carved sperm teeth were like trophies of the successful hunt; his carefully etched busk a tribute to his wife or sweetheart; his strongly cut clothes-pins a son's gift to his mother, with an ivory-headed cane a thoughtful present for father or grandfather. Each was a symbol of his faith in the ship and the loved ones at home. The use of time in these painstaking tasks was welcomed to break the monotony. As Captain William Reynard stated in his log of the New Bedford whaler *Abigail* in 1836: 'An idle head is the work shop for the devil. Employed scrimshon.'

Preparing the ribbed sperm (ivory) tooth or the tough right whalebone consisted of scraping and cutting and polishing. The fresh material was scraped with a broad-bladed knife, ground to a smooth surface with file and shark-skin sandpaper, and buffed with ashes from the tryworks

before it was ready for its design. Sometimes pumice and whiting were used to further prepare the surface. Softening agents ran the gamut from soaking the teeth or bone in brine to the use of plain hot soapy water. In later years, a small lathe was used for turning and buffing. There is a fine example of one at Mystic Seaport, Mystic, Connecticut.

Usually, the design was first outlined or scratched upon the surface. Often a picture from a book or periodical was pasted on the tooth or piece of bone and the detail transferred to the surface by pricking in the outlines. Patience was the key to the next step which was the actual engraving. The use of inks to complete the job was customary. Often India ink was not available and so paint, lamp-black, tar and even soot were utilized. Coloured inks provided excellent touches for the design, with scrolls and elaborations introduced for effect. Painstaking efforts many times produced outstanding pieces, although the earlier examples are invariably crude. Some whalers revealed an artistic insight which has made their scrimshaw handiwork collectors' items. A number of professional engravers ashore have tried their hand at this art but their product, while finely executed, lacks the primitive value of authentic scrimshaw.

3

4

3-4 *Two sperm whale teeth, showing the obverse and reverse decoration. The upper illustration shows the ship* Mechanic, *of Newport, Rhode Island, Commander, Capt. Henry Daggett, 1830, above the figures of Plenty and Justice. The lower illustration shows a U.S. naval frigate under all plain sail, and a typical* Lady Godey *book print transferred and engraved*

5 *Jagging wheels or crimping wheels*

6 *Cribbage board made of walrus tusk, c. 1850*

7 *Interior of Sallie Smith's workbox, showing clothespins, sewing 'egg', blocks, etc. Used on board the whaleship* Ohio

8 *Whalebone busks—frontal stays for ladies' corsets. Note the heart-shaped top of the smaller and the elaborately engraved work on the larger*

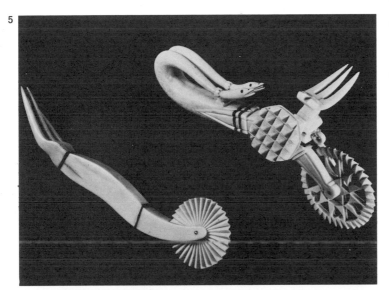

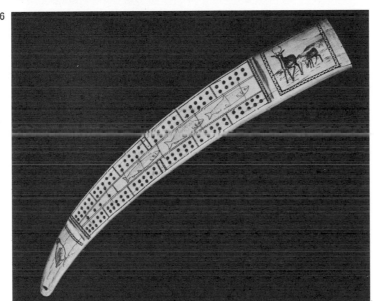

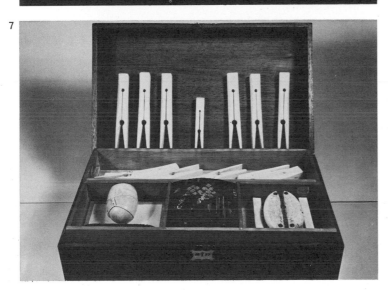

9 Swift of whalebone, used for winding wool. Ribs of whalebone, central shaft of bone with collars and casings of whale ivory; ivory clamp with mother-of-pearl inlay; ivory thumb screw and top

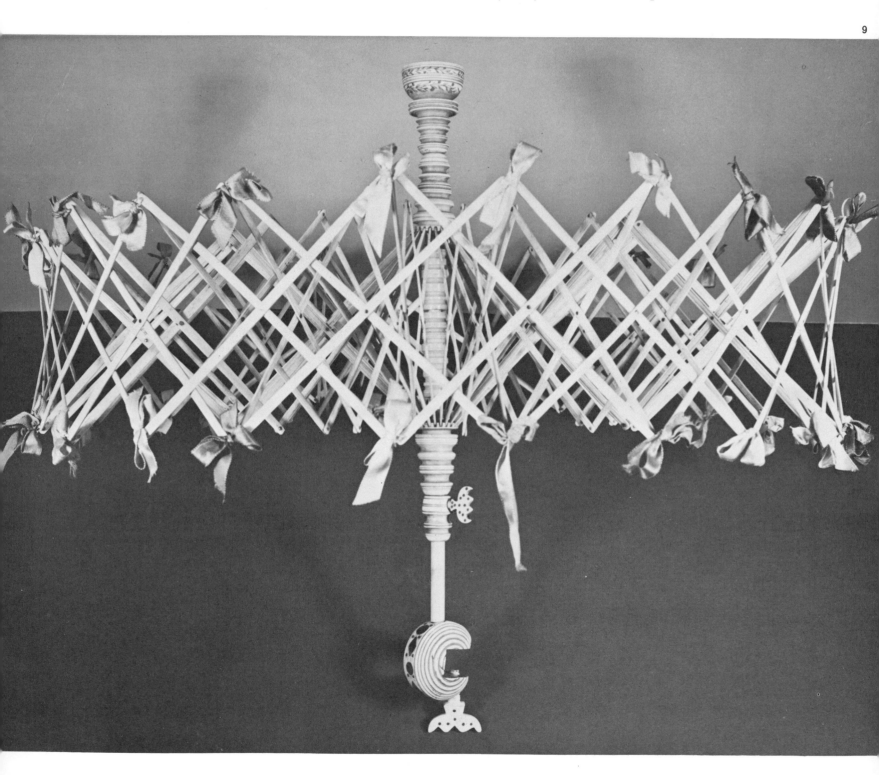

10 *Scrimshaw work on canes. Ball-in-hand of sperm ivory, mounted on ebony with brass band engraved with owner's initials. Elephant head of ivory mounted on whalebone, with elaborately designed brass fitting. Clenched fist of ivory on ebony with ivory bands*

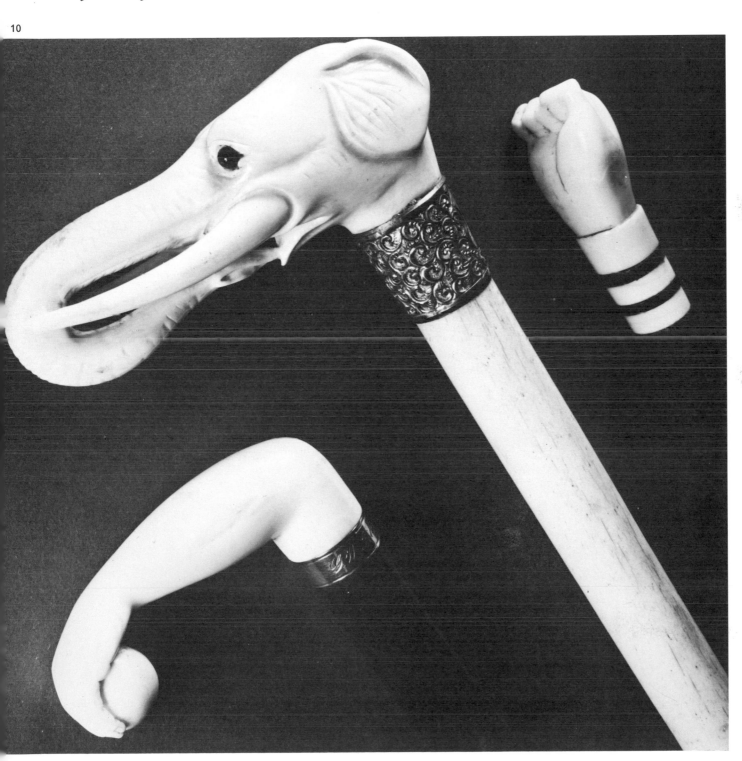

11 *Whalebone ditty or workbox, c. 1845, showing cooper's influence as well as scrimshaw etching. Copper and brass pins were used for fastening*

12 *A sperm whale tooth handle for a name-stamp. These were of wood inserted in an ivory handle*

13 *A sperm whale tooth seam rubber, for smoothing seams during the sewing of canvas aboard ship*

14 *Walrus tusks, c. 1855. These tusks were usually traded by Alaskan Eskimos to the whalemen, who did the scrimshaw work*

12

13

14

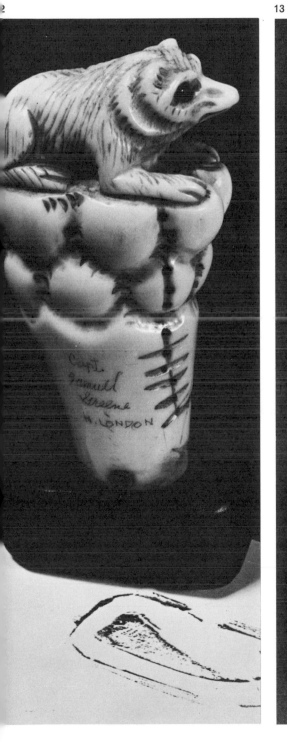

15 *This workmanship is primitive but interesting because it was done aboard ship on a panbone— part of the jaw—of a whale*

16 *Sperm whale teeth showing the Battle of Lake Champlain (top) and the Battle of Lake Erie. The craftsmanship of the engraver is well shown. Brought home by Capt. F. A. Butts, in the bark Bramin in 1852*

BATTLE OF LAKE CHAMPLAIN.—M'DONOUGH'S VICTORY.

BATTLE OF LAKE ERIE.—PERRY'S VICTORY.

CHAPTER XV

MARITIME ART OF THE AMERICAS AND PACIFIC OCEAN

C. A. BURLAND

Most of the native peoples of America arrived by land in pre-historic times. The route was across the Bering Straits either by ice-hunting tribes, or by peoples who found themselves in new hunting grounds after walking across the land bridge which once existed where the Straits now demand navigational skill. It is not therefore surprising that the Amerindians developed very little interest in boats.

The normal craft of the whole of the double-continent was a light framework covered by a skin, varying from the bull-boats of the Missouri and the bark-covered frames of the Fuegians to the beautiful birchbark canoes of the Indians of Canada and the eastern seaboard of the U.S.A. A height of skill in the construction of skin-covered canoes was reached by the Eskimos.

In forested regions the wooden dug-out was made, especially in the south-eastern U.S.A., parts of the Amazon, the Caribbean area and Mexico. A high point was reached in this field by the only truly maritime people of the Americas, the Indians who lived along the fiords and island chains of the north-western coasts of North America.

Rafts were known in a few scattered regions, but reached an important cultural standing only in Peru where the *totora*-reed raft and the deep-sea balsa raft permitted a highly original development which included the only aboriginal use of a true sail in all the Americas.

In all parts of the region there was some attention to art, with results sometimes of great beauty, but everywhere the motive was not beauty for its own sake but the conjuring of help from the spirits of nature. It was really vaguely felt prayer. A carving of a seal was part of an understanding that like attracts like. It was not to show the loveliness of the seal, but somehow to make contact with the spirit of the animals and make the hunter lucky so that the seals should come to the cooking pot. Beyond the limits of the vague and indistinct wishing of the primitives, the highly civilized peoples used images of humans and sea-creatures as a direct invocation to named deities to bring good fortune.

Running through the art of the whole region there is however a certain unity, a tendency to linear form and the use of ornament as a kind of symbolic writing. This is noticeably true of all American Indian art, and on the following pages the illustrations will range the continent from north to south,

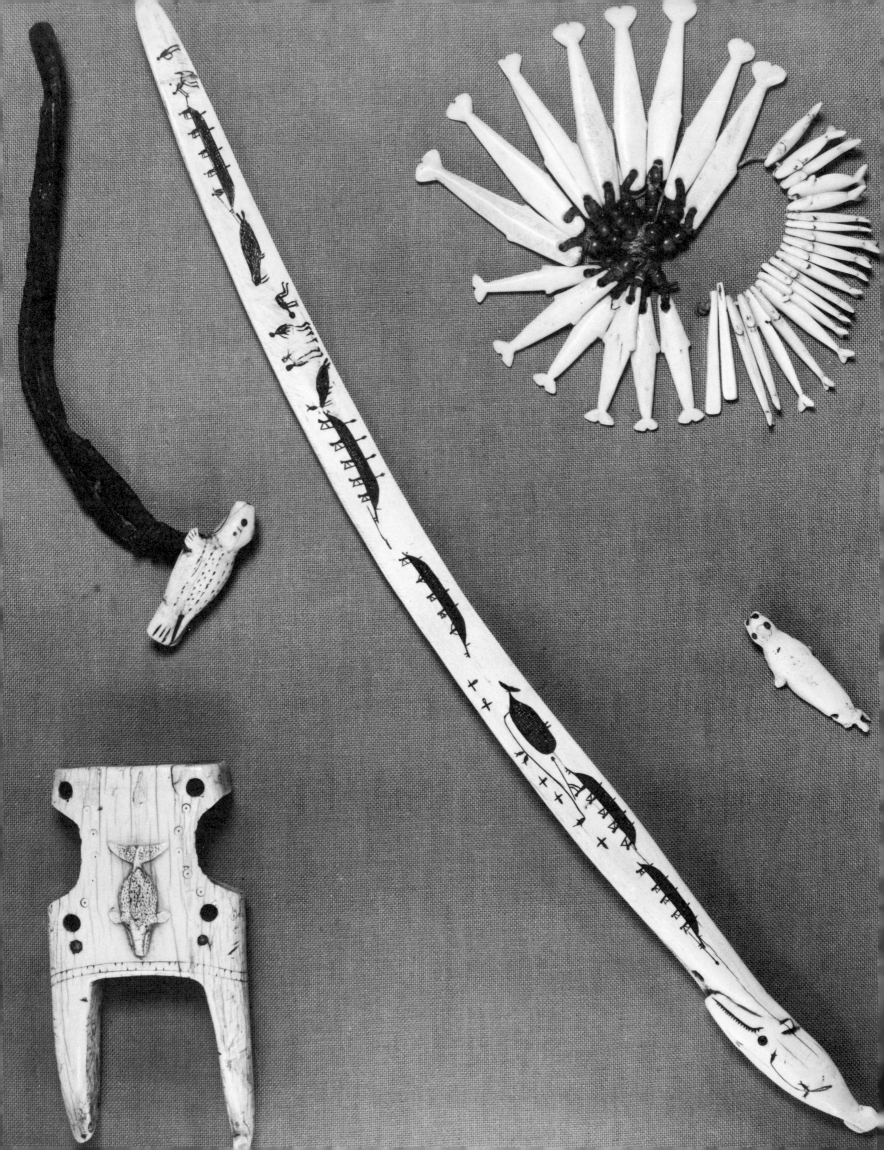

1 *Eskimo art in walrus ivory included all the fittings for the kayak, harpoon rests, toggles for securing lances in place, a snow beater for keeping clothes and equipment clear of ice, and of course good luck charms*

Seal toggle with thong

Snow beater with whale hunt in scrimshaw work

Ivory fish and whales carved to bring good luck when hunting

Harpoon rest with figure of whale in relief

Toggle in the form of a seal

2 *Arctic sea hunting equipment*
a *An Aleut hunter's eyeshade. This is made of a thin sheet of birch which is decorated with ivory carvings of the animals the hunter hopes to kill. They are shown by heads and tails, the parts which appear above the surface of the sea*

b *An Eskimo painted paddle. This also has magical properties, mainly aimed at helping the hunter's life force to manifest itself, hence the emphasis on hunting, success in fighting, and the conquest of women*

perhaps illustrating beauty, but more important, showing that the development of formal art grows with civilization and leisure. Formal art hardly occurs amongst the primitive peoples who have to spend all their time in the unremitting quest for food.

We have seen that the art of decoration of watercraft in native America was never far advanced except on the two areas of the Pacific Coast. The native civilizations had little need for the development of large boats. In their wars the land routes were of most importance. Trade was not sufficiently advanced to reward merchants who took more than a few large canoe-loads of goods along the Caribbean coasts, or balsa loads along the coasts from Ecuador to Chile. Dr Heyerdahl has shown that the balsa raft was practical for oceanic voyages, but the few Peruvian pots from the Galapagos Islands and the cultivation of *kumara* and the *totora* reed on Easter Island show that contacts were real enough, but neither frequent nor on a large scale. On the other side the Viking voyages to Delaware Bay and around Labrador seem to have made no impression on the skin kayaks of the Eskimo or the birchbark canoes of the Indians. In fact the work of constructing a plank-built ship with stone tools was perfectly feasible, but such a ship was of no use for coastal fish collecting, nor for river travel and portages. It did not fit into the Indian way of life and therefore could not be assimilated.

There is some evidence of Roman contact with Mexico, and more, but presumptive, evidence of West African–Arab contacts with Brazil, with similar lack of any real influence on American Indian cultures.

On the Pacific side there are plentiful rumours of ancient Chinese contacts, none of which has yet been proven, and a Marquesan legend of the construction of a huge canoe which, in the eleventh century, visited a land called Tefiti where there were great mountains, eventually returning home in the twelfth century.

Yet in spite of it all there may have been a single idea introduced, the use of a sail in Peru. This differed in many ways from the Oceanic sails, yet the idea probably came across the wide ocean.

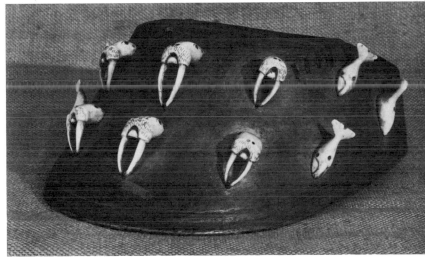

2a

2b

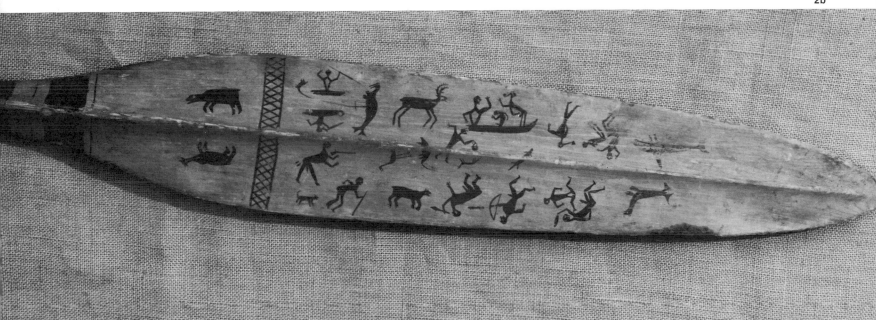

3a

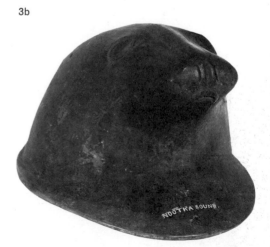

3b

3a *Cedar root plaited hat collected by Captain Cook off the coasts of British Columbia. It shows a whale hunt in progress in Nootka Sound*

b *The warriors of the rocky coasts around Nootka Sound wore their totem animal symbols on their helmets. Often the totems were sea creatures, like the seal on this cedar wood helmet (it is not a decoy)*

4, 4a *The canoes of the tribes of N. America were propelled by paddles, which were decorated with symbols representing the totem animals of their owners as clan badges. These are killer-whale (orca) totems*

b *Carved end of a wooden fid. The totemic carvings show a man, presumably of dragonfly totem, who is crushed by a killer-whale (orca)*

(*overleaf*)
Model Amerindian canoes

Haida Indian

Alonkian Indian

Siouan Indian

6 *Painted paddle (left) from the Eskimo of Bering Strait, showing sea creatures, contrasted with a painted paddle (right) from the Haida Indians which shows whale totem designs*

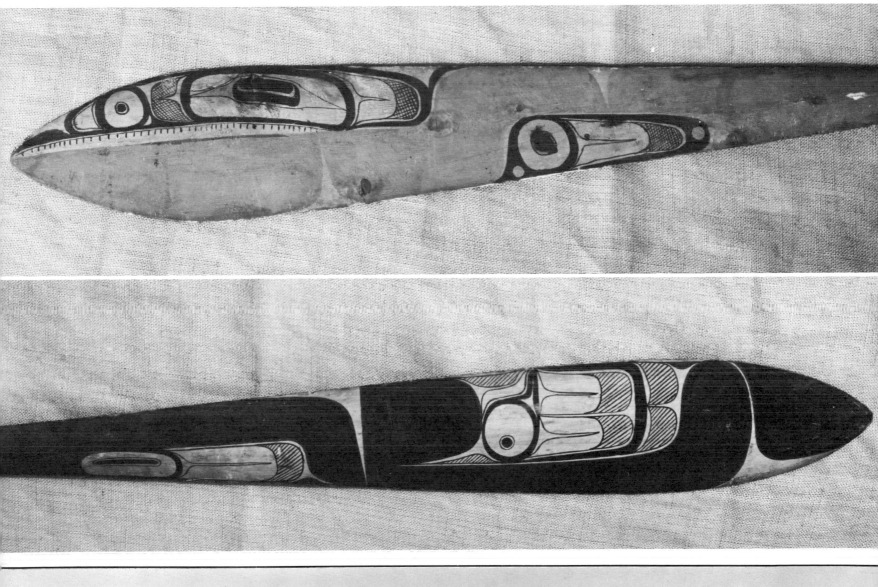

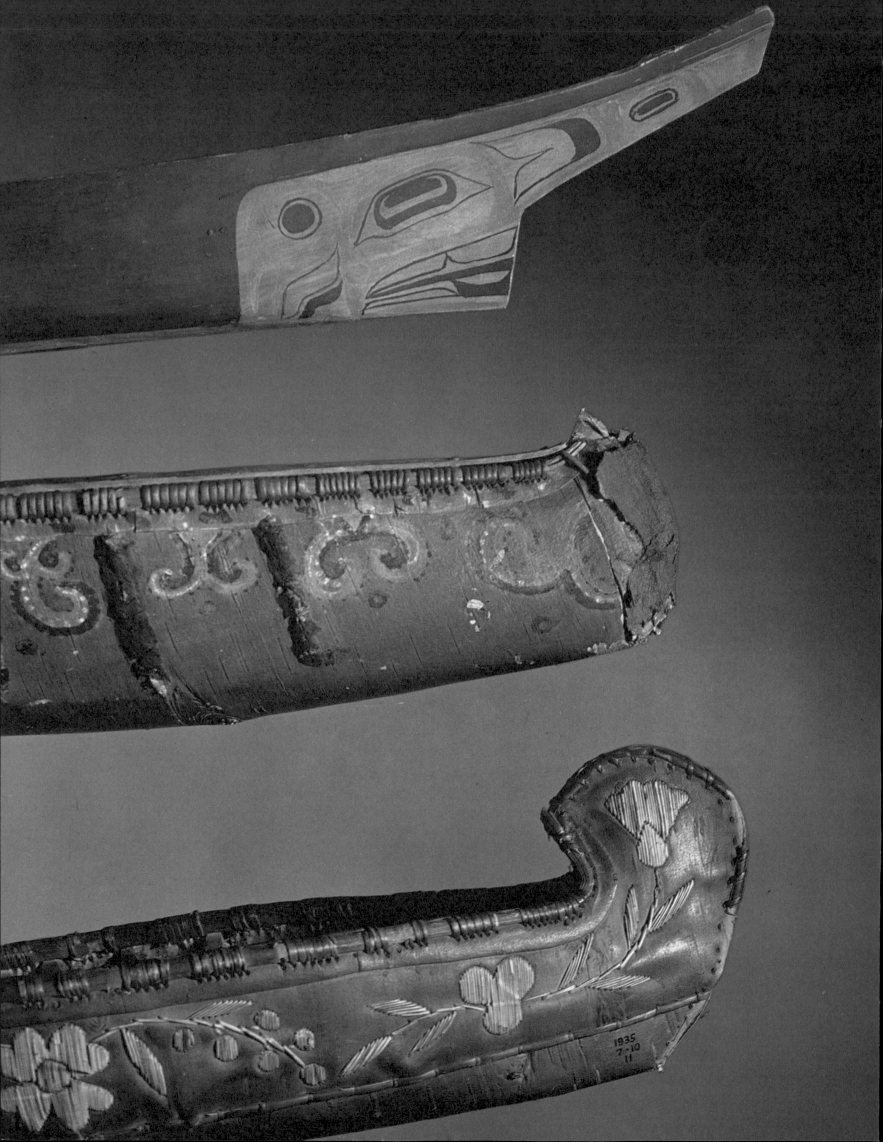

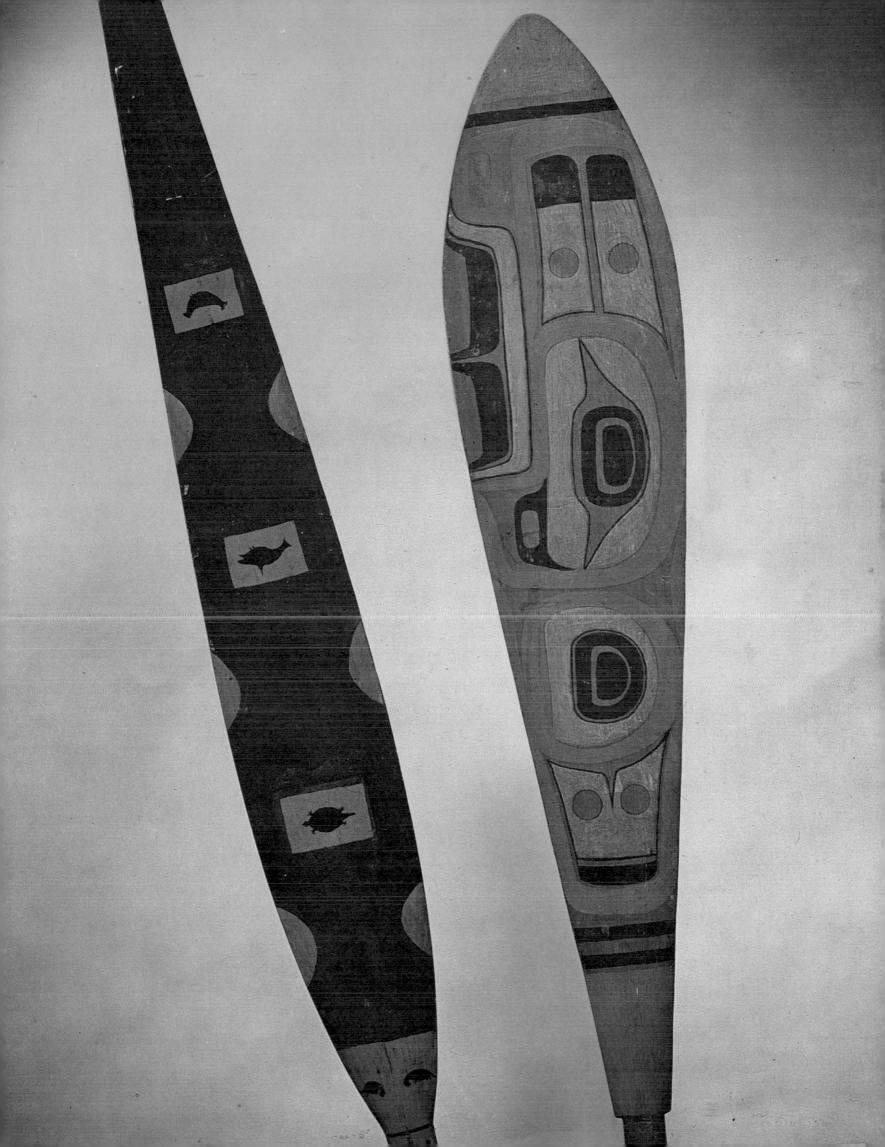

7 *Three model canoes from British Columbia. They show the style of painting which was used on the big canoes, often fifty or sixty feet long, and dug out from a single cedar tree. The decorations showed all comers which clan owned the canoe*

8 *Model birchbark canoes from the Indians of Canada and the north-eastern states of the USA. In olden times these graceful craft were severely practical, but later a little decoration was added. The models shown here were decorated with dyed porcupine quill embroidery for sale to the Europeans, although these geometric designs show no direct European influence*

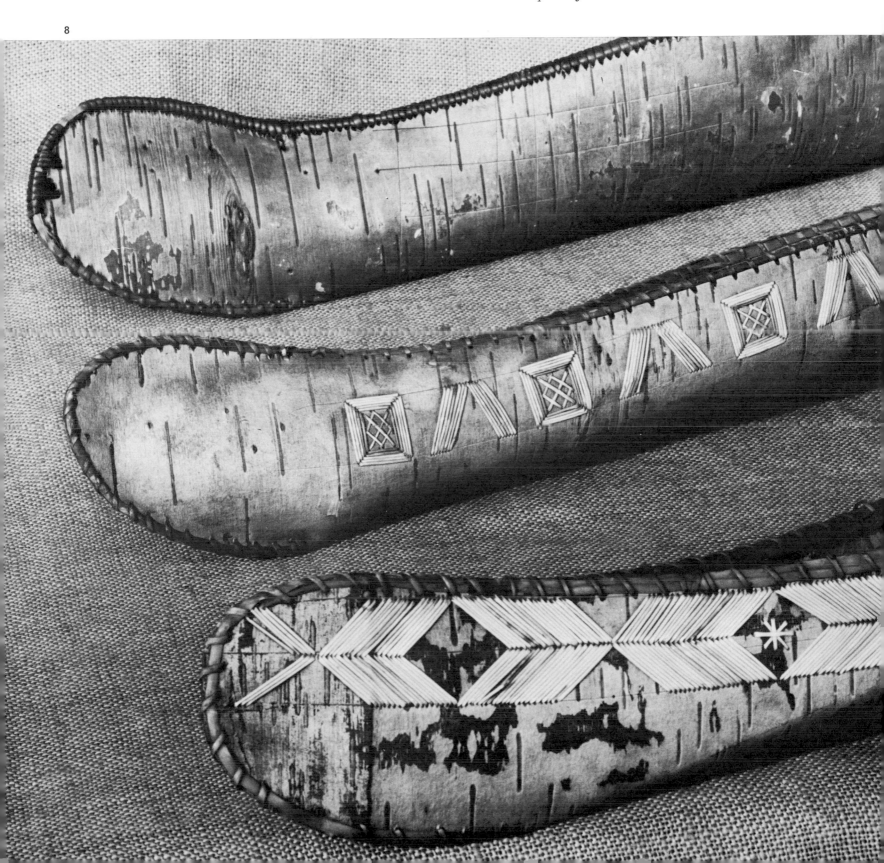

9 *Picture from the Mixtec Codex Zouche-Nuttall showing warriors crossing a lagoon in canoes. Note the great waves of the open sea*

10 *Carved wooden head of a centre-board, decorated with coloured mastic, from ancient Peru. Chimu, about A.D. 1200*

9

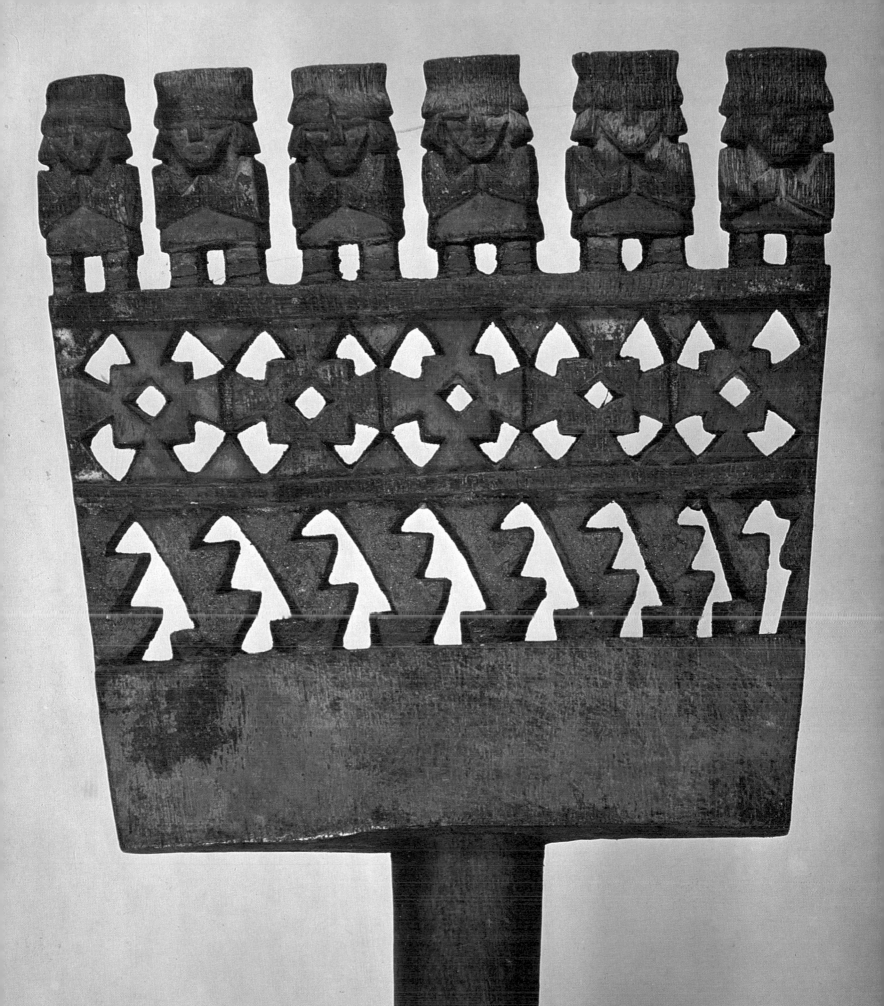

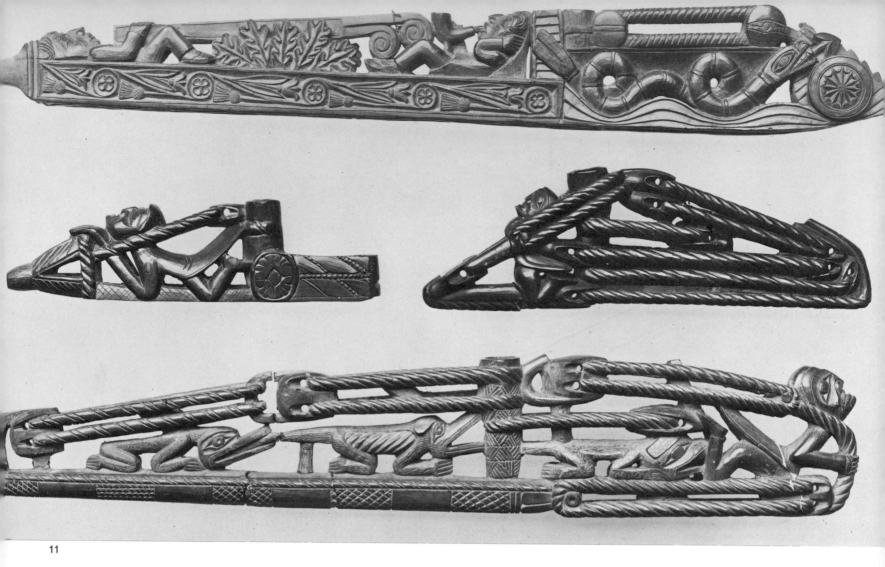

11

11 *When the white man came many Indians worked on ships. These tobacco pipes carved in argillite record an accident in which an Indian was killed through becoming entangled with ropes from a pulley. It aroused such a sensation at the time that it entered local folklore. The lower pipe includes the totems of the victim; the upper pipe depicts two white sailors and a sea serpent. The decorations are derived from the British emblems of the rose, thistle and leek*

12 *The Aztecs made dugout canoes of great beauty and the Maya of Yucatan made fine trading canoes, but no example of these boats is in existence today*

a *A drawing, c. 1550, of an Aztec canoe. Montecuzoma visits an island temple*

b *Native carriers bring parts of a prefabricated brigantine made for Cortes. They are using an Aztec canoe. Ixlilxochitl, Prince of Tezcuco, receives them*

c *A Maya deity paddles a canoe bringing merchandise. From the Dresden Codex (c. 1250)*

12a

b

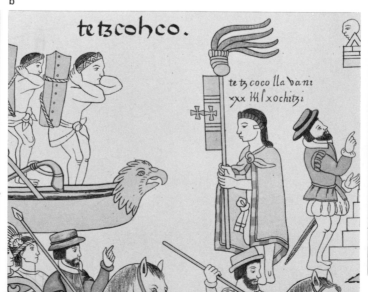

c

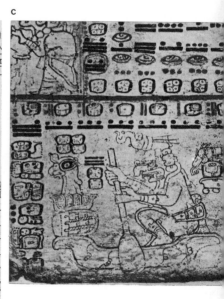

13 Cloth shirts decorated with appliqué pictures of boats. From the Chucunaque Indians, about 1924. The upper picture shows sailing ships, the lower steamers. These were collected by Mr F. A. Mitchell Hedges

14 An ancient pottery canoe from the Veraguas coasts before 1500. The canoe was the easiest means of travel in the mountainous country of Panama. It naturally attracted artists to depict it in clay

13

14

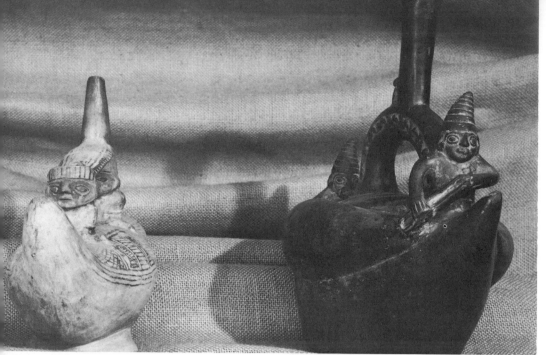

15a

15b

16

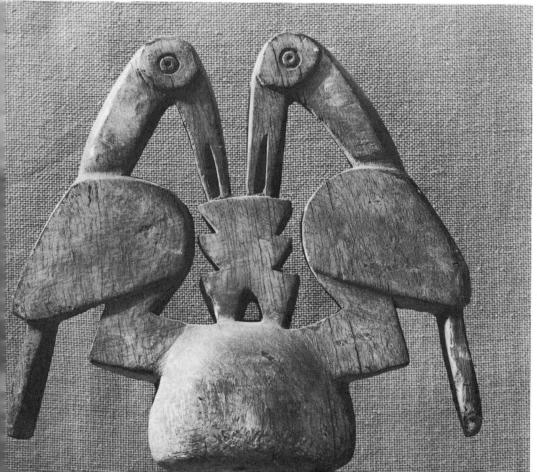

15 *In ancient Peru the commonest boats were made from bundles of* totora *reeds. They were used for coastal fishing, and apparently even took part in inter-tribal sea fights*

a *Models of fishermen in their reed boats*

b *Peruvian tapestry of about A.D. 1200 showing a fisherman holding his scoop-paddle. Below the canoe three centre-boards aid steering. The sea is full of fish*

16 *Head-of a beautifully carved paddle from a Peruvian balsa raft. The blade is tapered in cross section so that in normal use it can be held close to the side of the raft as an additional centre-board for steering; but in calms it could also be used as a paddle. The motif of sea birds expresses the wish for good luck in fishing and that the crew shall be as successful as the pelicans and gulls of the Humboldt current*

17a and b *Pottery jar of the Mochica culture of Peru c. A.D. 400. The vessel appears to be made of reed bundles but the dragon-heads at prow and stern must have been made of wood. It is large enough to carry a crew. On the deck a warrior dressed as the god Aiapayec wields a long club with a fork at the lower end. No relic of these larger vessels has yet been found archaeologically*

18 *There are no remaining balsa wood rafts from ancient Peru, but many finely carved centre-boards are still in existence. The patterns are usually geometric, representing the waves of the sea or rocky coasts. Human figures represent seated paddlers or standing officials. Chimu, after A.D. 1000*

a and b *The left-hand picture shows Chimu warriors wearing beaten bronze helmets. The right-hand picture represents squatting figures of Indians wearing woven turban-like caps*

PACIFIC OCEAN

19 *These three birds are decorations on the upper edge of the blade of the great paddle of which the top is shown in 16*

20 *The paddles of the River Amazon are the art objects associated with the river fishermen and traders. The canoes of the Indian tribes were either very simple bark trays, or plain but handsome dugouts. The paddle itself was a means of free expression, either in painting or very low relief carving*

We now turn to an almost opposite situation, the Pacific itself as the home of people who were as interested in watercraft as the American Indians were interested in land hunting.

The Pacific Ocean contains a variety of lands from continental Australia through the huge island of New Guinea and its neighbouring Melanesian islands, and thence into the immense area of open seas containing scattered volcanic island peaks and coral atolls, with only New Zealand big enough to support a large population.

At the time of the discovery all these lands were populated by people living in the Stone Age. The following pages will illustrate their amazing skills in carving and construction with simple tools.

The populating of the islands of the Pacific Ocean covered a long period. It is now understood that the greater part of the immigrant peoples came from South-East Asia, though occasional drift voyages from Peru and British Columbia may have taken place to bring other traditions to native Pacific cultures.

It is certain that the Tasmanians who were of Negroid Melanesian stock were the oldest immigrants, but their successors, the Australian aborigines, made their way via Indonesia and New Guinea tens of thousands of years ago. These people were simple hunters and had only the most primitive kinds of watercraft. Because their life was hard they had little room for art.

The next waves of invaders must also have come via the Indonesian islands. They are the various groups of dark-skinned Papuans and Melanesians. These peoples were all neolithic agriculturalists, living in settled villages and using watercraft as a means of improving their subsistence by fishing. In one area of south-eastern New Guinea inter-tribal trade flourished and fleets of trading double-canoes set forth on a ceremonial round of commercial visits each year. Naturally such a society was sufficiently well off to have leisure for art. A rich art developed based on symbols of fish, the frigate birds which prey on the fish, and the ripples of the sea by which birds, fish and men all obtained their living.

In other parts of New Guinea, and in the Melanesian islands, there was great diversity. Many tribal groups speaking many different languages occupied the coasts. They

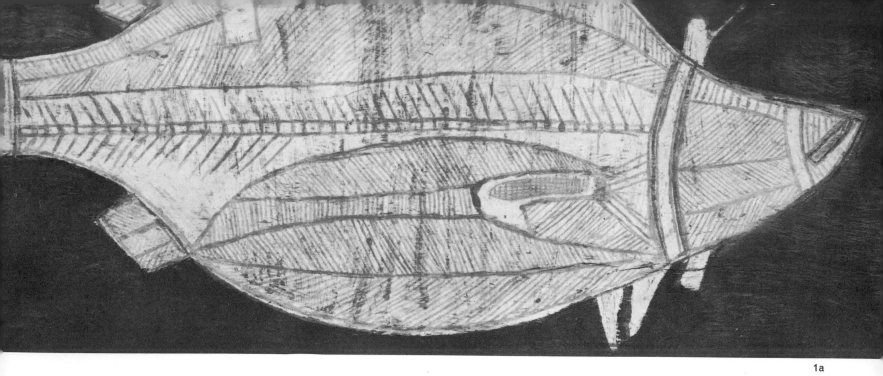

obtained much of their food from fish, which was eaten with taro, sweet potato and breadfruit. Their ornaments were often made of seashells. Their religious practice often called on the spirits of the ancestors to bring them success in the fisheries; and in this case sympathetic magic played a part in the frequent representation of the frigate bird which was thought to be lucky because of its skill in fishing.

The Melanesians made fine boats, which frequently made inadvertently long voyages when blown far away in storms, but they mainly kept within tribal territories. Inter-tribal war was common and not a few war canoes were made, in which, in the Solomon Islands particularly, small figure-heads in the shape of human heads carried by a warrior hinted at the grim purpose of head-hunting.

The Solomon Islands have a happier distinction in their unique discovery for the Pacific of the plank-built boat. These graceful single-hulled vessels with high prow and stern were often decorated with ornaments of cut pearlshell set in the black putty-nut paste which was also used with pandanus fibre as a caulking material.

The majority of Melanesian canoes were dug-outs balanced by outriggers on strong booms which sometimes supported a platform deck. Decorations on these boats were often brightly painted, for the islands produced red and white chalks and corals which were burnt for lime-based pigments.

The size of the Melanesian islands allowed farming tribes to remain comfortably within their own areas, even though they often raided each other. It was otherwise with the smaller islands of Micronesia and Polynesia. The small areas of the islands made a population reduction necessary from time to time, and it was popular for younger sons of chiefs to go voyaging with their followers in search of new homes. Thus the Islands were populated in the course of some fifteen centuries from the Micronesian sporades to Easter Island, and from Hawaii to New Zealand. It seems certain now that the Polynesian adventure originated in south China. The people, physically and linguistically akin to the Malayans, were skilled neolithic cultivators. Their religion conditioned

their art towards symbolic representations of the human body and sex organs. They believed in their physical descent from the gods, and realized the essential holiness of sex as the means by which lives were united through time.

Naturally they developed an aristocratic type of government and placed a premium on personal bravery and the spirit of adventure. In the twelfth century the Marquesan sailors discovered the coast of Peru and some of them returned to tell the story. Two waves of them discovered New Zealand in the eighth and thirteenth centuries. There seem also to have been more than one discovery of Easter Island, the last in the tenth century, which was recorded as the wild adventure of a Tahitian prince who took his ships and people away into the great ocean in a fit of pique because his love was unfaithful. But he was protected by the gods in the shape of the bird spirit Makemake who guided the ships to treeless Rapa Nui.

The most southern of the Maori peoples were those who settled in New Zealand. There they found the great kauri pine forests which provided material for enormous single-hulled dug-out canoes, which they ornamented with elaborate strakes and prow and stern ornaments. As usual their pride and bravery led the tribes to separate and then to fight each other, but this too produced a remarkable art in which the tattooed spirals on the face of the warrior appeared as decoration on all their brave and manly works of art.

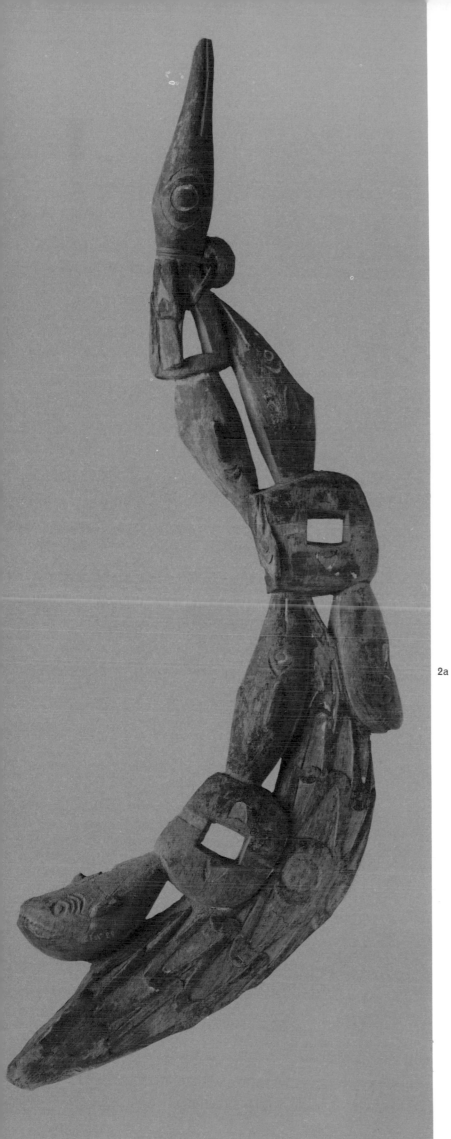

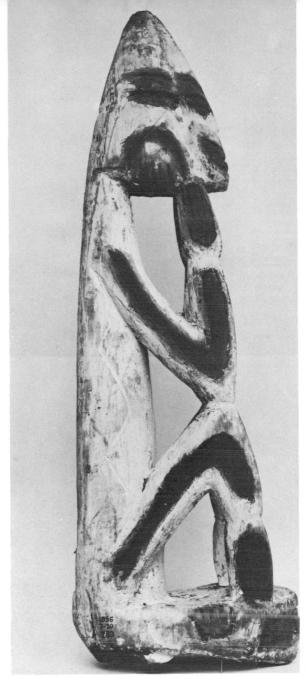

2a

2b

1a *A fish painted on a sheet of bark, from Arnhem Land. The local tribesfolk have a legend of a giant ancestress who walked through the sea. They now use simple dugout canoes copied from the vessels used by the neighbouring peoples of New Guinea*

b *The strange double raft of the Woroa of Western Australia. The two sections hold together by pressure alone. The little framework at the back is for holding the catch of fish*

2a *Canoe carving, perhaps a figurehead, from West Irian (S.W. New Guinea). The patterns represent a fishing bird, fishes and a human ancestor. It was carved with stone tools and is a remarkable expression of movement*

b *Canoe figurehead from the delta of the Kampong River, West Irian. Artistically it is interesting because of the presentation of the full face at the side as well as the front of the head, and the development of a foot pattern carved on the side of the base*

3 *Models of outrigger canoes from the Trobriand and Louisiade Islands, eastern Papua*

a *The larger type of vessel is similar to that used on trading expeditions, when it had a deck house for protection of the merchandise*

b *The smaller canoe for fishing and inter-island travel shows the arrangement of the traditional panels of sculpture on the vessel. Note the line of fish carved along the side strake. Collected on the Cook-Daniells Expedition, 1905*

4 *Traditional prow ornaments from the Trobriand Islands*

a *The designs are based almost entirely upon the frigate bird, seen here in its basic conventionalized pattern*

b *The more complex pattern will be seen to consist almost entirely of heads and beaks of the bird. These carvings were collected by Professor B. Malinowski*

5 *A group of three ceremonial 'standards' made from pieces of carved tridacna shell. They were mounted as emblems in the bows of head-hunting canoes in Vella Lavella, Solomon Islands*

3a   3b

4a   4b

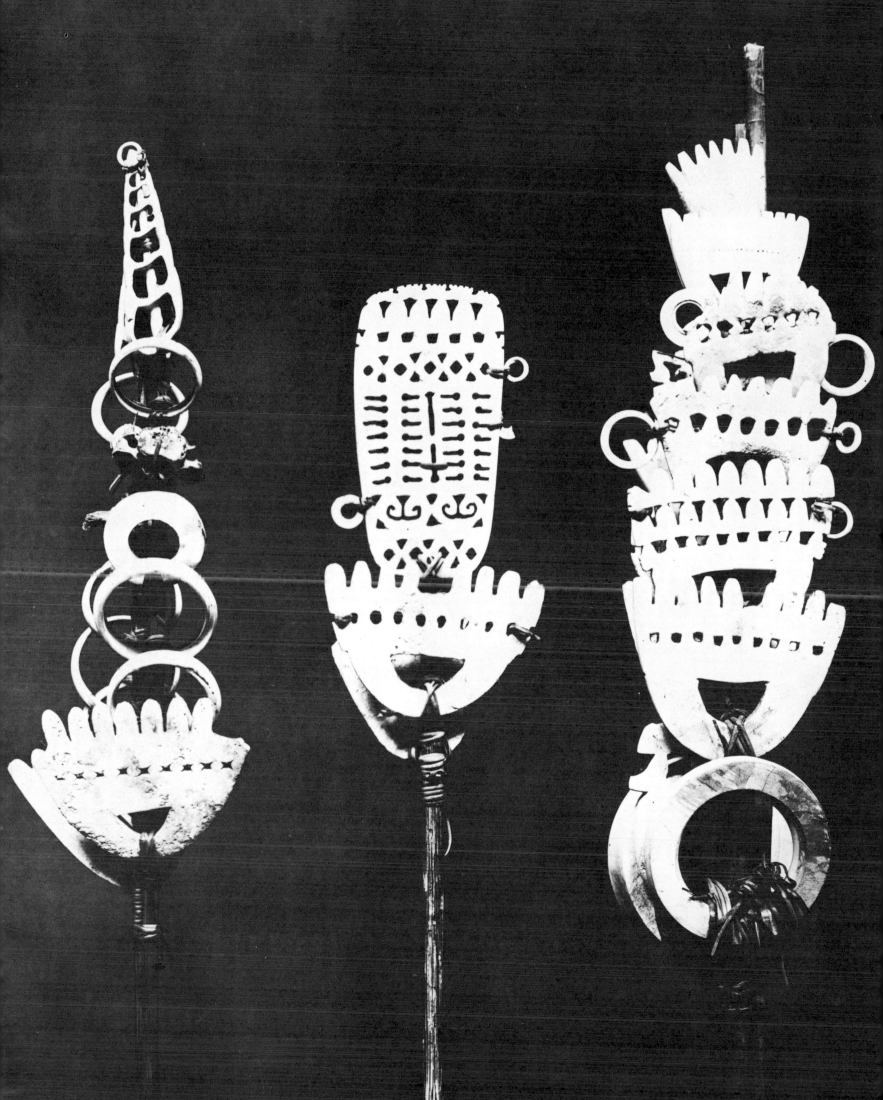

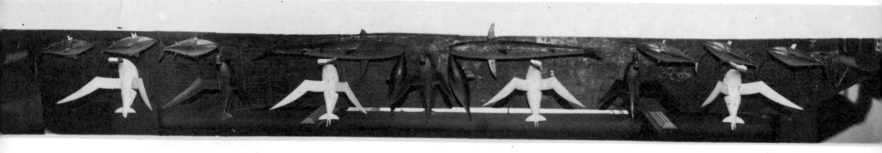

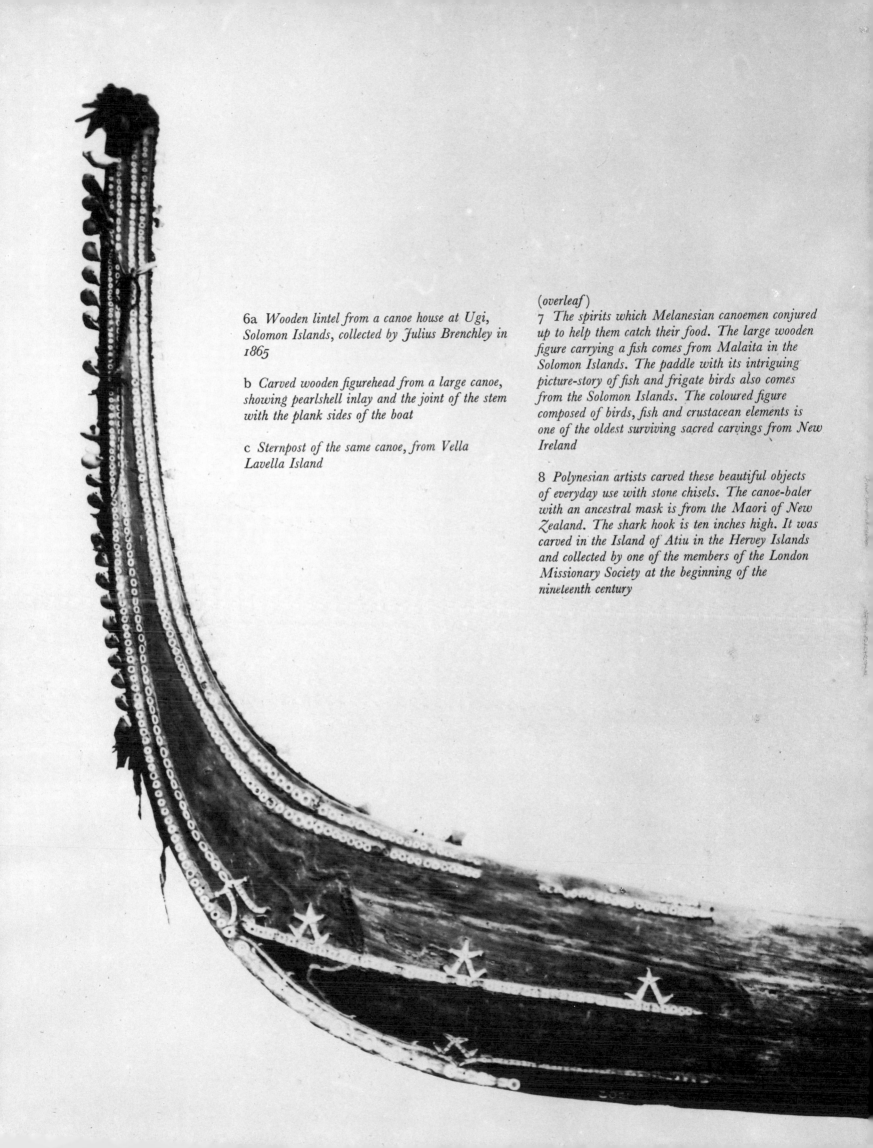

6a *Wooden lintel from a canoe house at Ugi, Solomon Islands, collected by Julius Brenchley in 1865*

b *Carved wooden figurehead from a large canoe, showing pearlshell inlay and the joint of the stem with the plank sides of the boat*

c *Sternpost of the same canoe, from Vella Lavella Island*

(overleaf)

7 *The spirits which Melanesian canoemen conjured up to help them catch their food. The large wooden figure carrying a fish comes from Malaita in the Solomon Islands. The paddle with its intriguing picture-story of fish and frigate birds also comes from the Solomon Islands. The coloured figure composed of birds, fish and crustacean elements is one of the oldest surviving sacred carvings from New Ireland*

8 *Polynesian artists carved these beautiful objects of everyday use with stone chisels. The canoe-baler with an ancestral mask is from the Maori of New Zealand. The shark hook is ten inches high. It was carved in the Island of Atiu in the Hervey Islands and collected by one of the members of the London Missionary Society at the beginning of the nineteenth century*

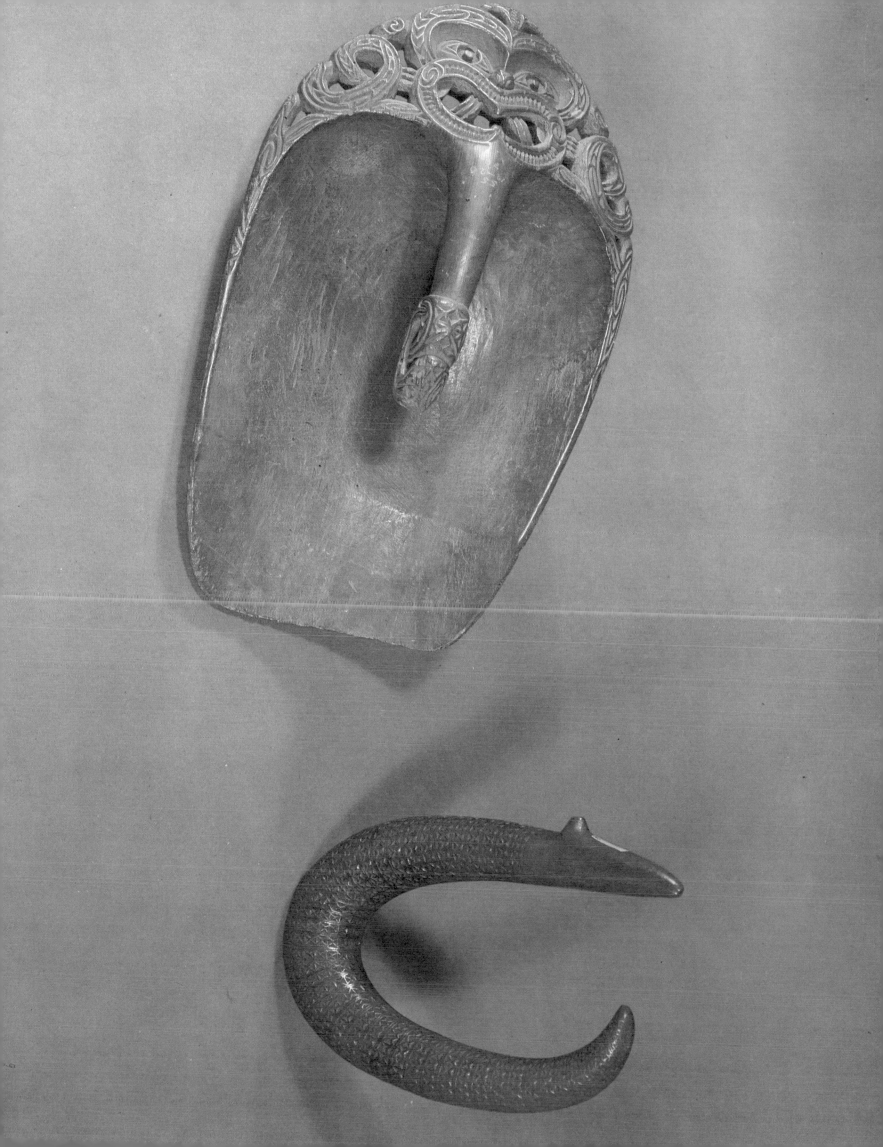

9a *Model of a large outrigger canoe with painted decoration, from the Anchorite Islands*

b *Carved and painted paddle blade from Bougainville, Solomon Islands*

c *Club, which in an emergency could be used as a paddle, from Bougainville, Solomon Islands*

d *Carved and inlaid model of a bonito, from Ulawa, Solomon Islands*

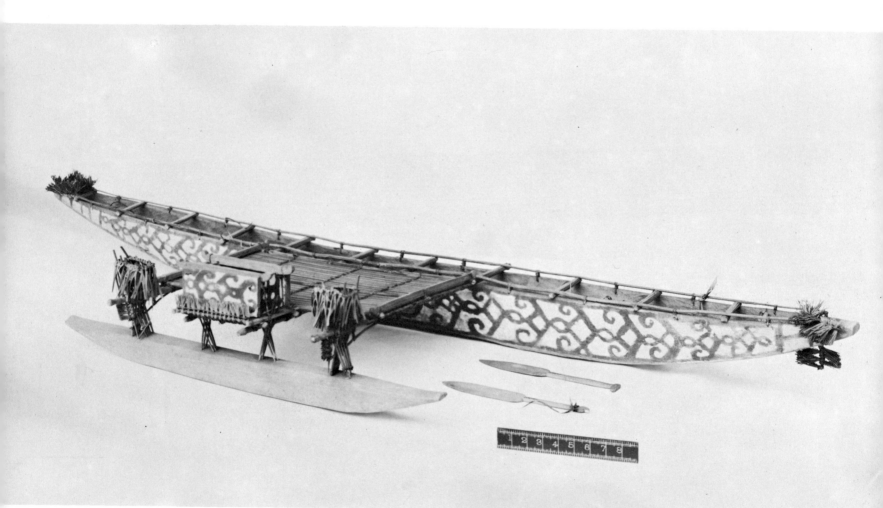

9a

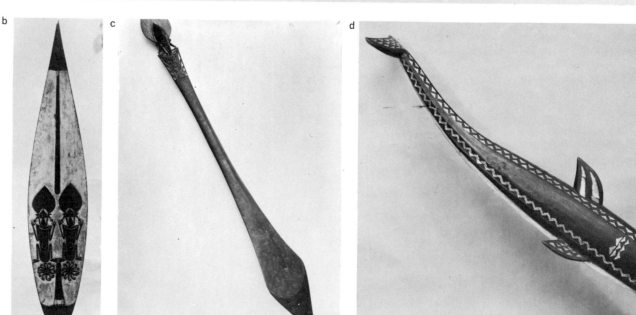

b

c

d

10a, b

10a *Carved and painted memorial figure from New Ireland showing the rich use of symbolism derived from fish and crustaceans*

b *Figure of a sea sprite from San Cristoval, Solomon Islands, combining characteristics both fish and human*

11a *Large food bowl carved and inlaid with tridacna shell, including representations of fishing birds. Collected by Capt. Henry Wilson in the Pelew Islands, 1783*

b and c *Fisherman's box from Tokelau, Micronesia, with a festival scene carved on the base*

11a

b

c

12a

b

12a *Rest from a Tahitian canoe showing two realist carvings of ancestors supported by an abstract female form*

b *Crouching female figure used as a spear rest; from a Tahitian canoe*

13a and b *A wooden four-seater dugout from Manihiki. The pearlshell and red grass decoration is traditional. The canoe is named after the Polynesian hero Maui who dragged the islands to the surface of the ocean*

c *Engraving of Tahitian war canoes*

13a, b, c

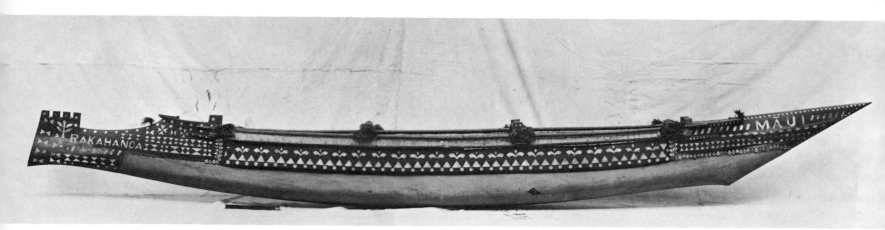

RAKAHANGA   MAUI

14 *The last of the sewn canoes of Polynesia. Collected in 1793 by Captain Wallis in the Tuamotu Islands. The prow points the way, the stern represents legs to help the canoe on its journey. The sennit stitching swelled when immersed in water and so minimized leaks. However, a baler was an essential piece of equipment in all Polynesian canoes*

15a *A canoe figurehead representing a warrior spirit to guide the boat on its victorious journeys. He rests his feet on the heads of conquered foes. Marquesas Islands*

b *Two spear rests from ancient Hawaiian canoes. The larger one was collected on Vancouver's voyage, and was worked entirely with stone tools. The smaller one was given to one of the members of the London Missionary Society a generation later*

16 *Carved sternpost of New Zealand canoe with interlacing patterns and symbols originally derived from human forms, but now representing the Manaia, or sea serpent*

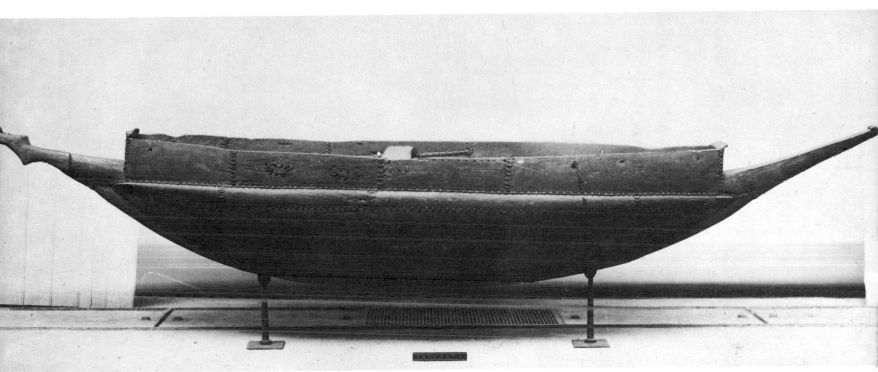

14

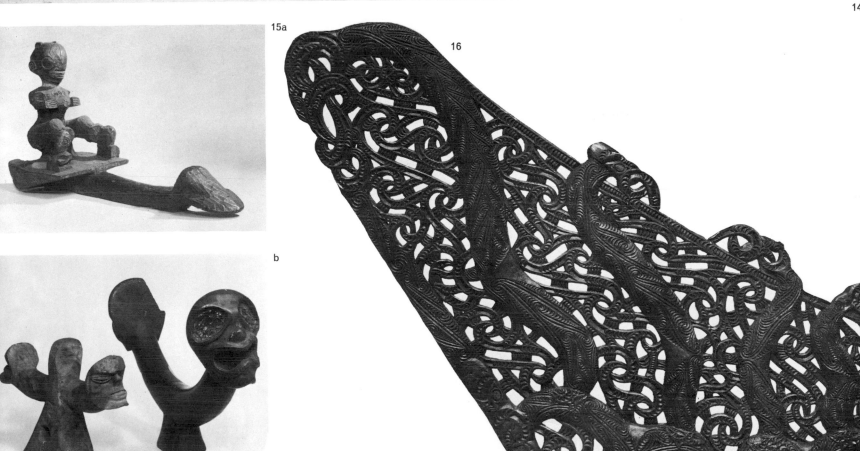

15a

16

b

17a and b *Maori canoe prow, New Zealand. The front shows a mythical creature, the Manaia, derived from a human figure. The head shows the tongue protruding in a grimace used by warriors in battle. The near figure represents an ancestress showing a woman's facial tattoo*

18 *Wood carving from Easter Island representing the god Makemake as a tropic bird. In this form he was said to have guided the canoes of the ancestors to make their landfall*

17b

18

CHAPTER XVI

MALAYSIAN CRAFT

CLIVE DALTON

There are few places in the whole world quite so interesting to the lover of boats as the numerous creeks and harbours of the Malay Archipelago. Nowhere else can be seen such a picturesque conglomeration of boats of every size, shape and colour, from the cockleshell canoes of the small boys to the rakish schooners of the Bugis from Celebes.

The Malay is by nature an amphibian and a born sailor. He swims as soon as he can walk, and often sooner, and as a boy he looks forward to owning his own canoe with the same certain expectation as an English boy looks forward to owning his first bicycle, and from his earliest days he looks upon a boat as an essential and integral part of his very existence.

To the Malays of the small islands—the *orang laut*, or men of the sea—the boats are a means of livelihood, and great pride is taken in their appearance. These simple fisherfolk do not concern themselves greatly with decoration for its own sake. They have an eye for clean lines and a good rig, and they like a boat that is good to look at. This will have a high tapering stem and tail which may be lightly carved and painted, but the Malays will not ornament their craft with elaborate figureheads as do the Dyaks of Borneo, nor paint her with intricate geometrical designs as do the men of Java. If we seek the spectacular then we must go farther afield, to Java and Borneo, Bali and Celebes.

The actual decoration of the Malay boat varies enormously according to region, for the Malays are a variegated race. There is a great deal of difference in tradition, culture and even religion between the peoples of different parts of the archipelago, and these things are inevitably reflected in their art and in the decoration of their boats.

Malay boats in general are of no great size. In the early days when piracy was rife, armed *praus*, which were often quite large, roamed the Eastern seas, but such ships are now only seen as models which figure in curious religious rites still practised in some of the islands. The modern Malay boat is seldom more than thirty feet in length, usually carvel-built, sailed or paddled and, in most cases, it has a shelter of palm-thatch as a protection against the weather.

The canoes in which the little boys learn their first lessons in seamanship are often hewn out of solid tree-trunks. They are beautifully symmetrical and finely balanced and a joy to handle. The slightly larger boats, commonly used for ferrying passengers from island to island, are slightly reminiscent of the Venetian gondola, with their high prows and the thatched roofing over the centre seat. Larger again are the river-boats which are the main means of transport in the dense jungle areas of the interior.

All these are good to look at but they are not highly decorative. The boats of Java are a great deal more striking, for the Javanese loves to paint his boat much as the gipsy loves to paint his caravan, in bold geometric patterns and vivid contrasting colours. He is not content merely to embellish the tailpiece and prow of his boat, nor to do his hull in a single plain colour. The whole boat must be emblazoned with stripes and triangles and scrolls and strange curling symbols which are purely Oriental in style, all in blazing colour of which the favourite yellow and red predominate. In addition he designs fanciful crutches to hold the lowered sail, and will even decorate the steering oar with the same sort of intricate work. In general the Javanese prefers the formal pattern and does not incorporate animals or birds into his designs as do the people of Borneo and many other parts. His patterns, although variegated and often highly original, are always symmetrical and perfectly executed, and yet, curiously, the overall effect of a harbour full of such boats, often quite uniform in their patterning, is one of riotous confusion.

In Bali, on the other hand, almost every boat is adorned with some representation of some mystical creature that could only have emanated from the twisted soul of Bali.

Bali is quite unlike the rest of the Malayan islands, and its people are unlike the rest of the Malay races. They alone of the Malay peoples embraced Buddhism, but not content with this alone, they confused it with Hinduism, mingled it with traces of even older religions from a forgotten past and merged the whole into a frightening hotch-potch which now weighs upon the people and their arts. It is reflected in the grotesque carvings of their temples, the tortured figures of their pictures, the ghoulish tales of their folklore and so, inevitably, in the decoration of their boats.

The Balinese use a curious sort of double outrigger, which most Malays would scorn, and these craft are nearly always decorated with the carving of a fabulous, nightmare creature, half-animal, half-fish; a blend of elephant and shark, some say, although elephants have never been seen in the island.

Fantasy is again evident in the carvings which the Dyaks of Borneo use freely in the ornamentation of their canoes, though here fantasy blends with realism in the production of dragons and more everyday creatures like fishes, reptiles and birds.

The Dyaks, until recently the dreaded head-hunters, are among the fiercest and certainly the most primitive of the Malay races, and are as unlike the simple fisherfolk of the islands around Singapore and Penang as the proud Javanese are unlike the dark-skinned Bugis. The Dyak boats are simple; for the most part a sort of flat-bottomed canoe, long, shallow and rather narrow, but often elaborately decorated with carvings which show a remarkably high degree of workmanship and skill.

Here are illustrated a number of interesting examples of this Dyak craftsmanship, for instance the quite extraordinary canoe prow depicting a monkey crouched inside the jaws of a crocodile. The same lively imagination and the same high degree of craftsmanship are evident in the various dragon heads and other carvings of beasts both real and mythical which appear in the boat adornments from the various parts of Borneo. The massive dragon face, the comparatively slender and even rather humorous figures from Kajamare, for instance, all show the same painstaking workmanship surprising in a people who until recent times were accounted amongst the most savage in the world.

The Bugis of Celebes are another fierce people, and it is generally agreed that they were the most feared pirates of Malayan waters in days gone by.

Here we encounter a surprising fact. The ships of Celebes are the largest and most Western in appearance of all Malay craft. They are, in general, of the schooner type, rigged fore and aft, and with high, square poops. There are no other boats like them in the whole of the archipelago.

It is believed that the explanation of this is that almost certainly the Bugis captured at least two or three of the Portuguese vessels which were the first European ships to reach these waters, and that having learnt to handle these, the Bugis eventually began to build ships of a similar type, or at least to incorporate some of the features of the Portuguese vessels along with their own to evolve a boat that was

1 *Small harbours on the coast of Java are gay with bright colours and elaborate designs of native boats*

2 *Sea-gipsies of the East Indies. Stems and tail-pieces of these boats are decorated with intricate floral patterns*

something between the two. These vessels are not so flamboyant in their decoration as the Javanese boats, but they do favour the bright colourings and bold designs of their neighbours. Generally there is a single broad stripe of a contrasting colour along the full length of the hull, and the square stern pieces are decked out with scrolls and floral patterns in vivid hues. Sails, too, are sometimes striped, although in general the Malays do not favour decorated sails, preferring to concentrate on the actual vessel.

Still farther east there sometimes appear traces of a slight Polynesian influence, as can be seen in the delicately carved canoe prow ornaments embellished with shells from Timor-Laut. And here again is the same painstaking workmanship that tells of time and thought lavished on a job that was done well for its own sake.

All these things: the Dyak carvings, the Javanese paintings, and even the twisted creations of Bali are the expression of a deep-felt love of boats and the sea inherent in all island peoples. And the boy who paints his sailing dinghy in two colours is, deep down, in tune with the native of Borneo who cuts himself a dragon figurehead and decorates it with human hair.

3 *Typical Javanese designs embellish the tail-pieces of these boats*

4 *This Siamese state barge might have been designed for a Hollywood epic*

5 *More picturesque than decorative; the Javanese of Madura still adorns his boat-home with fanciful designs*

4

5

6 *The double outrigger commonly used in Bali*

7 *Kenyah figurehead*

8

8 *An armed Malay prau of the type that once terrorized the Java Sea. These ships are no longer seen, but models of this type are sometimes used in the observance of old religious rites still carried out in the smaller islands*

9 *Characteristic figurehead of Balinese outrigger.*
This mythical creature is half fish and half animal

10

11

12

13

10 *A remarkable carving of a monkey in the jaws of a crocodile decorates this Dyak canoe*

11 *An example of the dragon-type figurehead from Borneo*

12 *This fantastic carving of a dragon is also typical of the type of figurehead used on the boats of Borneo*

13 *Heavy figureheads representing dragons and fabulous beasts used by the Dyaks of Borneo*

14

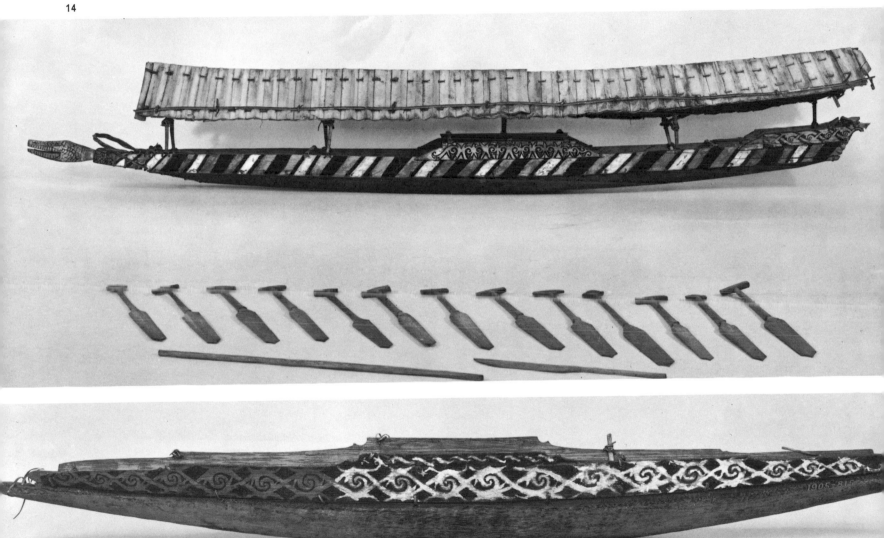

15

14 *A model boat, showing characteristic covering of palm-thatch, and a set of paddles*

15 *This model boat shows the type of decoration which may be seen around the coasts of Borneo and Sarawak*

16 *Fine carvings from Timor-Laut which form the decorations of canoe-prows*

17 *These almost Western-type schooners are Bugis vessels, originally copied from captured Portuguese schooners*

16

17

VESSELS OF THE ORIENT

Capt. DONALD MACINTYRE, R.N.

East of Suez and north of the equator, ocean-going craft comprise two main types, the Arab dhow and the Chinese junk. The former, with the graceful, crescent-shaped yard of its lateen sail, is of a design which gives pleasure enough to the aesthetic sense. The far-roaming seamen and merchants of the Semitic races never showed much interest, however, in decorating their craft. The raised transoms are often ornamented with conventional carvings of rope designs, but coloured decorations are rarely seen, painting being confined to giving the vessel a light-coloured bottom and black sides relieved by two white bands of unequal width, while the numerous windows or ports of the poop are picked out to form a chequerboard design in the style of the old wooden sailing ships of the West.

The sea-going craft of India are mostly variations of the dhow and are similarly drab and colourless. To find any noteworthy examples of the decorator's art one must turn to the ceremonial barges of Indian princes who travelled in gorgeous state on their inland waters.

The Burmese similarly lavished their decorative art mainly on ceremonial vessels of state, as seen in the picture by a nineteenth-century French traveller of the Imperial Burmese barge. From the same artist's brush comes a picture of a craft which he describes as a Burmese war canoe. The European naval officer seated in the bow under an umbrella and the curious arrangement of the oarsmen on the port side are puzzling features, but the decorated stern is well illustrated.

The ornamental barges were rare exceptions, of course, and their decoration was in honour of their august passengers; whereas the true decorative art of the mariner was applied in loving care for and pride in the ships themselves. This undoubtedly was the source of inspiration for the brilliantly coloured, striking designs to be found decorating the many varied types of Chinese sailing craft.

Even here the Westerner today may be denied the sight of the craft which illustrated the Chinese love of colour and artistic sense. Apart from the fact that most of the coast of China now lies behind the 'bamboo curtain', through which the non-communist can pass only with difficulty, much of the colour and traditional decorative art vanished with the passing of imperial splendour from the Chinese scene in favour of republican drabness, and the coming of Western influence with its steamships and commercial bustle. The junks best known today, those to be seen in their hundreds in the waters round Hong Kong, trawling in pairs or beating their way up the coast on trading voyages with their brown lattice sails spread, are second to none in their sturdy beauty of design; but they were never greatly ornamented, their plain brown or dark red varnished hulls being relieved only occasionally by brighter colours—reds, yellows and greens—picking out the galleries round the high sterns.

An earlier generation, on the other hand, enjoyed the sight of gaily decorated junks in the harbours of Canton and Hong Kong which originated in provinces farther north. From Fukien, for example, came the Foochow Pole (or Stock) junk which was mainly used to transport cargoes of wooden or bamboo poles. Their brightly painted hulls varied in colour scheme according to the village of origin, but all had in common the conspicuous 'Eye' on either bow, the red-serpentine good-luck sign on each quarter and the fantastically ornamented transom stern.

The 'Eye', so often considered a peculiarly Chinese whimsy based on the charming notion that 'ship have no eye, no can see', is, in fact, believed by some authorities to have its origin in the Eye of Osiris worn by ancient Egyptian boats and brought to China in the great days of Arab trade before Mohammedanism banned such pagan emblems, when flourishing trading posts existed on the China Coast. In support of this theory it is pointed out that vessels from north of the Shantung Peninsula, beyond which the Arabs never penetrated, did not carry the 'Eye'.

The intricate design of birds and dragons, with the phoenix usually conspicuous, was to be found decorating the sterns of other types of ocean-going junk such as the big trading junks from Ch'uan Chow, the Zaytun of Marco Polo. These were distinguishable by their white hulls, the topsides of which were a bright red in the bow, sometimes with green panels as background for the conspicuous Eye. Further aft, the black topsides were picked out in white and ornamented with red squares against square white panels. A portion of a panorama of the waterfront of Canton, painted at the beginning of the nineteenth century, illustrates several of these craft.

A huge and most decorative example of the ocean-going junk, named the *Keying*, was sailed to London in 1848, the first junk to round the Cape of Good Hope; she made a great sensation when she appeared in the Thames. (See Fig. 12.)

From Wenchow, in the province of Chekiang, sailed junks with quite a different decorative scheme. That illustrated has a red, white and black bow plate, white water-line strakes and red topside picked out with blue and white and a green panel as background for the 'Eye', though the general layout varied in detail from boat to boat. The fishing junks were ornamented with the same gay abandon as the traders.

The province of Chekiang, indeed, with its several busy seaports and the heavy traffic amongst the islands of the Chusan Archipelago, offered a number of examples of the decorative art of the Chinese seaman. The traditional junk of Ningpo, already in the first quarter of this century a rarity and probably no longer in existence, was as picturesque as any ocean-going craft of the Orient. Big ships, of some 100 feet in length, their high, flat sterns were painted a bright blue with red facings. Their gracefully curving quarters were usually picked out with scarlet chevron-shaped borders.

A more modern type of 'Ningpo Junk' that was to be seen in considerable numbers both fishing and trading in that busiest of Chinese sea areas, between Hangchow Bay and Shanghai, would be more accurately styled 'Chusan Junks', as Chusan Island was their place of origin. Faster-sailing, handier craft than the old-fashioned Ningpo trading junk, they were ornamented less elaborately with plain, contrasting colours and an absence of fanciful design.

Less than a hundred miles from Chusan, a type of junk very different both in design and ornamentation was developed. This was the Shaohsing or Hangchow Bay junk illustrated in Fig. 9. Its flat bottom, curving upwards to meet the wide, wedge-shaped stem, was in sharp contrast to the graceful Chusan junk; but even more conspicuously different was the grotesque yet artistic decoration of the flat stem with a form of stylized, grinning face. Perhaps because this naturally provided the ship with its 'Eyes', the position on either bow usually reserved for this feature was occupied by the 'Pakua', very common Chinese good-luck charms or talismans. The hull, brown varnished or black,

1 *Udaipur state barge*

2 *Calcutta state barge*

would usually be embellished also with a brilliantly coloured phoenix on either quarter while the high bulwark, running the full length of the ship, and often painted red, would be decorated with intricately designed panels in blue, red and yellow according to the taste of the junk-master. The whole picture gave an impression of pride and loving care for a ship which was also a sea-going family's home, perhaps only to be compared to the gaudy decoration of barges on English canals.

The inland waterways of China, such as the Yangtse Kiang and the Yellow River, also had their share of gaily decorated craft until the age of steam came to rob the junk sailors of the cream of the river traffic, leaving them to a less prosperous, drab, workaday way of life. One of the prettiest of river craft in those distant days was the 'Mandarin Boat' with which the rivers were policed.

Lightly built, with elegant lines, Mandarin Boats were by far the fastest craft on the water when propelled by their numerous oarsmen, sometimes as many as twenty a side, in pursuit of smugglers or other breakers of the law. At other times they might be navigated under sails spread on their two masts, gaily ornamented with little flags and pennants and golden balls. Their hulls were decorated with neat carving and fancywork and smartly painted, usually with bright blue topsides and white below.

In spite of its gay appearance, however, the Mandarin Boat was no pleasure craft. Its armament might include several small swivel guns to enforce the law and punish wrongdoers, with the rowers protected by a thatched roof and the flag indicating its authority flying from the yard-arm.

China's inland waters teemed with many different types of craft; for not only were they great water highways along which were transported merchandise, foodstuffs and passengers, but they also bore on their placid surface a large population which made its home afloat. Where the waters were broad and easily navigable, junks similar to the sea-going types plied. On narrow, more sheltered waters, oars or punt-poles propelled flat-bottomed boats and barges which, for all their cumbersome design, were often gaily and even lavishly decorated.

The houseboats and passenger craft belonging to high-ranking mandarins or rich merchants naturally lent themselves to the attention of artists, as is shown in the delightful bone model. Elegant also were the floating teashops and restaurants and the famous 'Flower Boats', seraglios in which beautiful and talented 'Sing Song Girls', able to compose and recite poetry and romantic tales as well as sing to the music of the lute, catered for the leisure hours of their well-to-do customers.

A particularly picturesque craft to be seen wherever communities lived by sheltered or inland waters was the Dragon Boat. This was purely for semi-religious ceremonial use on the annual Dragon Boat Festival which commemorated the tragic death of the famous poet and statesman Ch'u Yuan in the fourth century. Having been unjustly accused and dismissed from his government post, he committed suicide by drowning himself in the Yangtse Kiang. Sympathizers put out in boats and searched in vain for his body, and a re-enactment of this search became an annual ceremony on the anniversary of Ch'u Yuan's death on the fifth day of the fifth moon. Offerings of boiled rice in bamboo tubes to appease his spirit were thrown into the river. His apparition then appeared, however, to complain that all these offerings were being eaten by an ill-natured dragon, and said that, to frighten off the dragon, the rice should in future be wrapped in silk and tied with five-coloured threads.

With the passing of time the boats which put out in symbolic search for the poet's body came to be constructed with a dragon's head and tail.

Often, however, they were designed to take part in races on the day of the festival, long and narrow and rowed or paddled by a large crew. Amidships were stationed a drum and a gong, from the beating of which, as well as from the gesticulations of a man in the bow armed with a flag, the rowers were expected to take their time. The instruments were beaten and the flag waved with true Chinese abandon and a minimum of co-ordination; but in spite of this a fair degree of rhythm was achieved.

Whether the Japanese in the age of sail indulged to the same extent as the Chinese in the use of decoration for their ships is hard to determine. For in the seventeenth century a virtual prohibition of communication with the outside world was imposed under the Tokugawa régime, which persisted until 1853. The Japanese had no cause during this period to

3

build ocean-going ships and little is known of their ships prior to it; but that her navigators had absorbed from Western contacts considerable knowledge of the distant oceans can be inferred from the 'Sho' Map which dates from 1645 and can now be seen in the British Museum.

Nevertheless, as art in all its forms flourished in Japan, chiefly under Chinese influence, it is likely that ornamentation of ships followed Chinese example. That some of this survived can be seen from the model of a Japanese whaling sampan. A rare and beautiful example of a marine subject chosen by a Japanese artist is the boatload of minor gods carved in ivory.

4

5 *Foochow junk, stern*

6 *Foochow junk, broadside*

5   6

7 *Wenchow trader*

8 *Chiman Cheo junk*

7

8

10 *Small mandarin (police) boat*

9 *Hangchow Bay junk*

11 *River junk*

THE CHINESE JUNK, KEYINC, 其衣喊揆烔知 CAPTAIN KELLETT.

The first Junk that ever rounded the Cape of Good Hope, or appeared in British waters.

Mainsail	9 Tons
Mainmast 85 feet long from Deck	
Upper Mainyard	67 feet long
Lower	61 "
800 Tons Burthen, Chinese Measurement	

14

15

16

12 (*opposite*) *The* Keying *in the Thames, 1848*

13 (*opposite*) *Waterfront of international settlement at Canton showing Ch'nan Chow junks,* c. *1810*

14 *River craft*

15 *River craft*

16 *River craft*

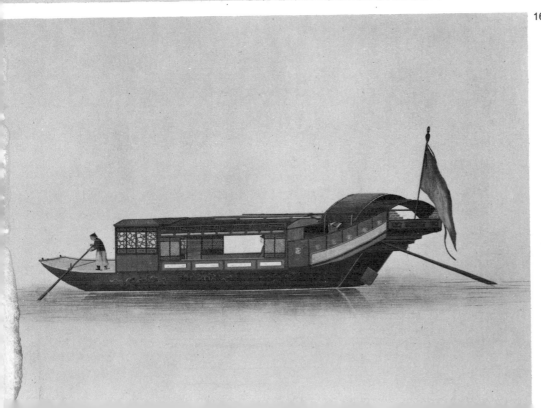

南京運糧船

17 *River craft*

18 *Flower boat*

19 *Mandarin's pleasure boat*

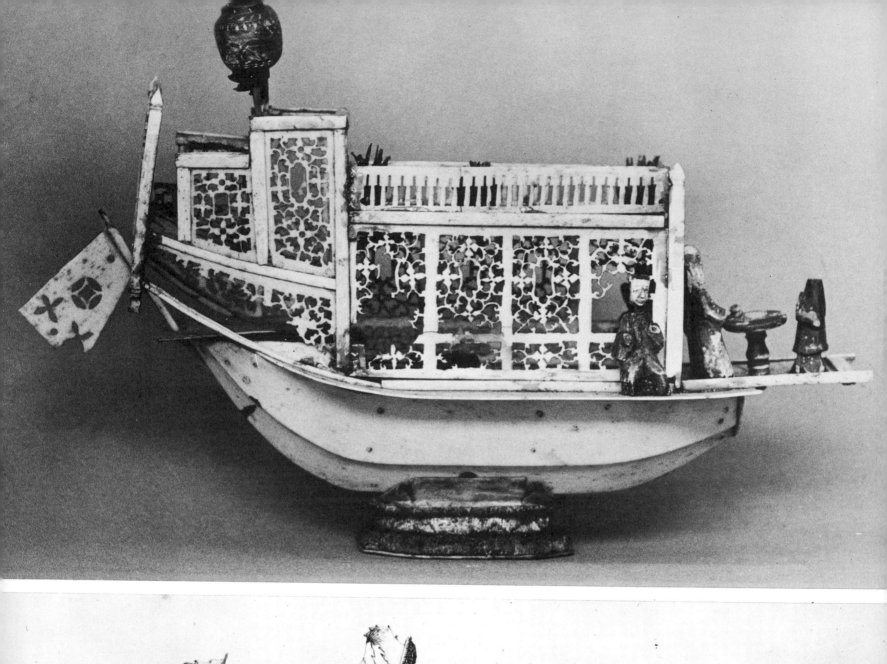

22

23

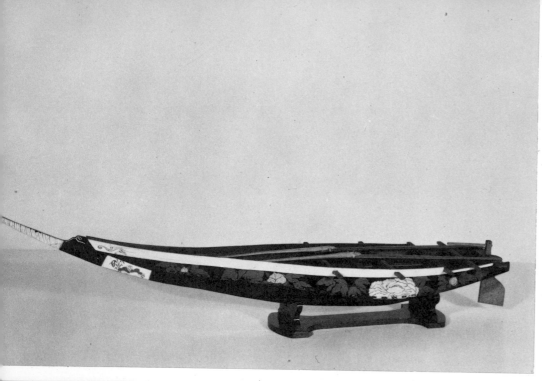

24 *Japanese whaling sampan*

25 *Japanese ivory model of a boatload of minor gods*

26 *'Sho' map. Japanese, dated 1645*

25

26

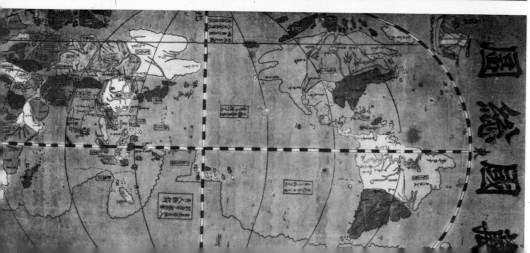